W9-ADO-214

DISCARDED
JENKS LRC
GORDON COLLEGE

The Information Web

Ethical and Social Implications
of Computer Networking

JENKS L.R.C.
GORDON COLLEGE
255 GRAPEVINE RD.
WENHAM, MA 01984-1895

The Information Web

Ethical and Social Implications of Computer Networking

EDITED BY

Carol C. Gould

Westview Press

BOULDER, SAN FRANCISCO, & LONDON

TK
5105.5
.I494
1989

All rights reserved. No part of this publication may be reproduced
or transmitted in any form or by any means, electronic or
mechanical, including photocopy, recording, or any information
storage and retrieval system, without permission in writing from
the publisher.

Copyright © 1989 by Westview Press, Inc.

Published in 1989 in the United States of America by Westview
Press, Inc., 5500 Central Avenue, Boulder, Colorado 80301, and in
the United Kingdom by Westview Press, Inc., 13 Brunswick Centre,
London WC1N 1AF, England

Library of Congress Cataloging-in-Publication Data
The Information web : ethical and social implications of computer
  networking / edited by Carol C. Gould.
    p. cm.
  Includes index.
  ISBN 0-8133-0699-X
  1. Computer networks--Moral and ethical aspects. I. Gould, Carol
C.
TK5105.5.I494 1989
323.44'83--dc19   88-23199
                                                              CIP

Printed and bound in the United States of America

 The paper used in this publication meets the requirements of the
American National Standard for Permanence of Paper for Printed
Library Materials Z39.48-1984.

10   9   8   7   6   5   4   3   2   1

In memory of I. Richard Lapidus (1935-1988),
scientist and humanist

Contents

viii

Preface

Second only in importance to the computer revolution itself is the current rapid development of computer networking. The present book is the first to deal with the major ethical and social implications of this most far-reaching technological development. In this collection a number of leading thinkers--philosophers as well as computer scientists and researchers in the natural and social sciences--address some fundamental philosophical questions posed by the new technology.

A computer network connects any number of independent computers, often at geographically remote locations, so that they can communicate with each other and share programs, data, and hardware. This novel combination of communication and information resources makes possible new modes of scientific collaboration, new techniques of management and control, and new forms of political participation and governance. It thus presents opportunities for more fully realizing such norms as scientific cooperation and efficiency in management and production and such ethical ideals as democratic participation and social cooperation.

At the same time, the network revolution poses several major ethical and social problems: the protection of individual privacy against the accessibility of personal information in a network; the question of whether

programs and certain other information accessible in a network constitute forms of property and the question of what laws would be appropriate for the protection of such property;
moral questions arising from the wide sharing
of scientific data and research results and
the access to the ongoing research activity of
others through the network (e.g., questions of
authorship and priority, of plagiarism, manipulation of others' data, and so on); the
problem of the abuse or manipulation of information when networks are used in the political
process (e.g., in computerized voting); the
growing problem of computer crime; the new
question of who is morally responsible for
computer or program errors and harms, which
the computer makes possible; and the more
general question of whether computer networking requires new moral principles and
norms of practice. These are the issues that
the contributing authors discuss and on which
they break new ground.

Many of the papers presented here are the
result of a collaborative research project
sponsored by the National Science Foundation
program in Ethics and Values in Science and
Technology.* The others were solicited for
their relevance to the general theme of the
research project.

As recent as these papers are, it is a
sign of the rapid development in the field of
computer networking that new problems and
issues have arisen since they were written.
For example, there is the new phenomenon of
so-called computer "viruses," which can be
surreptitiously and subversively planted in a
"host" program or file via networking and
which can then spread and destroy information
in the computer system. More generally,
networking has proliferated so widely in the
past few years that the papers collected here
have become even more widely relevant and find
more complex applications than ever before.

----

*NSF/EVIST Grant # R11-8410360, 1985-1987.

I would like to express my thanks to Dr. Rachelle Hollander, program director of the National Science Foundation program in Ethics and Values in Science and Technology, for helping to focus the project as it developed; to my colleagues at Stevens Institute of Technology who were members of the collaborative research team under the NSF grant--Professors Rodney Andrews, Frank Boesch, M. Peter Jurkat, Arnold Urken, and the late I. Richard Lapidus, whose untimely death cut short an active scientific career at the frontiers of physics and biology; to my work-study assistants, Igor Shapiro and Drew Lange, who helped with the preparation of the manuscript; and to Dawn Madak. I would also like to thank the administration and my colleagues at Stevens for their cooperation in this project.

Carol C. Gould

1

Network Ethics: Access, Consent, and the Informed Community

Carol C. Gould

Introduction

Computer networks may be considered as the nervous system of the society of the future. The network becomes a means by which information can be communicated to and from all nodes of the system, by which resources such as data and programs can be represented, stored, and transmitted, and powerful computational processes can be widely shared. But no matter how it is technically defined, what a network ultimately networks are human beings with minds. Therefore a network cannot simply be defined electronically or in terms of information and communication without a knowing subject. Rather, it must also be understood as a set of social and cognitive relations among persons. It is precisely such a context of social interaction that gives rise to ethical issues. Thus the implementation and uses of computer networks present a range of moral and policy questions for those who use the network and for those who are used or abused by it.

Before addressing the specific issues that are the focus of this chapter, it may be useful to suggest how important a development computer networking is. The point was made rather dramatically a few years ago by Stanley Winkler (conference governor of the Sixth International Conference on Computer Communication). He wrote (somewhat grandly):

In 1972, I suggested, albeit tentatively,

that the impact on the 21st Century of the innovation of computer communications would rank with the impact of Newtonian mechanics on the 17th and 18th Centuries, and with that of the Boltzman-Gibbs concept of a contingent universe on the 20th Century. I would no longer consider that suggestion as tentative. There can be no doubt about the significance and revolutionary impact of computer communication.[1]

The twenty-first century aside, it is already clear that computer networking is playing an increasingly important role in a variety of fields--scientific research, management, defense, government, and politics--as well as in the more informal contexts of the computer culture and subculture.

What is a computer network? We may briefly define a computer network as an interconnected set of autonomous computers that can communicate with one another and can share resources such as programs, data, and hardware. Thus, networks permit the exchange of information among computers and the distribution of computer capabilities among geographically remote locations. A central feature of such networks is that they make possible multiple and remote access to system resources.

In this chapter, I will focus on the ethical and social implications of computer networking. The ethical values I will explore include <u>privacy, property, equality,</u> and <u>cooperation.</u> The introduction of computer networking gives rise to conflicts among these values--for example, between the right to privacy and the demands for social cooperation--and creates the need for a conceptual clarification of the meaning of these normative terms in these new contexts. Such conflicts of values will be considered here in terms of two main contexts of computer networking that will serve as case studies for analysis--the contexts of scientific research and of citizen-government interaction. The principles of ethical choice that I will propose later are general principles that apply not only to these two contexts but to other applications of computer networking as well. But the emphasis on these two contexts from among all those in which networking is developing (e.g., management, banking, health care, education) is prompted by the fact that the ethical conflicts that emerge here are particularly instructive and, moreover, have not yet been widely studied.

In this chapter, I approach the question of how to resolve these conflicts of values by introducing two basic principles that I take to be central in considering the ethical and social implications of computer networking. Principle I is that of _free and informed consent_, and Principle II is that of _equal access_. These are, of course, general ethico-social principles whose applications extend beyond the domain of computer networking. For example, the principle of free and informed consent has been of central concern in the contexts of curative medicine and experimentation with human subjects. Likewise, the principle of equal access has been central in the domains of social and economic justice—for example, in issues of equal rights of access to education and to employment. However, these principles have not yet been considered in the context of computer technologies. I propose to show how they apply to this field and to suggest a distinctive interpretation of these principles. In addition, it will be seen that in each of the two contexts for the case study—scientific research and citizen-government interaction—a basic norm governs ethical choice within its domain. In the case of scientific research, the norm is that of free and open scientific communication; in the context of citizen-government interaction, it is the norm of increased political participation in democratic decision-making. I will suggest how in each of these cases the application of the two general principles serves to satisfy these norms.

4

Value Conflicts in Computer Networking

The Context of Scientific and Engineering Research

Let us turn to some of the specific contexts in which value conflicts arise in the use of computer networks. In the case of scientific and engineering research, there is a conflict between (1) the value of free and open communication within the scientific community through the use of computer networking, and (2) the values of confidentiality or privacy in one's personal research, as well as the proprietary rights in research and development contexts in which the scientist uses the facilities of a computer network. In addition, there is a conflict between the value of equal access to networking and to the informational and computational resources it makes available for research, on the one hand, and the criteria of ability to pay and of competence or relevance of one's research, on the other. The economic criterion of ability to pay refers here both to the institutional costs of participating in a network, such as ARPANET or even the less expensive BITNET, and also to the costs paid by individual research grants, which limit funds available for network use. Thus, whether the differential ability to pay is in terms of hard money or soft money, it has led to a have and have-not situation in which there is unequal access to the network facilities.

In order to explore these conflicts and the ethical questions to which they give rise more concretely, it is useful to note which scientific research networks we are referring to and what their actual and potential uses are. A convenient summary and history of networking in this context appears in a 1986 article by Dennis M. Jennings et al.[2] The major operative wide-area networks used in scientific research are of course ARPANET, sponsored by DARPA (the Defense Advanced

Research Projects Agency); CSNET (Computer
Science Research Network), which now includes
over 165 university, industrial, and government computer research groups; BITNET, a
university-based computer-assisted communications network for academic purposes; and
MFENET (Magnetic Fusion Energy Network), sponsored by the Department of Energy, as well as
some others. There are also state networks
and campus networks, that provide access to
shared computing facilities and communication
among researchers. The major new project is
NSFnet, a so-called "internet" or a "network
of networks," which, according to Jennings et
al.,

> will probably have the most impact on
> science of all networking activities in
> the United States at this time. Being
> based on new and existing networks, it
> will provide both high-speed access to
> supercomputers and communication between
> scientists in all disciplines throughout
> the nation. Although initially designed
> for supercomputer users to gain access to
> supercomputers and to communicate with
> each other, NSFnet is expected to be a
> general-purpose computer communications
> network for the whole academic research
> community and associated industrial
> researchers.[3]

A taxonomy of the uses of computer networking for scientific research may be outlined as follows:
1. An individual researcher of the
facilities of a network--including advanced
computational facilities, access to programs,
databases, and consultation with other research or technical personnel.
2. Joint or collaborative research may
be done by means of a network. In this case,
two or more researchers can be in communication from their computer workstations at locations that are remote from each other and can
engage in simultaneous or sequential collaboration in actual research activity, jointly

using the data and program capacities of the
network for computation, simulation, graphics,
and so on. Thus, the stimulation of collaborative research becomes widely available to
scientists irrespective of their location or
institutional affiliation.

3. The results of research can be made
public by means of a network, in the form of a
bulletin, newsletter, or "journal" disseminated through the network. Work in progress
may be circulated through the network for comments or even for editing or revision by colleagues in the network. Some current opinion
speculates that this form of electronic publication and dissemination will come to replace
printed scientific journals.

4. The computer network can also be used
for scientific seminars or conferences involving groups of researchers. Such conferences,
which may be either one-shot affairs or
ongoing or episodic, differ somewhat from collaborative research in that they are primarily
addressed to the sharing of individual research activities with others in an organized
agenda.

Specific ethical issues that arise from
the use of computer networks in scientific
research may now be considered more fully.
Though these issues may have analogues in more
general questions of the ethics of science,
the network-related ethical values and problems have a specific configuration. Thus, a
general ethical norm in scientific research is
the free and open exchange of ideas and information among members of the scientific community, all of whom are taken to be equals, if
not with respect to their competence or
achievement, then at least with respect to
their equal freedom to pursue scientific inquiry and their equal right of access to the
information required for such research. This
norm is what Robert Merton has referred to as
the traditional _ethos_ of science, in which the
scientific community is described as itself a
kind of "democratic republic." Within this
framework, such values as truth, open sharing
of information, and publicity of results char-

acterize the internal norms of the practice of scientific research and thus are intended to regulate the behavior of scientists in their relations with one another. These ethical norms mark off as disvalues in scientific research such practices as fraud, deceit, plagiarism, and the withholding of the results of research from others. It is in fact on these grounds that ethical questions arise with regard to classified research at university research centers as well as secret industrial research that affords competitive advantage; such situations involve limited access to results and to classified or restricted information. There are also conflicts between the traditional ethical values of science and other social values (i.e., national security in one case, profit or competitive advantage in the other). In such cases, the fundamental ethical norm of scientific research is not met, though other ends related to scientific research may be achieved, such as practical efficacy or social utility.

In the scientific use of computer networks, the norm of a free and open scientific community becomes achievable in a more encompassing way than ever before. For example, the general ethical value in science of free and equal access to information is realizable to a hitherto unimaginable degree in a wide-area networked situation. Likewise, intellectual cooperation and collaboration in research, which are traditionally counted among the highest values of the _ethos_ of science, are enhanced by the availability of means of communication that far exceed any previous capacities and permit interactive research in real time among widely dispersed scientists. It is true that traditional written communication and information sharing through the mail or by publication as well as by telephonic communication and personal travel have all functioned to these same ends in the past and will continue to do so. However, the changes that networking makes possible in the magnitude and scope of the accessible information, the speed of transmission, the instantaneously available and shareable computational facility, and the possibilities for wider interaction and communication with a much larger pool of research colleagues, introduce not only quantitative but qualitative changes in the nature of research activity. In effect, the scientific community becomes much more closely knit at the same time that the number of scientists who can participate increases.

Yet, this great increase in access to information and interaction poses the problem of preserving the privacy of the scientist's own creative thought and research activity, inasmuch as this privacy is also a value. Scientists using computer networks in individual or collaborative research may inadvertently make the results of their activity or their private conjectural or analytical procedures available to eavesdroppers on the network. Thus, the ease of unauthorized snooping made possible by the wider and freer access to the network may result in an invasion of the privacy of the scientist's own research.

A concomitant problem is that of maintaining proprietary rights in research and development contexts to protect the scientist whose work may be subject to theft or unauthorized appropriation. Or there may be problems of maintaining the identity of an individual scientist's contribution to research and ensuring that the scientist receives credit for his or her own work. Even the case of intentional publication and dissemination of one's work through computer networks raises problems of preserving copyright and also of protecting one's text against tampering or malicious distortion. Thus, the ethical issues of theft, deception, fraud, and plagiarism, and the question of scientific integrity--all of which are already problems in normal research and publication contexts--are exacerbated by the new technology. The opportunities for covering one's tracks while perpetrating such acts are multiplied by the technical complexities of the network and the difficulties of securing it against such abuse.

In these various ways, there would seem to be a conflict between the values of a free and open scientific community and the concomitant possibilities of increased social cooperation, on one side, and the values of privacy and property (i.e., intellectual property) as individual rights on the other side.

However, there is still another sense in which these two values conflict here. In addition to the problem of inadvertent disclosure of researchers' thoughts or results and unauthorized access to their communication, there are cases where the normative demand for full and free sharing of information among scientists stands in tension with the demand for research privacy and the denial of such access to other researchers. Clearly, there is a need for some ethical guideline for determining the demarcation between these two positive values.

There is another major benefit of networking in science and engineering, namely, one that concerns the value of equality. This is the fact that the network provides for the widest distribution of resources for research. Equality as a value in the democratic republic of science means that one is not disadvantaged in access to resources by the accidents of location or financial ability. The network, by making access independent of geographical location, and by minimizing by several orders of magnitude the unit costs of information, computation, and communication, can radically increase the degree of equality of access to scientific resources. However, the actualization of these potentialities for equal access will depend on the allocation of computer network resources and on criteria for priorities of access. For in the short term, at any rate, these network facilities will be a relatively scarce resource, at least in the financial sense that not all prospective users will be able to afford the costs, and hence there will inevitably be differential, rather than equal, access. In their recent article, previously cited, Jennings et al. write about the ARPANET experience as follows:

The major lesson from the ARPANET experience is that information sharing is a key benefit of computer networking. Indeed it may be argued that many major advances in computer systems and artificial intelligence are the direct result of the enhanced collaboration made possible by ARPANET.

However, ARPANET also had the negative effect of creating a have-have not situation in experimental computer research. Scientists and engineers carrying out such research at institutions other than the twenty or so ARPANET sites were at a clear disadvantage in accessing pertinent technical information and in attracting faculty and students.[4]

This financial limitation on equal access to informational and computational facilities is compounded by another limitation, namely, that of social utility as a criterion for differential allocation of network access. That is to say, the funding of research or even the selection among funded projects may depend upon decisions as to which projects are most important from the point of view of their satisfaction of either national, industrial, or scientific needs. Thus, for example, government funding of networking and of research using networks would be based on what are seen as national priorities; the major wide-area network ARPANET was originally developed as a Department of Defense research project. NSFnet, on the other hand, has as a major consideration of social utility the development of basic research in the sciences themselves. In the industrial case, the market is supposed to serve as the means of determining relative social utilities. Even in the case of university research, however, major university centers that command larger financial resources, whether of endowment or funding, generally will also enjoy significantly greater access to expensive network facilities. Ethical guidelines for policy in the allocation of

university funding by government agencies,
therefore, would have to take into account the
trade-off between equalizing access for the
smaller or financially weaker universities and
the value of building on the strengths of
existing facilities or on perceptions of past
achievement.

Yet another criterion that may enter into
considerations of limiting access is that of
the relative competence of researchers, which
enters into judgments about the feasibility of
their proposed research. That is, the relative social or scientific utility of a project
may be judged in large part on the basis of
the reputation of the researchers and on the
expectation that the proposed results will
therefore be forthcoming. In these various
ways, a conflict emerges between the ethical
and intellectual value of fully equal access
to computer networks, on one hand, and the
social utility of the use of networks, which
suggests unequal allocation of what is seen as
a scarce resource, on the other hand. Thus
the question of access to networks, and thus
to informational, computational, and communi-
cational resources, can be framed as an ethical question concerning competing views of
distributive justice.

The Context of Government and Politics

The conflict of values in the scientific
use of computer networking has its counterpart
in the arena of political life. Here, the
greatly enhanced social cooperation and political interaction that would be afforded by
prospective computerization and networking of
citizen-government interaction (as well as
citizen-citizen interaction) should lead to a
wide development of democratic participation
in decision-making and thus to a realization
of the democratic ideal itself. However, this
same technology may also permit more effective
electronic manipulation of voter opinion and
may lead to violations of privacy on a large
scale. Even in the present situation, the
threat of violations of personal privacy and

freedom by government agencies is raised by proposals to combine existing government data-banks (e.g., social security, tax, and crime) in a single network (in the interests of increased efficiency and cooperation among government agencies). Such a proposal has been blocked by Congress in the past, but it may well come up again.

Some of the proposed uses of computer networking in relations between citizens and the government or among citizens themselves may be reviewed briefly here. One such development is the use of interactive computer-based communications systems, in which citizens can be electronically polled on various political issues. An example of such a networked system utilizing cable television outlets is the QUBE system, which was tested in Columbus, Ohio. Another example is the prospective development of an interactive computer network that would link representatives and their constituents, which would make possible direct and immediate communication between these parties and permit consultation with constituents in any geographical location. It may be argued that such communication is already possible by telephone, by mail, or by personal travel. But what makes the networking case distinctive is the extraordinary increase in both the scale and the speed of such interactions, such that they could become a routine part of representative government, as well as the immediate access to relevant background information that would becom possible. An operational example of such an interactive system was the so-called Constitutional Network set up for use in the 1978 Hawaii Constitutional Convention. This system involved the use of computer conferencing and polling to permit the citizens to be in frequent and direct contact with the delegates to the convention.[5] Another example is the congressional pilot project, in which constituents in five House districts can communicate directly to their representatives' electronic mailboxes through their home computers.[6] Still another use of networking that has been proposed is the development of computer conferencing for the purpose of democratic participation on the town-meeting model, in which groups of citizens can engage directly with one another in political deliberation and decision-making. Related to this is the proposed use of computer conferencing or other interactive communications to facilitate referenda on questions which could be put to citizens for their immediate response. On a more modest scale, computer networking opens up possibilities for the development of interest groups, which, through this means of organization, could expand their political activity and engage in grass-roots lobbying. This range of applications of computer networking, together with other uses of telecommunications to facilitate democratic decision-making, has given rise to the phrase "electronic democracy" in the current literature.[7]

It has also been suggested that networked systems may be used to disseminate information to citizens or to make it accessible to them at will. This would involve a vast increase in the accessibility of currently available data, such as the Congressional Record and other government publications.[8] Computer networks are also being used within government agencies, not only to provide information but also to increase coordination between levels of government. Such networks are coming into increasing use among law enforcement agencies at the national, state, and municipal levels, as well as in other kinds of agencies (e.g., the U.S. Weather Service). It has also been proposed that such network uses be extended to regulatory agencies. Such a system would permit central monitoring of the applications of regulatory policies in local contexts concerning questions of compliance, violations, and effectiveness. All of these ways in which government agencies manage and use information presumably contribute to the effectiveness and efficiency of the government in serving its citizens. But they also raise serious ethical questions concerning what sorts of information about citizens the government should collect,

what uses should be made of it, and who controls or regulates such information and its
uses.

In this brief summary, I have mainly
discussed prospective uses of computer networking and their potential impact in increasing democratic participation and interaction
between citizens and their representatives.
All this points to positive outcomes of such
technology. However, in the recent literature
on "electronic democracy" (most of which does
not deal with computer networking per se but
with other forms of telecommunication), a number of reservations have been voiced about the
effects of this technology on democratic processes and on its actual and potential misuses. One general point is that the technology taken by itself does not determine whether
its political effects are to enhance wider
citizen participation in democratic decision-
making or, on the contrary, to limit it and
increase the power of political bureaucracies.
In his article "Technology and the Federal
System," William Dutton writes:

> Dramatic visions of the political impacts
> of computers and telecommunications make
> useful rhetorical devices. However, the
> effects of technological change remain
> constrained by the social, political,
> economic, and historical contexts of
> American governance. If viewed as one
> aspect of a larger and more complex
> social setting, the impacts of changing
> technology on the federal system should
> be seen as marginal, subtle, often
> countervailing, and unlike the sweeping
> visions that blame national centraliza-
> tion or decentralization on the develop-
> ment of an electronic communications
> network.[9]

Dutton goes on to argue that "the new technologies have reinforced the ascendance of professional managers and information elites."[10]
Thus the effect would seem to be the further
bureaucratization rather than the democratiza-

tion of the political process.

Similarly, it has been pointed out (e.g., in the Aspen Institute Conference report) that many of the current uses of the new technology are a top-down or one-way communication from representatives to constituents and that in their use of this technology, "many congressional offices are little more than reelection organizations run at government expense."[11] The same report goes on to observe that the primary effect of the new communications technology in the context of political interest groups has not been to recruit citizens to active participation but rather simply to mobilize citizens to carry out agendas set by the leaders of such groups. The Aspen report proposes that an important policy question to be addressed is

> how technological resources could be allocated to enhance the public's involvement in politics. Neither government nor special interests have invested heavily in uses of computers and telecommunications designed to enable ordinary Americans to play a larger political role. Society's resources have been concentrated on building one-way downward communication systems and creating a small class of information specialists rather than in developing a technologically "literate" population and establishing two-way horizontal and vertical communication systems. The latter arrangement, of course, would cost much more and take longer to develop than the arrangement that is in place.[12]

These reservations and qualms about "electronic democracy" suggest a general value consideration with respect to the use of computer networking in interactive, or in polling, contexts: Should the technology be used in a merely instrumental way to manipulate opinion or to elicit response with respect to questions or policies already formulated in a top-down way? Or instead, should the technol-

ogy be used in a way that permits the citizens
not only to respond to but to formulate the
questions and not only to react to an agenda
set by others (e.g., in public opinion polls)
but to play an active role in setting the
agenda themselves?[13]

These are, in fact, rhetorical questions
since they presuppose a norm of increased
democratic participation, which defines the
good of political practice. This suggests
that the implementation of computer networking
in citizen-government contexts needs to be
guided by such a norm, for as we have seen,
the technology itself can go either way. This
norm also suggests that whatever the political
values may be of leadership by experts, managerial efficiency in government, and coherent
public support for government policies, these
are to be subordinated to the value of the
widest democratic participation.[14]

Even in its positive implications in
realizing the norm of greater democracy,
computer networking gives rise to a set of
distinctive ethical issues. Some of these
issues arise out of the conflict of values
between the increase in opportunities for
participation and cooperation in political
life, on the one hand, and the rights of privacy and confidentiality which may be in-
fringed by the uses of this technology, on the
other. Thus it would seem that the realization of one value is at the expense of the
other. It is the special feature of combining
computerized data with communication networks
that creates the problem here. For example,
in the case of government databanks--for
taxes, social security, and law enforce-
ment--it would seem prima facie plausible that
networking these databanks would lead to an
increase in efficiency that would benefit all
the citizens and would facilitate cooperation
among government agencies. Yet it is this
very efficiency of centralization that has
been seen as posing a most serious threat to
the rights of individuals. Again, in the
particular uses of computer networking described earlier--where there is interaction

between political representatives and their constituents via the network, or where there is electronic polling or referenda--the benefits of enhanced democracy entail the risks of violations of the confidentiality of political expression, inasmuch as information about the political choices that individuals make may be accessible through the network to unauthorized snooping. Protection of privacy of expression in these circumstances is technologically very difficult and prospectively very expensive.

The relation between the technology and its social and ethical impact can therefore be studied in terms of how alternative models of the organization of network use or the management of computer conferencing either satisfy or fail to satisfy the joint ethical desiderata of democratic participation and individual privacy. In this connection, it would be important to consider how alternative group decision procedures map onto alternative network conferencing structures; that is, how aggregative decision procedures may be organized to maximize democratic participation. Just as in parliamentary procedures, rules of order, such as Roberts' Rules, serve to structure democratic and fair participation in debate and decision-making, so for interactive discussion and decision-making procedures using computer networks, something like a Roberts' Rules of order for electronic meetings would be necessary.

A second ethical issue that arises in these particular uses of computer networking concerns the possibilities of manipulating information through a network so as to affect opinion in unauthorized and undetectable ways. Just as the network technology makes possible wide access to information and cooperation among users, it is also vulnerable to computer fraud and to what we may call computer forgery. That is, information in a network can be more easily tampered with or changed without being detected than is the case with the mail or the telephone, so that false or deceptive information can be substituted without the knowledge of the recipients or users. In

the political context, this could make possible the perpetration of political fraud and
interference through tampering with polls,
referenda, and the information being communicated. Clearly, ethical questions arise here
concerning coercion, deception, and fraud, as
well as evasion of responsibility for actions.
Furthermore, certain programs for the organization of network use would permit centralized
control of information and its communication
and therefore would invest great political
power in whoever could exercise such control.
A similar problem of centralized control
arises in the case of large government databanks, in which personal information, if not
properly protected, can be used for purposes
of manipulation, coercion, or political
blackmail.

The third area in which ethical issues
arise in these contexts is that of the distribution of access to computer networks.
This bears on the values of equality and
justice. In a society in which information
becomes a major commodity and which has been
called "the knowledge society," the availability of or accessibility to information becomes
a condition for competent participation in
political life and for the ability to utilize
social resources. As networking proliferates,
access to computers and to networks becomes an
important requirement for democratic equality.
It would be possible then to speak of informational poverty or deprivation for those who do
not have means of access to the databanks or
information resources on which an increasingly
computerized society will rely. The ethical
issues here concern equal rights of access to
information and justice in the distribution of
social and technological resources.

Similarly, where networks are used for
interactive decision-making or for polling,
lack of access to the system can skew the
results and give unfair advantage to those who
have such access. An example of this took
place in the use of the QUBE system in
Columbus, Ohio, in which the QUBE audience was
polled by the city government on the question

of whether the citizens would be willing to
pay more taxes for better city services, in
view of the fact that there were many complaints concerning the lack of such services
(e.g., snow removal) in certain areas of the
city. Because the QUBE system was distributed
principally in the more affluent areas, which
were already well served, the QUBE vote went
against the proposal. As one former resident
put it, this served to subvert the electoral
process. In this way, the use of the QUBE
cable network ostensibly to increase political
participation in fact resulted in an undemo-
cratic procedure because of the unequal access
to the system.[15]

Two Ethical Principles
for Computer Networking: A Proposal

One way to approach such a conflict of
values would be simply to admit that there is
an endemic and ultimately irreconcilable conflict between mutually exclusive claims of
individual rights and social goods. According
to this view, the only way to handle such a
conflict is to adjudicate specific cases on an
ad hoc basis, with no further or higher principle that can be appealed to in order to
guide the choice other than the practical requirement to come to a decision (or to fore-
stall one) so as to keep things going. This
is not the approach I am proposing. Rather, I
suggest two principles that can serve to guide
decisions and thus to help resolve the appar-
rent conflict between social and individual
values in the computer-networking cases we
have examined. These are the principles of
free and informed consent and equal access to
information. I will discuss these shortly.
However, these principles themselves may be
seen to be normatively grounded in a wider
philosophical framework in which the conflict
between the individual and the social is re-
solvable. I will briefly note this framework
here, having discussed it at length in other
writings.[16]

This philosophical framework may be characterized as a social ontology; that is, as a theory of the nature of social reality, which takes the fundamental entities that make up social life to be individuals in relations, where these individuals are understood to be agents, that is, capable of deliberation and free choice, and where their relations are social relations that partly constitute these individuals as who they are. For example, scientists, in this view, would be understood as being in the first instance as particular individuals who carry out their projects through the exercise of their individual agency and deliberation. At the same time, what makes them scientists, and thus constitutes them in part as who they are, is their relations to other scientists and to the institution and practice of science--that is, a social relation in which they are recognized as scientists and in which they engage in a common activity with others. More generally, such individuals, beyond the context of their scientific identity, both have projects and choices of their own and need to realize these in social interaction with others.

This social ontology has as its ethical import first of all that the essential individual agency and capacity for free choice that characterizes all human beings as human needs to be protected by individual rights, which include those of privacy and of property (understood as a right to the conditions for exercising one's agency), among other rights. Second, since a principal condition for the exercise of individual agency is sociality and, thus, the opportunity for cooperation and for participation in common activity with others, the social good does not stand in inherent opposition to individual good but rather can complement it. In this framework, there is no endemic contradiction between the protection of individual rights and the value of social cooperation. The idea that there is a necessary conflict between individual and social values arises from a contrary view of individuals in which they are taken as funda-

mentally isolated, asocial beings whose relations with one another are essentially anta-
gonistic.

The social ontology that I have sketched
as a general theory of the nature of social
reality and of individuals-in-relations thus
points to how the apparent value conflicts
between individuality and sociality can be
resolved on an abstract theoretical level.
This does not yet show how such a theory can
be interpreted for the concrete situations
that I have considered in the context of computer networking. The task here is to provide
principles that can serve as heuristic guides
in applied cases of value conflict. One such
principle, as noted earlier, is that of free
and informed consent. This principle has been
developed as an ethical guideline for other
contexts, especially those of medical treatment and of experimentation with human subjects, as a principle safeguarding the individual rights and freedom from coercion of the
clinical and experimental subjects. However,
it has not been applied to the case of the
protection of privacy as an individual right,
either generally or in the specific context of
computers and computer networking.

The Right to Privacy

In order to understand what this right is
that needs protection, we may begin with a
brief analysis of the nature of privacy. It
is clear that privacy is a major ethical
question in the domain of computer networking
and of databanks. The questions here are:
What kind of an ethical question is it? And
what are the grounds for privacy as a value or
as a right? There is an extensive discussion
about the general nature of privacy and of the
right to privacy in the contexts of both law
and moral philosophy, and there is also an
extensive literature on the threats to privacy
posed by computer databanks. Space does not
allow for a full treatment of these legal,
ethical, and security questions in this chapter. But it may be helpful to briefly summar-

ize   some of the alternative interpretations
of the right to privacy and its foundations.

In the law, privacy has been interpreted
in tort law as a right to control information
about oneself. It has also been seen to have
a basis in constitutional law as implicit in
the First and Fourth Amendments which protect
individuals against unwarranted intrusions by
the government. Similarly, the Ninth and
Fourteenth Amendments, as well as the idea of
"penumbras" associated with specific guaran-
tees in the Bill of Rights, have also been
interpreted as protecting privacy. Of these
constitutional protections, only the Fourth
Amendment has been applied explicitly as a
protection against invasions of informational
privacy, specifically, in the case of wiretap-
ping. The others have been applied primarily
to decisions relating to privacy interpreted
in terms of domestic life and to questions
concerning the rights to one's body. In addition, there are explicit statutory protections of informational privacy, most notably
in the Fair Credit Reporting Act of 1971, the
Family Educational Rights and Privacy Act
(1974), and the Privacy Act of 1974, which
relates to the protection of privacy in the
keeping and use of government records. At
present, federal legislation concerning the
protection of privacy of digital communication, such as electronic mail, is under consideration. Thus the law does not present a
uniform and coherent approach to privacy protection, but rather, a variety of different
approaches and a situation of flux.

Likewise, the philosophical discussion of
the concept of privacy and of its moral foundation has been intense over the past decade.
Among these various analyses of the concept,
some have seen it as reducible to or derivable
from other rights taken as more basic, such as
property rights or rights of bodily security.[17] Others, by contrast, have seen privacy
as itself an irreducible right, not derivable
from other rights. In one such approach, privacy has been defined narrowly as "the condition of not having undocumented personal

knowledge about one possessed by others."[18] Alternatively, the right of privacy has been interpreted more broadly as a requirement for the development of interpersonal relations of love, friendship, and trust, which are taken to be essential to being human;[19] or as a social practice or ritual by means of which the social group recognizes an individual's existence as his or her own.[20] Other views conceive the right of privacy in relation to individual liberty or personal autonomy, in which it is a condition for the exercise of such values.[21]

Without entering into any discussion or criticism of these philosophical views here, I simply want to suggest that one of the main grounds for the value of privacy is that it serves as a condition for freedom in the exercise of one's agency in individual projects or in various forms of social relations; for privacy provides the protection of that psychic space required for individual reflection and deliberation, which is necessary for the rational exercise of an individual's agency. The freedom realized in the course of such individual and social activity is understood as self-development, that is, as the positive freedom to realize one's projects or purposes--and not only as negative freedom or freedom from external constraint. Moreover, the right to privacy allows one to choose whether others will be permitted or invited to share in one's activity or in one's deliberations. In this sense, privacy is a protection against unwanted imposition or coercion by others and thus a protection of one's freedom of action. In linking the value of privacy with that of freedom, I would suggest that the recent legal effort to discern a constitutional basis for privacy rights in the penumbra of the Bill of Rights is an appropriate move on both legal and philosophical grounds.

Apart from the issue of what the moral basis is for the right to privacy, it seems clear that an essential aspect of its meaning is the right to control information about oneself. This brings us directly to the ways

in which the right of privacy is centrally
involved in the development of computer technology and, in particular, of computer networking. The right to privacy interpreted as
the right to control information about oneself
is most obviously open to violation in the
context of databanks, where, as noted earlier,
personal information is stored. With the
development of networking, it becomes possible
to link the information from various databanks
and, as a number of critics have pointed out,
to form composite portraits of individuals
from information concerning banking and
credit, health, telephone records, travel
records, and so on. In this way, it is possible to create a dossier on a given individual that even tracks his or her personal and
professional life dynamically through time.
Though each particular type and piece of
information may be by itself relatively innocent and voluntarily given, the compilation of
all of these together may yield a composite
picture that the individual has not knowingly
or willingly consented to give. In this way,
individuals lose control over information
about themselves, and their privacy is system-
atically violated in ways of which they are
not even aware. Such dossiers are already
being compiled by various organizations and
for various purposes in both the public and
the private sector. As David Chaum puts it in
a recent article on systems designed to protect privacy against such intrusions, "The
foundation is being laid for a dossier
society, in which computers could be used to
infer individuals' life-styles, habits, where-
abouts, and associations from data collected
in ordinary consumer transactions."[22]

So too, in the potential uses of computer
networking in polling or in other interactive
political contexts, anonymity of political
opinion as a privacy right to control information about one's views can be violated through
snooping or undercover surveillance. The government's past record in this area has come
under sharp criticism and scrutiny by congressional oversight committees. For covert sur-

veillance of the political views of American
citizens was carried out by a number of federal agencies in the name of national security, in direct contravention of constitutional
protections.

The violation of informational privacy is
also likely to become an issue with the proliferation of the uses of computer networking
in scientific research. Here the information
to be protected is not personal in the previous senses, but concerns the personal research activity and scientific ideas and
results of the individuals who use such networks as research instruments and as a means
of communication with other scientists. The
threat here involves those violations of the
scientific ethos which we noted earlier, such
as fraud, plagiarism, and malicious tampering
with network information.

The Principle of Free and Informed Consent

The protection of informational privacy
requires a principle to serve as a guideline
in both the practices and the structuring of
institutions with respect to computer networking as well as in the use of computers
more generally. The principle that would
satisfy these requirements is that of free and
informed consent, or informed consent for
short. The principle may be stated in a first
approximation as follows: No personal information about an individual may be acquired by
any other person or organization, or stored or
transmitted or any other use made thereof,
without the free and informed consent of that
individual. By free consent is meant consent
given without any force or coercion or threat
of such force or coercion. Furthermore, consent is informed when clear and complete information is openly given concerning the fact
of the acquisition of such information, and of
its storage, transmission, and all uses or
purposes to which it will be put. This condition is a very strong one, but with appropriate interpretation, it may be seen to be
feasible. It might be objected that at the

time a person is asked to give informed consent there can be no complete account of all
the uses to which the information might be put
in the future, but only those uses that are
already planned. However, fully informed
consent can be preserved if a person's consent
is required prior to any new or unanticipated
use of the information.

This informed consent principle, as a
protection of informational privacy, is an
alternative to weaker protections that either
now exist or have been proposed. The most
common form of such protection is the right of
individuals under the Privacy Act of 1974 to
be notified, upon their request to a government agency, as to whether there exist any
records of personal information on them, and
the further right to have access to these
records and to be able to correct or amend
them. The act also requires the agency to
obtain prior approval from the individual for
any nonroutine use or transmission of such
records. Despite the fact that this act provides penalties for failure to comply, it has
not been effectively implemented in several
respects. Apart from this, its main weakness
is that it requires the initiative of individuals to request such information about their
records and, indeed, to find out which organizations are keeping records on them.

An alternative, but still weak, principle
for the protection of informational privacy is
that proposed by Arthur Miller. It is what he
calls a principle of fiduciary obligation, as
applied to information handlers in whatever
context they may operate, whether public or
private. Miller characterizes it as "a human-
istic notion of good faith, fair dealing--to
the data subject. The information handler
owes the subject a duty of care to make sure
that the information is germane, that it is
current, and that it is verified."[23] This
puts the burden of protection of privacy
either entirely upon the thin reed of good
faith or upon legislation that would permit
suits to be brought against violators of such
good faith and penalties to be imposed upon

those violators.

The principle of informed consent, by contrast, imposes upon the institution or agency that has or wants the information the burden of seeking the consent of the subject and of informing him or her. Thus, the information remains under the control ab initio of the person whom it is about. Clearly, the implementation of an informed consent policy raises complex questions that will still need to be addressed. But such a discussion is beyond the scope of this chapter.

The question may be asked, however, as to what constitutes the general normative ground or justification for this principle of informed consent? The answer clearly is that the principle derives its force from its recognition of the freedom and autonomy of human beings as agents and, consequently, their right to participate in decisions that directly affect them in their person, either with respect to their well-being or to what belongs to them. As such, unless they freely consent to actions by others that affect them, such actions are impositions of the will or choices of others on these agents and thus delimit their freedom. Furthermore, because consent is blind in the absence of knowledge of the consequences or intentions of the actions to which the consent is being given, the effects of these actions remain outside the control of the agent and thus also delimit his or her freedom. While there may be no obligation to generate such knowledge for individuals, there is an obligation not to withhold it from them if it is available and relevant to their deliberation and choice. A general conceptual difficulty in the formulation of such a principle is where to draw the line between those actions by others which demand consent and those which do not, since, in a certain sense, the range of those actions by others that affect one personally is so wide and diffuse that a general and unlimited requirement would not be feasible. However, in practice, the principle is always applied in particular contexts that serve to suggest the limits of its applicability or feasibility.

The context in which the principle of free and informed consent has been most explicitly developed recently is that of medical treatment and experimentation with human subjects. Here it forms a cornerstone of contemporary medical ethics. In this regard, it concerns the patient's right to know the probable consequences of a procedure or treatment and to consent to such treatment without coercion or undue influence, to make an informed decision rather than to consent out of ignorance. Similarly, in the case of experimentation with human subjects, it is the probable or known effects and the degree of risk involved in the experiment that the subject has a right to know. Here again, consent has to be given without coercion.

Yet it may be objected that this case differs in principle from that of informed consent in informational contexts. For example, in the medical case, the consent is given with respect to actions that invade the privacy of one's body or that remove or make use of parts of one's body, which presumably belong to one exclusively. In the case of personal information, the consent does not seem to concern an action done to one (as, for example, a surgical procedure might be) or the use of a part of one's body or of something that belongs to one exclusively. Rather, it is consent to the obtaining and use of information about oneself. However, in this case too, the consent is required to preserve the right of privacy, not the privacy of one's body but of personal information, which, as in the case of the body, one has a right to control. And here too, knowledge concerning the risk involved in permitting the use of such information is also a condition for informed consent. It should be recalled here that what counts as personal information subject to informed consent includes not only databank records but the content of personal communications and one's own research activity, insofar as this information is accessible in networks

used for scientific research. Obviously, it
also includes the information about one's
opinions or political communications that may
be involved in the use of networks in citizen-
government interaction.

The discussion so far has emphasized the
nature of the principle of informed consent as
an ethical principle. As such, informed
consent can also serve as a guide for social
policy and for legislative safeguards for
informational privacy. However, it may also
serve as the goal to be achieved by means of
technical developments in the security of
systems. The aim of such a security system
would be to give individuals the technical
means for controlling information about themselves and for giving and withholding consent
to the use of such information. One such
proposal concerning security systems using
"digital signatures" is given in a recent
article by David Chaum.[24]

The Principle of Equal Access

A second major principle that should
serve as a normative guide for the resolution
of value conflicts in computer networking is
that of equal access to information and to
computer networks. This principle is grounded
first of all in the value of equality and in
the concomitant notion of equal rights. Here
the argument, which I will simply state but
not develop, is that all human beings have
prima facie equal rights to those conditions
that are required for their self-development,
or the concrete realization of their freedom.[25] This abstract idea has a particular
application in the contexts of our discussion.
The general ethical value of equality may be
interpreted here as a prima facie equal right
to information, inasmuch as access to information may be counted as one of the conditions
that are required for the carrying out of
individual or common projects. On one model,
one may say that information is a principal
capital good of production, whether such production is technological or purely cognitive.

In the specific case at hand, the value of equality is interpreted as justifying an equal right of access to information and the use of systems of computer networking.

Yet, the general equal right of access to information is subject to qualification on several grounds. First, the right of access to information is context-relative. That is, an equal right of access to the relevant data-bases and to the use of computer networking in scientific research is clearly a universally equal right not for just everyone but rather for those who are engaged in such research and who are in this sense competent to use the facility. Likewise, even in the wider context of citizen-government interaction, an equal right of access to the facilities is nevertheless limited to the relevant individuals, namely citizens, or the particular consti-tuency relative to some representative. Thus, one may say that the right of equal access is qualified by the relevance of the informa-tional access to a given community of users. Second, though it may be true that information itself is a conserved quantity through trans-formations--that is, the wider sharing of informational content or data does not require a proportional decrease in the amount of in-formation each one may have (that is, does not use it up), and thus the same information can be shared more widely without loss--neverthe-less, access to this information, as well as its storage and communication, does require means or channels, and these are commodities of relative scarcity. For even if the unit cost decreases rapidly with technological innovation, it is nevertheless a cost of some economic significance at present.

This suggests therefore that there is some need for principles of just distribution of access to this relatively scarce resource. The prima facie principle of justice here would be straight equality, in which case there would be less for everyone equally, with no differential or privileged access. Alter-natively, access might be differentially allo-cated in terms of the users of the resources that produce the greatest good or satisfy the widest social needs. In this case, there would have to be some criterion of the relative productivity of access. Obviously, this approach would lead to difficulties in determining who shall decide rights of access and how these priorities are to be arrived at. A third principle of distribution could be the simple market criterion of the ability to pay (or "them as has, gets"). But this principle would not satisfy the value of equality. Rather, it would simply carry over into the informational-computational domain those social inequalities of wealth or power that exist in the community at large.

What does such a principle of equal access to information and to computer networks imply for policy decisions that arise in the contexts of scientific research and citizen-government interaction? Without elaborating this issue here, one may suggest that the principle implies that there should be the widest possible distribution of rights of access in the face of those factors that tend to increase the inequalities and deny access to some who, though they meet the criteria of relevance and competence, do not have the ability to pay. Such economic disadvantage, whether of institutions or individuals, which prevent the fullest sharing of information and computational facilities, can be overcome through some degree of public subsidization of equal access. What would be required would be different in each case. For example, in the case of scientific research, what may be required is subsidization by federal or state agencies of the costs of joining or using the networks for those who are relatively financially disadvantaged in this respect (whether poor institutions or underpaid scientists). In another case, where participation in interactive computer networks becomes a condition for political participation in general, then equal access to the means of such communication is crucial. And just as voters who cannot get to the polls are entitled to receive help with means of transportation, so too, in interactive electronic democracy, there may be a need to subsidize the economically disadvantaged in order to insure their equal rights of participation (e.g., by having accessible centers for electronic polling or interactive communications, or by placing appropriate units for such networking in their homes).

Finally, a peculiar value conflict may arise in this regard. The principle of equal access to information might seem to justify access to personal information about other individuals, and hence violate the privacy right of such individuals. But one may respond to this as follows: Equal rights of access to information does not mean the same as rights of equal access to _all_ information. Specifically, the information that would be available under equality of access would be limited by privacy rights with regard to personal information.

Finally, if we take the two principles that I have introduced--namely, free and informed consent and equal access to information--and consider them in tandem, then I would claim that we have a normative guide for dealing with the value conflicts considered earlier in this chapter. Thus the guarantee that the values of social cooperation will not conflict, or will conflict minimally, with the values of individual privacy and property rights is a policy of free and informed consent by all those individuals who participate in networked activities concerning the uses of information about themselves; and a policy of equal access to information among those who interact reciprocally through informational networks. This last condition assures that one person is not disadvantaged with respect to another on the basis of inequalities of access to needed information. (What cannot be assured is that equal use will be made of the accessibility.) If these conditions are met, then the social cooperation that networking permits may in fact enhance individual liberties and self-development rather than conflict with them.

Thus, I conclude by proposing a general

principle of network ethics that is formed from the complementation of the two normative principles I have discussed. As a heuristic principle, it may be stated as follows: Maximum sharing of information and maximally equal access compatible with the preservation of the value of privacy, as protected by the requirement of free and informed consent.

Notes

1. Stanley Winkler, "The Quiet Revolution Revisited," Computer Networks 7 (June 1983), pp. 169-172.
2. Dennis M. Jennings et al., "Computer Networking for Scientists," Science 231 (28 February 1986), pp. 943-950.
3. Ibid., p. 943.
4. Ibid., pp. 945-946.
5. Starr Roxanne Hiltz and Murray Turoff, The Network Nation (Reading, MA: Addison-Wesley, 1978), pp. 199-201.
6. Thomas E. Patterson, "Toward New Research on Communication Technologies and the Democratic Process," Report of the Aspen Institute Conference on Communication Technologies and the Democratic Process, in Communications and Society Forum Report (New York: Aspen Institute, 1985).
7. Some of these uses of computers and of telecommunication in the context of democratic participation are discussed in Benjamin Barber, Strong Democracy (Berkeley: University of California Press, 1984), pp. 273-278; and Alvin Toffler, The Third Wave (New York: Morrow, 1980).
8. Cf. Michael Margolis, Viable Democracy (Middlesex, England: Penguin Books, 1979), pp. 158-170.
9. William Dutton, "Technology and the Federal System," Proceedings of the Academy of Political Science 34, no. 4 (1982), p. 111.

34

10. Ibid., p. 119.

11. Norman Ornstein, cited in Thomas Patterson, "Toward New Research on Communication Technologies and the Democratic Process," p. 4.

12. Ibid., pp. 10-11.

13. Ibid., p. 4. Cf. also C. B. Macpherson, The Life and Times of Liberal Democracy (Oxford: Oxford University Press, 1977).

14. This is not to say that democratic participation is the supreme value. For its authority may be overriden when it is in violation of certain fundamental rights. For further discussion of this, see Carol Gould, Rethinking Democracy: Freedom and Social Cooperation in Politics, Economy, and Society (Cambridge: Cambridge University Press, 1988).

15. Personal communication from Devon M. Thein and Gary L. Thein, (20 January 1985).

16. Cf. Carol Gould, Rethinking Democracy: Freedom and Social Cooperation in Politics, Economy, and Society; and Marx's Social Ontology: Individuality and Community in Marx's Theory of Social Reality (Cambridge, MA: The MIT Press, 1978).

17. Judith Thomson, "The Right to Privacy," Philosophy and Public Affairs 4, no. 4 (Summer 1975), pp. 295-314.

18. William A. Parent, "Privacy, Morality and the Law," Philosophy and Public Affairs 12, no. 4 (Fall 1983), p. 269.

19. Charles Fried, An Anatomy of Values: Problems of Personal and Social Choice (Cambridge, MA: Harvard University Press, 1970), Chapter 9. A related conception is developed by James Rachels, "Why Privacy Is Important," Philosophy and Public Affairs 4, no. 4 (Summer 1975), pp. 323-333.

20. Jeffrey H. Reiman, "Privacy, Intimacy, and Personhood," Philosophy and Public Affairs 6, no. 1 (1976), pp. 26-44.

21. Cf. Stanley I. Benn, "Privacy, Freedom, and Respect for Persons," in J. R. Pennock and J. Chapman, eds., Privacy (New York: Lieber-Atherton Publishers, 1971); Alan Westin, Privacy and Freedom (New York:

Atheneum, 1967).

22.   David   Chaum,   "Security   Without
Identification: Transaction Systems   to Make
Big   Brother   Obsolete," Communications of the
ACM 21, no. 10 (October 1985), p. 1030.

23.   Arthur   Miller,   "Computers   and
Privacy," in W. Michael Hoffman and Jennifer
Mills Moore,   eds., Ethics and the Management
of Computer   Technology   (Cambridge,   MA:
Oelgeschlager, Gunn & Hain, 1982), p. 106.

24.   David   Chaum,   "Security Without
Identification."

25. This principle is developed at length
in my Rethinking Democracy: Freedom and Social
Cooperation in Politics, Economy, and Society.

2

The Public-Private Status of Transactions in Computer Networks

Deborah G. Johnson

The ubiquity of computers has been noted many times, along with comments and cautions about the social impact of such widespread use of computers. More often than not these social commentaries lump together a broad range of uses of computers and fail to distinguish effects resulting exclusively from the use of computers from those that result from a con-glomeration of forces that were at work in our society long before the advent of computers. Little has yet been written specifically about the social implications of computer network-ing, though this capability (a more recent technical development) enormously magnifies the scope of computer usage.

Tanenbaum has defined a computer network as an interconnected collection of autonomous computers. Computers are connected if they are capable of exchanging information.[1] The exchange of information may involve data of various kinds stored in a database. It may involve access to programs, or it may involve the communication of thoughts and ideas of persons as they occur. Although the defini-tion is simple and straightforward, the range of possibilities of kinds of networks is extremely broad and complex. The variations involve a number of variables, including types and numbers of users, types and numbers of machines, and types and quantities of infor-mation. In addition, there are a variety of configurations for exchanges, with information flowing in complex patterns. These patterns have received a good deal of attention in the technical literature on networking, as the possibilities are built into the software and hardware.[2]

Though the analysis has much broader implications (even beyond networking), the focus in this chapter will be on computer conferencing--a form of networking involving direct communication of thoughts and ideas among individuals. My aim is to contribute to our understanding of the ethical implications of networking by examining one of the conceptual muddles surrounding computers, namely the distinction between private and public. However, in the first part of the chapter I will hardly mention networking. Rather, I will try to understand just how computers, and other new technologies, create moral puzzles or raise seemingly new moral questions and how these moral issues come to be resolved. In the second part of the chapter, with a framework in hand for understanding the ethical issues raised by computers, I will argue the following points about conferencing: (1) the public-private status of communications within computer conferences is very unclear at present; (2) clarifying the status of such communications may be difficult because the public-private status of comparable noncomputerized communications is often unclear; (3) the values at stake in computer conferencing are dependent on the context, as is the importance of privacy; and (4) it would be good, in general, to require the informed consent of participants in computer conferences to the public-private status of these conferences.

A Framework for Computer Ethics

Recent work in computer ethics, as well as in other fields of applied ethics, has frequently elicited a question about the uniqueness of the issues raised. Are not the moral issues posed by computers really just the same old moral problems, involving power,

privacy, property, and conflicting obligations, interests, and ideals? The question
can easily be proffered about most new technologies. Don't new medical technologies and
nuclear power, for example, really just raise
the same old problems in new forms? What is
the value of human life? How can we balance
one life against another? How can we balance
increased risk against other goods? To be
sure, with or without computers, social life
creates complex situations involving rights of
privacy, rights to property, and access to
power. Computers may simply aggravate old and
already troublesome moral dilemmas.

This question about the uniqueness of
issues raised by new technologies has a kind
of nagging persistence. In the case of computers, the issues seem unique in some senses
and not in others. For example, computer programs have never existed before, and the particular problems involved in trying to prevent
infringement of the proprietary rights of program creators are new. On the other hand, the
issues do not seem to be fundamentally different than for other technologies. Copyright,
trade secret, and patent law are filled with
examples of inventions that are difficult to
protect because they pose both practical as
well as conceptual problems. Likewise, protection of personal privacy is an age-old
problem, and although computers make new kinds
of intrusions possible, these particular
threats to personal privacy are just additions
to a long series that has included the
development of printing technologies, photo-
graphy, and telephones.

Perhaps the question itself--about the
uniqueness of issues raised by new tech-
nologies--will seem odd to some in that an
account of how new technologies pose new moral
problems seems somewhat obvious. New technologies create new possibilities for events
to occur that could not have occurred before
(e.g., nuclear holocaust), new possibilities
for systems to be put in place which could not
have been put in place before (e.g., connecting all government databases for purposes of

surveillance), and new possibilities for individual actions that were not open to individuals before (e.g., I can now give away my
organs for transplantation when I die; I can
now press a button on my home computer and, by
using my finger in this way, buy something,
send a message to someone, create a work of
art, destroy something, etc.).[3] These new
possibilities need, then, to be evaluated
morally and as such might be thought to raise
"new" moral questions.

This account seems quite accurate and I
do not want to deny it. In keeping with this
picture, James Moor has suggested that computer ethics is needed because computers
create a vacuum.[4] Moor argued that there is a
vacuum in the sense that there are no rules,
conventions, or policies with regard to the
new possibilities. On one hand, there often
does seem to be a gap in our understanding of
how we should behave with regard to computers
and other new technologies: Should I copy
this piece of software? Should I treat communications that take place in a network as
confidential? Should I give my organs for
transplanting?

On the other hand, there is something
misleading or lacking in this picture of computer ethics. For one thing, it emphasizes
the character of the solution, not of the
problem. It suggests that we are lacking a
remedy, that is, rules or conventions about
how to behave. In this respect, this approach
does not give us a sense of the nature of the
problem and how we are to decide upon specific
rules to cover these new problems. Moreover,
in most of the situations created by the use
of computers, although there may be a vacuum
in the sense of no explicit or agreed-upon
specific rules, rarely is there a vacuum in
any other sense. Rather, there seems to be
confusion from mixed signals and a graying or
blurring of acknowledged moral rights, obligations, or responsibilities. This is so
because most of the actions, transactions, or
relationships that take place by or on computers were carried on in some form before

computers. Information about individuals was
gathered and exchanged, individuals communicated with one another via a variety of
mechanisms, and tools and techniques for
solving problems were bought and sold. Conventions, rules, and laws applying to these
noncomputerized transactions and relationships
are generally known, though individuals are
often not aware of, or have not thought much
about, the higher order moral principles on
which this these rules are based. The introduction
of computers to mediate or facilitate these
transactions and relationships may make the
old rules obsolete, but the moral principles
reflected in these rules rarely become obsolete. The simplest example to illustrate this
point is the case of computer crime. Everyone
knows that it is illegal to physically break
into someone's office, open a locked file
cabinet, and read what is there, but the laws
prohibiting this type of action do not explicitly address online, unauthorized access to
files. It might be true to say that we need a
new law here (and in this sense there is a
vacuum), but it would be a mistake to jump to
the conclusion that we find ourselves in a
moral desert, and need a whole new "ethics" or
a whole new set of moral principles. The
general moral principles that applied before
still apply. And, in this particular case, it
is not all that difficult to figure out how
they apply to the "new," online situation.
Breaking into a file cabinet and breaking into
a computer file are roughly comparable.
     Most situations created by the use of
computers seem, then, not to be generically
new, but rather to be new species. For example, when it comes to the privacy of computerized records, we have to say that records
were kept and individuals had relationships
with information-gathering bureaucracies long
before computers existed. In the case of computer conferencing, too, communications of the
generic kind that take place in a network took
place before computers. The scale may change
and this in turn may change the meaning or
implication of an individual transaction such

that the rules need to be changed, but the
point is that the issues posed by computerization are not generically new.

So, Moor's account is right in identifying what is needed to resolve many of the
moral issues raised by computers, but his
account is wrong insofar as he means to suggest that there is a moral vacuum in the context in which computers are used. Situations
created by the use of computers are often
morally perplexing, but this is so not because
we find a moral vacuum, but rather because we
have not yet figured out how our norms and
values apply to the new details of the computer situation.

I do not mean to suggest that the moral
puzzles created by the use of computers are
easy to solve. Indeed, they are often very
difficult problems. Rather, the point here is
to try to understand just how or why the
issues arise and why they may be difficult to
solve. The process by which we arrive at conventions, rules, and laws for new technologies
involves uncovering the generic nature of the
situation, identifying the values at stake and
the principles that apply, and then fitting
rules to the special details of the new technology. Moreover, we often look at how we
have worked out the generic problem in similar
situations--in other species, so to speak. So,
for example, in trying to arrive at privacy
rules for computer use, we might look at how
we have dealt with privacy and telephones, or
in working out rules for the ownership of programs, we might look at how we have handled
proprietary rights to other types of invention, and so on.

When we look to the familiar cases to
help us figure out the new species, sometimes
we find help and sometimes not. Often, that
is, the rules or conventions we have established in the noncomputer case are muddled.
The rules may not be clearly formulated, formalized, or widely known, or the rationale for
the rules may not be well understood. Indeed,
the computerization of a particular activity
often forces us to clarify and formalize norms

that were only vaguely understood or acknowledged before. A good example of this type of situation is privacy and medical records. The public-private status of these records was not nearly so well defined until computerization of recordkeeping. It is not that noncomputerized medical records had no public-private status, but rather that there was not as great a need to formalize this status because the possibilities for exchange were limited.

We look to the rules we have developed in other cases both to maintain some kind of consistency in the principles we apply as well as to find a model for how, practically, to achieve certain norms and to balance conflicting values in the new species. However, in doing this, it might be argued, we reinforce the status quo. That is, in patterning the rules for the new technology on the model of old technologies, the process might be said to be inherently conservative. Although there is some truth to this objection, I believe that the opportunity to make change is created, if for no other reason than that the process involves attention to fundamental values and ideals, or general moral norms. Protecting these values and realizing these norms, rather than simply being consistent with past solutions, becomes our aim in creating rules for the new technology. So, for example, if a question were to arise about the just distribution of computers in our society, the question would call upon us to look at how we have distributed other technologies, as well as to look at our ideals of justice and equality of access, past experience with these other technologies might provide a model of how to distribute computers fairly or point to pitfalls to be avoided. That is, we might find that past solutions have not achieved what was aimed for, and so we have the opportunity with the new technology to create rules that come closer to realizing our moral norms and ideals.

The important point for our purposes here is not to decide whether or not the process is conservative but simply to understand that in creating rules or laws for a new technology, we can and should look at the values and norms that we believe in and consider how they apply to situations in which technology will play a role. Then, we can and should look at other species of the situation and examine how we have interpreted or balanced our norms and values in these cases. In the case of computer networking, we have to look at the moral norms and values at stake in establishing certain rules and determine how we have interpreted these norms and balanced these values in noncomputerized species of the generic situation.

Applying the Framework
to Computer Conferencing

The process by which new technologies are assimilated into a society seems to involve at least two fundamental stages. First, there is what might be called a transition period, during which conceptual and moral puzzles arise and there is a need for explication of specific rules, conventions, or laws to tell us how to behave with regard to the new technology. This stage is probably one that we are still in with regard to computer networking. The second stage is the period after we have finally digested the new technology and have developed (formally and/or informally) fairly clear rules of behavior. The first stage, or transition period, is important because it determines how the technology becomes integrated and how it does or does not get used. This stage is also the most interesting one from a philosophical perspective because the conceptual and moral puzzles created by new technologies, as has already been suggested, often call upon us to uncover and make explicit fundamental moral norms.

Computer networking creates a broad range of new possibilities for human communication, and many of these possibilities will, no doubt, be exploited. One of the most important ethical issues in computer networking, and in particular in computer conferencing, concerns the public-private status of trans-actions that take place in a network. The rules we adopt will define this status and, in turn, will determine which conferencing capa-bilities are exploited and how.

There seems to be little doubt that the status of communications in computer confer-ences is now unclear. For example, consider the following cases.

1. A political scientist decides to participate in a special one-day online discussion of a somewhat controversial topic on which she has already published. Participants are able to sit at their terminals, read what has just been said (typed in) by other participants, and respond immediately. The political scientist is very taken by the discussion and responds quickly to many of the ideas expressed. The next day as she is reading The Wall Street Journal, she dis-covers that what she said in the forum has been quoted (and attributed to her) by a newspaper reporter.

2. A small group of scientists from across the country, while at a con-vention, decide to set up an ongoing com-puter forum on the topic of their common specialty. One of the scientists sets up the system and others tie in. They ex-change ideas and discuss the results of research still in the formative stage. Several months later, just as one scientist is about to send a manuscript off to a journal for review, he notices an article, just published, by a parti-cipant in the forum. As the scientist reads the article, he realizes that it contains many of the ideas that he had originated and presented on the forum months ago. Indeed, it contains many of the same ideas as the paper he is about to send off for publication.

3. Students at a university are each given small personal computer

accounts on the university-owned
mainframe. Through the student chapter
of the ACM (Association for Computing
Machinery), a forum system is set up.
Any student with an account can sign on,
read what has been entered into the
forum, and add his or her own comments.
A discussion of sexual behavior develops.
One student briefly describes a pornographic questionnaire that has been distributed among students. The questionnaire asks in graphic detail whether a
person would or would not do certain
things on a first date. The student also
announces that he has put the questionnaire in one of his files and has
accessed it to a particular signon i.d.
He gives the signon i.d. so that those
who want to see the questionnaire can.
He warns those who might be offended that
the questionnaire is crude. Several
weeks later the student is called into
the Dean of Student's Office and
threatened with expulsion. The university had heard about the questionnaire
and had traced it to him through his
comments in the forum.

These three cases have a number of
features in common, but the most striking is
the fact that all three individuals were surprised to find that their communications in a
computer conference were treated in a way they
had not expected. Their communications were
treated as being much more public than they
had presumed. If our primary concern were to
attribute blame or responsibility, we could
say that the individuals were, at least partially, at fault for not inquiring into the
status of their communications in the conference before they participated. And, indeed,
as computer conferencing becomes more familiar
to us, people will probably seek more and more
clarification about the status of conferences
before they participate.

Nevertheless, the point is that without
explicit specification, it is not clear what
the public-private status is of such communi-

cations. This situation seems precisely to
fit Moor's idea that computers create a
vacuum. There are no rules or conventions
telling us how our communications will be
treated. In some sense this problem is an
easy one to solve. All we have to do is
create rules. Once we decide what the rules
should be, it will be fairly easy to ensure
that user/participants know them, for they can
be flashed on the screen when any user signs
on. Still, it is not as easy as it may seem
to decide just what the rules should be. When
we begin trying to figure out this dilemma, we
find (instead of a vacuum) many important
norms and values that must be balanced against
one another and any number of comparable
situations giving mixed messages about what
the rules of computer conferencing should be.

Consider the first two cases described
above (the political scientist whose entries
in the forum were quoted by a reporter and the
scientist whose ideas were published by
another scientist). One significant value at
stake in these conferences is the advancement
of knowledge. A robust exchange of ideas
allows scholars to critique and build on one
another's work. Computer conferencing could
serve this value enormously by increasing
communication among scholars. Computer conferencing facilitates this communication by
making it possible for many scholars to exchange ideas with one another informally
(rather than in writing), quickly, and frequently, without the burden of traveling to
one central location, and without the financial or time constraints involved in
traveling. However, there are other ways to
promote the creation of new knowledge. In our
society we have adopted a system that encour-
ages the development of new knowledge by
granting credit to those who create it and put
it into the public realm. In addition, we
often grant proprietary rights to the creators
of new knowledge, giving them the potential to
benefit economically from their creations.
This system is aimed at producing an atmos-
phere of healthy competition with rewards for

those who succeed, and it discourages individuals from publishing their ideas before they
have reached a certain degree of certainty
about them.

These strategies for encouraging the
development of new knowledge seem to conflict
with the type and degree of exchange made
possible by computer conferencing. As explained above, computer conferencing makes
possible frequent, informal exchange among
many scholars. But the system of scholarship
in our society is such that if communications
in computer conferences are not private in a
certain way, scholars will have to take great
risks in participating. They will have to
risk being quoted long before they are ready
to go public with their ideas (which might
reflect poorly on them), and they will have to
risk having their ideas stolen. They are not
likely to participate under such conditions.

Notice that in the analysis of cases (1)
and (2), privacy is revealed to be of importance not in itself, but because of its role
in a particular system. Privacy is revealed
to be important because it gives individuals a
kind of control of their ideas, which is
desirable in that system of scholarship. In
another system, privacy might be less important. I will return to this theme later. For
now, it is important to note that these conferencing cases can be seen as species of communications that could also take place without
computers. Thus, we might look to other
species of the generic kind in order to identify rules or patterns that achieve the result
aimed for with these computerized conferences.

First, we have to decide what noncomputer
situations best fit these computerized conferences. One important species of communication
between scholars and scientists is, of course,
publication in professional journals. It is
probably the most important vehicle by which
scholars and scientists communicate and have
their ideas critiqued and transmitted. Conferencing might be seen according to this model.
Indeed, as journals become available online,
the distinction between conferencing and

publication could become blurred. Similarly, participating in a computer conference might be seen as analogous to presenting at a professional meeting. Are these the best analogies? Or is conferencing more like sending an early draft of a paper out to a few close colleagues for comments? Or like having an informal discussion of a topic in your office with a few colleagues who are bouncing ideas off one another? These situations all seem to be species of the generic form of communication. All are aimed at the productive exchange of ideas.

If computer conferences are treated according to the model of publishing in a journal or presenting at a professional meeting, then communications within conferences should be viewed as highly public. One would not be shocked to see one's published article or one's presentation at a professional meeting quoted in the newspaper, and one would be surprised to have ideas expressed in these forms used or quoted by others without proper crediting. If we treat conferencing in this way, we can map the rules or conventions of journal publication or professional meetings onto conferencing. However, if we follow this route, we will lose many of the advantages of conferencing, for scholars do not release their ideas to the public until they are well developed and proven. If conferencing communications were considered to be highly public, then the kind of informal input that is helpful at the formative stage of research, and that is made possible in an increased degree by conferencing, would not take place in computer conferences. Indeed, online journals and computer conferences would become identical.

On the other hand, we might view conferencing as more like sending a rough draft of a paper to a colleague. This approach might come closer to serving the goals we want to achieve with conferencing--an open and informal exchange. Such exchanges are often limited to only a few colleagues because individuals do not want to lose control of who has

access to their work. Thus, if we go this
route, the rules would not fully exploit the
potential of computer conferencing. Moreover,
we would have to map new territory, as the
public-private status of these exchanges is
not at all clear. Scholars generally expect
written ideas, even if unpublished, to be
credited, but conventions for exchanging rough
drafts are not well established or formalized.
Likewise, if we treat conferencing like throw-
ing ideas around in one's office, we recognize
the activity as informal, but we get little
help from this noncomputer analogy because the
rules are even less clear here. For example,
I would not be surprised to find that an idea
that I had come up with in the course of a
casual discussion in my office was not
credited to me by a colleague; on the other
hand, others might expect such credit to be
given.

Comparing computer conferencing to these
other species helps us to identify what is at
stake in using conferencing in the context of
scholarship and makes us aware of patterns or
rules that have been used in this context, but
as I have already noted, such an examination
does not always provide clarity. Furthermore,
it is important to emphasize that "context is
all." That is, the norms to be protected or
realized will be different when conferencing
is used in business, government, the nonprofit
sector, or, as in the cases just discussed,
for scientific or scholarly exchange. To further illustrate the importance of the context,
it may be helpful to consider the third case
described earlier, the student forum case.
Here we have a different context and different
issues concerning public vs. private communications.

The student who ultimately got in trouble
with his university administration seemed to
be treating the forum as public. That is, he
did not bring the pornographic material into
the forum itself, which would have, in some
sense, forced students to see it who did not
choose to do so. Rather, he informed students
of its availability so that only those who

wanted to see what they knew was pornographic, would see it. This approach seems to agree precisely with how we handle noncomputerized pornographic literature. We do not allow public displays or advertisements or distribution by mail to consumers who did not request the literature, but we do allow those who so choose to have access. For example, we allow individuals to enter bookstores that sell pornography but do not allow those bookstores to display their "wares" in windows. Putting the case in this context might, then, generate a number of principles to follow in dealing with conferencing that are not unlike the principle to which the student seemed to adhere.

Nevertheless, in this case, there is yet another layer of public-private concern, in that the computer on which the forum took place was a university-owned computer. The university administration thought of the forum as private, not in the sense that the communication between students was confidential, but rather in the sense that it took place on campus under the control of the administration. Thus, the administration saw the communication in the forum as comparable to communications that take place in meetings on campus. To give the administration the benefit of the doubt, they might have reasoned that although it is good to allow freedom of expression (an important value on college campuses), they should always retain the right to censor what is communicated--in buildings, on campus, in the classroom, and in the computer. Censorship too might serve educational interests.

To work out this case further, we would have to bring out the values at stake in an educational setting, in communications involving pornography, and the relevance of the ownership of computers and accounts. This task would involve classifying this situation as a generic kind (or perhaps as falling into several generic kinds) and identifying the special details that accompany computerization. The values to be served in the particular context are critical, and it is for this reason that it is difficult to develop rules (especially rules for public-private status) that cut across all contexts. In order to see this difficulty more clearly, it will be helpful to try to develop a cross-cutting rule.

A first attempt at a principle applying to all computer conferences would be to advocate a principle of honesty in conveying the public-private status of communications. That is, when individuals are informed about the status of communications in a computer conference, it seems that they ought to be truthfully informed. According to this principle, it would be deceitful to specify that a conference was private in a certain way and then intentionally make the contents available to those whom participants thought were excluded. It would also be a matter of negligence if a conference was said to be private but was not adequately protected from unauthorized access. This principle imposes an obligation on those who set up and maintain computer conferences to be honest. Such individuals might be called "gatekeepers," as they control who has access to a conference and who does not.

The honesty principle is sound, but it is not special to gatekeepers or conferencing, as it would apply to all persons. Moreover, it is not a very strong solution because it does not require that gatekeepers inform participants of the status of communications and seek their prior consent. It only requires that they be honest if asked about the status. The claim that gatekeepers have an obligation to obtain the informed consent of individuals to the conditions of a conference before they allow individuals to participate would be much more powerful.

Can such a claim be defended? It is tempting to argue for such an obligation on moral grounds. We might claim that this principle is derivative from a principle of respect for individuals and their autonomy. If a person is to have control over his or her ideas and over who hears them, then a person must know the public-private status of his or her communications. However, although it is probably true to say that one needs to know the status of one's communication in order to control who hears one's ideas, one does not necessarily have a right to this control, nor do others have an obligation to ensure it. Autonomy has not been traditionally understood to entail control over who hears (or reads) one's ideas. Moreover, one can retain the control in question simply by refraining from participation in computer conferences. Thus, the case for informed consent cannot be made in this way.

Still, although informed consent cannot be defended as a moral right in all computer conferences, it may be defended in particular contexts. For example, if our society were computerized such that one could only vote in political elections by expressing one's vote in a computer network, then the claim to informed consent to the public-private status in the network (and to privacy), would be very powerful. In another context, however, the claim might be very weak. For example, if employees of large companies were expected to exchange ideas with employees of the company at other locations, they would not need to know the public-private status of the communications. The company could protect them however they wished.

The desirability of informed consent in conferencing is tied to the importance of privacy, and the role of privacy also varies with the context. Some conferences may be about such trivial matters that individuals will not care whether they are public. Other conferences may involve information that is so personal that individuals would not want to communicate about it, no matter what degree of privacy is guaranteed. For business transactions, privacy is important to protect competitive advantage and trade secrets. Thus, the importance of privacy will vary. Nevertheless, adherence to a principle of informed consent is likely to facilitate participation, because when one knows what the public-private status of a conference will be, one can evaluate the risks and benefits of participa-

tion. Individuals are more likely to participate under such circumstances.

It is for this reason that adherence to a
rule requiring that participants in conferences be informed of the public-private status
of their communications would be a good thing.
It is not a matter of right, but rather of
benefit--the benefits of conferencing. Informed consent would encourage the use of conferencing and allow us to take advantage of
the benefits it offers. Moreover, as there is
now a good deal of ambiguity about the status
of communications in conferences, participants
are vulnerable to exploitation. Gatekeepers
or other participants may take advantage of
the ambiguity and allow participants to believe conferences are more private than they
really are. If the ambiguity remains, participants are likely to avoid computer conferencing. The informed consent requirement
would protect participants from this risk by
ensuring that they know the risks of their
participation ahead of time.

In conclusion, this analysis shows that
when we look at computer conferencing, we do
not find a moral vacuum. Rather, we find
situations that are both like and unlike other
situations in which there is no computer. To
understand the morality of computer cases, we
have to figure out the generic nature of the
case and compare it to noncomputer species.
This approach helps us to see what general
norms are relevant and what values are at
stake. Sometimes the noncomputer comparables
provide a model for balancing values or expressing norms. Other times, they are not so
helpful. Informed consent in computer conferencing is a good thing because individuals are
more likely to participate when they know what
the public-private status of their communications will be. However, informed consent cannot be claimed to be a moral requirement of
all conferences. Its role depends on the
context.

Notes

1. Andrew S. Tanenbaum, <u>Computer</u> <u>Networks</u> (Englewood Cliffs, NJ: Prentice-Hall, 1981).

2. See for examples: Vijay Ahuja, <u>Design</u> <u>and</u> <u>Analysis</u> <u>of</u> <u>Computer</u> <u>Communications</u> <u>Networks</u> (New York: McGraw-Hill Book Company, 1982); Robert L. Ellis, <u>Designing</u> <u>Data</u> <u>Networks</u> (Englewood Cliffs, NJ: Prentice-Hall, 1986); and Mary E. S. Loomis, <u>Data</u> <u>Communications</u> (Englewood Cliffs, NJ: Prentice-Hall, 1983).

3. Emmanuel G. Mesthene, "The Role of Technology in Society," in Albert Teich, ed., <u>Technology</u> <u>and</u> <u>the</u> <u>Future</u>, 4th ed. (New York: St. Martin's Press, 1986).

4. James Moor, "What is Computer Ethics?" <u>Metaphilosophy</u> (1985), pp. 266-275.

3

How to Invade and Protect Privacy with Computers

James H. Moor

Probably no other issue in computer ethics stirs emotions more than the threat of computerized invasions of privacy. For example, Swedes protested vigorously when they discovered that a team of sociologists had been rummaging through computerized files on approximately 15,000 citizens.[1] For a period of 20 years, Swedish sociologists had used various databanks to compile profiles on individuals, including information about their families, school grades, test scores, and employment histories. In the interest of social research, the government had allowed the sociologists access to health and criminal databanks that are normally closed to public inspection. Activities like those in Sweden present an Orwellian nightmare of science, government, and technology conspiring to invade the privacy of individuals.

How can individual privacy be protected in a highly computerized society? This question is particularly important as computer networking develops. As more and more computer data bases are linked by networks, the opportunities and temptations for invasions of privacy increase. Obviously, a Luddite leveling of machinery or a complete prohibition on gathering information about individuals would not be a viable policy for our complex technological society so dependent on computers and information. Science requires information for good research, and government requires information for good decision-making. In our technological society it is neither possible nor desirable to forbid collecting and computerizing information about individuals. Therefore, it is important to look for ways of accommodating the legitimate needs of science and government for gathering information about individuals while respecting the right of individuals to privacy. In this chapter I propose a procedure for science and government to gather information about individuals that is both ethical and practical.

What Is Privacy?

Although many Americans take the right to privacy to be fundamental, in fact privacy is not explicitly guaranteed by the U.S. Constitution. Moreover, before 1890 no U.S. court ever granted relief based expressly on the invasion of privacy. Since the publication of a seminal 1890 law review article by Samuel Warren and Louis Brandeis[2] many have struggled to define and defend a right to privacy. Over the years the notion of privacy has evolved in many directions. For example, in tort law there are four different conceptions of privacy: (1) intrusion into one's solitude, (2) publicity of one's name, likeness, or private information, (3) placing one in a false light, (4) and commercial appropriation of one's personality.[3] Philosophically the debate continues about the proper conception of privacy.[4]

My strategy in this chapter is to focus on the concept of informational privacy, the concept that seems most relevant to concerns about computerized invasions of privacy. I am sympathetic with attempts by others to limit the concept of privacy to informational privacy,[5] as so many diverse concerns have been lumped under the concept of privacy that it has become a catchall. But I also recognize that accounts of privacy solely in terms of information are overly restrictive.[6] For instance, I may in an ordinary way regard the bombardment of my office each spring by loud music emanating from the dormitory across the street as an invasion of my privacy, although such an invasion has nothing to do with collecting information. Thus, I take informational privacy to be a central feature in any adequate account of privacy and it is the focus of this chapter, but I readily grant that it does not exhaust our ordinary conceptions of privacy.

A person has a right to (informational) privacy in a given domain if and only if that person has the right to control access to personal information in that domain. A domain may be a physical place such as a person's residence or, more broadly speaking, a domain may be a kind of situation. For example, being examined by a physician and confessing to a priest are domains in which a person has the right to privacy. Even though in these domains a person shares information with another, the physician or priest is not at liberty to divulge the information publicly. I will use the phrase "sphere of privacy" to capture the various domains in which persons have a right to privacy. A sphere of privacy is a normative notion. Within a sphere of privacy an individual is granted legal or moral protection. Within a sphere of privacy a person has the right to decide how much of his or her life will be revealed and to whom.

Undoubtedly, the size of the sphere of privacy varies from society to society. The sphere of privacy for individuals in Britain is much greater than it is in the Soviet Union. The fact that the dimension of the sphere of privacy varies from culture to culture does not diminish the fact that for most, if not all, cultures, privacy is an important norm. But because privacy is only one among many values, different societies have to work out what the appropriate sphere of privacy is for them. Indeed, a sphere of privacy is dynamic within a culture. The domains in which people are granted a right to privacy may change over time. Social unrest is one force that may influence the domains in which people are granted a right to privacy.

If a society is going through a period of chaos, then its members may be willing to trade a little privacy for social order. Technological innovations can also lead to adjustments in the boundaries of a sphere of privacy. When telephones were integrated into our society, a decision had to be made whether to include the contents of phone conversations within the sphere of privacy.

Why Is Privacy Important?

Why is privacy important to us? In considering this question, a number of _instrumental_ answers immediately present themselves. If people have privacy, they can avoid certain harms that others might cause them and can avoid some embarrassments. James Rachels suggests further that privacy allows people to form varied relationships with other people.[7] Certainly privacy allows us to avoid some harms and permits an intimacy with some people that would be difficult without privacy. But is there not something deeper about the value of privacy? Deborah Johnson thinks so.

> So, not only does the loss of control of information about one's self have some possibly serious negative consequences, such as no protection from misuses of the information, it also means a loss of autonomy. The latter may sound like just one more negative consequence, but it is not. Loss of autonomy means loss of one's capacity to control one's life. It is a reduction of one's status as a moral being. A right to control information about one's self is fundamental to being a self-determining and responsible being.[8]

I think Johnson is right to see autonomy as an important right. People need to be autonomous in order to plan and execute their personal projects. But her justification, though more fundamental, still views privacy as an instrumental good rather than an intrinsic good. In her view privacy is important because it facilitates autonomy. Without privacy people are not self-determining and responsible beings.

I think these instrumental justifications of privacy are encouraged by the way the question is asked. Given the question, "Why is privacy important?" it is difficult not to suggest some good to which privacy leads. But this sort of answer overlooks another possible position about the value of privacy--that is, that privacy is a good in itself. Of course, privacy is instrumentally good, but some people, and I am one of them, regard privacy as something worth having in itself. I think this point is an important one, for if privacy is only instrumentally good, then justifying a right to privacy is less secure. Put another way, if whatever privacy accomplishes can be accomplished without it, and if that end is privacy's only value, then why protect privacy itself? In fact, in situations in which privacy is lost but our lives remain otherwise unchanged, we still think something important has been lost.

Consider a thought experiment about Tom, an electronic eavesdropper. Suppose that Tom likes to peek at your life. Tom is very clever and discreet in his observations. He uses the best computer technology to gather information about you. Because Tom likes to know about you in detail, he decides to engage in a computer search of your financial records. He knows exactly what you buy and how much it costs and how late you are in paying for it. He knows how much you earn and how much your mortgage payments are. Of course, you don't know that Tom has been using his computer to search your financial records. Tom is so careful that nobody knows he has entered and snooped about in the computer files accessed by his own computer over networks. The more Tom learns about you financially, the more Tom wants to know about you. He searches your health records and criminal records. He knows about those persistent hemorrhoids and the DWI charge from many years ago. He uses electronic equipment to pick up your conversations when you are outside and to record your phone conversations when you are at home. He becomes so fascinated by you that he miniaturizes and employs television equipment that automatically records your daily actions no matter where or how personal. Tom's computer equipment assembles the information so that Tom can watch and listen to it when he comes home. For Tom, watching your life is like following a soap opera--The Days of Your Life. He gets enormous enjoyment out of this activity, especially watching some of those instant replays, but you, of course, never know about Tom or his hobby and your life is never affected by it.

In this thought experiment your privacy is clearly invaded but the invasion has absolutely no consequences for you. Tom doesn't harm you, and because you know nothing of Tom's activity, you suffer no embarrassment and your relations are as diverse as ever. Your autonomy is not jeopardized. You do exactly what you would have done if Tom had never existed. Privacy has no instrumental value in this case, and yet something of value is lost when privacy itself is gone. I think most of us would prefer to lead our lives without Tom's peeping than with it.

The view of privacy as an intrinsic good as well as an instrumental good is based on an empirical claim about people's basic values. Not everyone may view privacy as a basic value, but I think many do. Moreover, treating people ethically requires respect for their basic values. Thus, for me the roots of privacy are found in respect for the dignity of people; it is not a value generated, for example, from a hedonistic utilitarian calculation. In fact, this view of privacy is in opposition to classical utilitarian doctrine. Given a choice of two worlds--one world like the thought experiment in which Tom enjoys his clandestine peeking at you and the other world just like it except that Tom doesn't peek--the classical utilitarian may well favor the world

in which Tom peeks. In fact, the more Tom enjoys peeking, the better it is for the classical utilitarian!

Privacy has value not merely because it
leads to pleasure and avoids pain, though it
may do that, and not merely because it en-
hances autonomy, though it may do that too,
but because privacy is something that has
value in itself. People value a sphere of
privacy in which they have the right to control access to information about their lives.
Moreover, once privacy is regarded as a fundamental value and not just as a means to other
ends, then privacy concerns are not easily
overridden by other considerations. Privacy
is on a firmer foundation.

A Closer Look at the Swedish Study

Recall that in the Swedish sociological
study researchers gathered data on about
15,000 citizens. Details were collected about
the lives of these people, who were all born
in Stockholm in 1953, and information on education, employment, marriage, children, social
background, health, alcohol-related difficulties, and criminal activity was entered into a
computer over a twenty-year period. Why, exactly, is this an invasion of privacy?

The mere gathering of information about
people and storing it on a computer does not
constitute an invasion of privacy. Some information about people is clearly public, and
Sweden considers many types of information to
be in the public domain. Sweden gathers more
information on its citizens than most countries and has had a tradition for open access
to public records that dates back at least a
century and a half. According to Joseph
Lelyveld,

> In the computer age it is a relatively
> simple matter, for instance, for any
> Swede to look up the income that any
> other Swede has reported to the tax
> authorities and what taxes he has paid;

or to discover the extent of his property holdings; or even, for about 40 cents, to buy from the authorities a photograph of any holder of a Swedish passport or driving license.[9]

Even with this openness, the sociological study constituted an invasion of privacy. Though the Swedish sphere of privacy is different from the one in the United States, a sphere of privacy does exist in Sweden. Many records, such as health and criminal records, are closed to public inspection. Swedes would normally assume that this kind of information is protected within their sphere of privacy that it is kept private unless the people involved have granted permission for its release, and hence, on these grounds, an invasion of privacy did occur in this sociological study.

In defense of their activity, the sociologists pointed out that parents of the subjects knew about the project because at the beginning of the project they had given consent to the collection of their children's academic records.[10] The researchers also argued that their project was public knowledge, contrary to newspaper headlines that suggested that the research was done secretly. Since the project's inception in 1966, over twenty reports from the project have been published.

These rebuttals still do not justify the methods of the study. Consent given by parents about academic records would cover, at most, early academic records. Such consent would not cover nonacademic records or any information about the subjects after they were grown. Real consent was missing, and moreover, so was public knowledge about what was happening. The Swedes for the most part did not know, through published reports or otherwise, about the existence or the scope of the investigation. Indeed, some of the research methods were simply deceptive. For example, individuals were sent questionnaires about such matters as their political preferences and their television-viewing habits without being told that the information was part of the study.

Given that the Swedish project did invade privacy, why was it wrong to conduct such a study? It did no obvious harm. No information gathered in the study was ever used against anybody. Moreover, nobody's autonomy was taken away. Everybody did exactly what he or she would have done without the study taking place. The answer is that the study did not show respect for people and their right to privacy, and privacy, as I have argued, has intrinsic value.

Protecting Privacy with Computers

What is the best way to protect people from such invasions of privacy? In the Swedish case, once the general public became aware of the study, the Swedish government moved to protect privacy by ordering the destruction of all information that would identify the subjects of the study. This action terminated the project and the follow-up studies that had been planned, such as a study of the marital patterns and psychological health of women who have had abortions. I have no doubt that the Swedish government made a good decision to stop this invasion of privacy, but a general predicament remains. Sometimes it is desirable and justifiable for science and government to gather information about individuals. In general, a public policy based on accurate information about people is likely to be a better policy than one based on hearsay or speculation. Therefore, sometimes it may be in the public interest to support a scientific investigation that collects private information. Could a project, perhaps even on the scale of the Swedish project, which fulfilled a legitimate need to investigate social problems, be conducted ethically?

One approach would be to obtain informed consent from all subjects. This approach, however, although highly desirable, may be practically impossible. Carl-Gunnar Janson, the sociologist who headed the Swedish project, suggested that the cost and difficulty of obtaining such permissions would have crippled his research project. He also pointed out that one purpose of the project was to study the relationship between social background and criminal deviance and that those who were of special significance to the project would have been unlikely to consent.[11]

The difficulty in obtaining informed consent can be further illustrated by epidemiologic research, which depends heavily on searching various files for information. By linking files of hospitals, physicians, employers, and municipalities, it is possible to discover the dynamics of diseases. For example, it has been shown that occupational exposure to asbestos increases the risk of cancer; smoking increases the risk of cardiovascular diseases; taking oral contraceptives increases the risk of stroke, and so on. The nature of the research often precludes knowing in advance what information will be useful. Consider the discovery that when mothers had taken diethylstilbestrol (DES) during pregnancy to prevent miscarriage, their daughters had an increased risk of developing a rare vaginal cancer.[12] The person taking the drug did not get the disease, only the female offspring developed it some fifteen to twenty years later. Thus, different records of different people had to be checked to discover the connection. In this situation it was not clear whose records needed to be checked and from whom consent needed to be obtained without first checking the records. Moreover, the practical problems of obtaining consent would be severe. As one epidemiologist stated, "If such use of medical records had been prohibited, or had been permitted only with consent of the patient, this study--perhaps the first demonstration in human beings of transplacental carcinogenesis--would have been extremely difficult or impossible to carry out.[13]

The problem is simply this: Information is needed for good decision-making, but sometimes obtaining consent from individuals in order to gather information is not realistic and gathering information without such consent invades people's privacy. For such situations a computer approach deserves consideration. A computer can be used to code information as it is gathered so that no researcher ever knows the true identity of the subjects. In other words, a computer can be used to protect privacy. Consider the collection of data as a three-step procedure: A source supplies the data, a computer analyzes and codes the data, and a research team receives data that is purged of any identifying marks. The key is the middle step. A computer must be programmed to search data files and to find the required information. The program in the computer--let's call it a privacy program--would know how to associate various identifiers for one individual, such as name and social security number. In this way information from various data files could be gathered by the computer even though the files would not use the same identifiers. In fact, the computer could continue to search various data files over time. Periodically, the privacy program would report information, but the information reported would be labelled only with a subject number, which the program would generate. No identifying information would be released. The programmers of the privacy program would never see the actual source files and would have nothing to do with the research project. Once the privacy program was completed and operational, it would serve as a black box to convert the data source files to the deidentified research files. The researchers themselves would see only the purified data. They would never have contact with the original information.

Does this plan to use a privacy program constitute an invasion of privacy? Strictly speaking, I think it does. It involves access to information about people in a sphere of privacy for which the people have not given consent. Indeed, the computer gathers and keeps identifying information. But, because the invasion is a machine invasion and not a human invasion, the access is done with respect for the individual. Although personal information is taken, and used, identities are not ultimately revealed, and thus, spying by other humans is not possible. This procedure uses the invisible operations of a computer to keep the identities of individuals secret. Only the computer knows, and it's not talking. Because identities would not be revealed, consent, though desirable, would not be required. However, because some invasion of privacy would take place, justification for the activity would still be necessary. It would have to be shown that the benefits of this approach in a particular situation were worth the infringement on people's right to privacy. Gratuitous invasion of people's privacy by computers is not justifiable.

Several objections to this approach are worth examining.

The Technical Objection. The privacy program cannot work because no computer system is so smart that it can travel through any file in any format and pick out the right information. Some information is not computerized at all.

Reply. Many privacy programs may be used. There doesn't have to be one program that does it all. A privacy program can be tailored to the specific formats and requirements of a particular research project. The programmers can be given dummy samples of the source files to test and modify the privacy program. Of course, there may be situations in which the records are in a form that a computer or scanning device cannot read and the program would not work. However, if privacy is considered important enough in such a case, these records could be converted to a machine-readable form.

The Leaky Program Objection. The privacy program may be presented as a black box, but there is always the possibility that information that identifies individuals would leak

out once the program is running. Such leakage
may occur through oversights in programming or
by prying by skillful hackers.

Reply. I think this objection is very
serious and care must be taken not to dismiss
it too easily. In fact, it is always possible
that the most carefully coded and protected
information is eventually revealed. If the
information is sensitive, e.g., psychiatric
records, then revelation of personal information may cause enormous harm. That is why
care must be taken in designing the program to
reduce the risk of revelation as much as possible. Moreover, given such risk an adequate
justification of the invasion of personal records, even by computer, must be established.
It must be shown, preferably in a public
arena, that the evils eliminated by the information gained by the computer invasion of
private records outweigh the risk of potential
revelation.

The Erosion of Privacy Objection. If the
use of privacy programs were to become acceptable, then research projects into the private
lives of people would become commonplace. Our
right to privacy would be eroded.

Reply. Increased use of privacy programs, according to this plan, would require
justification in each case. There must be
significant benefit, say in the area of epidemiologic research, to warrant the intrusion
into private files. Such an increased machine
invasion of privacy is possibly justifiable,
but requests for using privacy programs should
not be given granted automatically.

Use of privacy programs may, in fact,
increase privacy. The types of investigations
into private files that are currently being
done would be less open to revelation if privacy programs were used. Moreover, humans
interviewed by other humans, for example, in
national censuses, might feel their privacy
was better protected if the information was
given directly to a privacy program.

I think that using computers to protect
privacy while accommodating the legitimate
informational interests of government and

research interests of science is a policy
worth considering. Privacy programs show respect for the privacy of individuals and
yet permit us the benefits of informed
decision-making and fruitful research.

Notes

1. Joseph Lelyveld, "Worried Swedes
Questioning Wide Reach of Researchers," The
New York Times 135 (11 March 1986), p. A1.
2. Samuel D. Warren and Louis D.
Brandeis, "The Right to Privacy," Harvard Law
Review 4 (1890), pp. 193-220.
3. William L. Prosser, Handbook of The
Law of Torts (St. Paul, MN: West Publishing,
1955), pp. 635-644.
4. Ferdinard D. Schoeman, Philosophical
Dimensions of Privacy: An Anthology
(Cambridge: Cambridge University Press, 1984).
5. William A. Parent, "A New Definition
of Privacy for the Law," Law and Philosophy, 2
(1983), pp. 305-338; and "Privacy, Morality,
and the Law," Philosophy and Public Affairs,
12 (1983), pp. 269-288.
6. Judith W. DeCew, "The Scope of Privacy
in Law and Ethics," Law and Philosophy 5
(1986), pp. 145-173.
7. James Rachels, "Why Privacy Is
Important," Philosophy and Public Affairs, 4
(1975), p. 323.
8. Deborah G. Johnson, Computer Ethics
(Englewood Cliffs, NJ: Prentice-Hall, 1985),
p. 66.
9. Lelyveld, "Worried Swedes," p. A3.
10. Vera Rich, "Swedish Action Will
Terminate Big Social Study," The Chronicle of
Higher Education 32 (19 March 1986), p. 1.
11. Lelyveld, "Worried Swedes," p. A3.
12. Leon Gordis and Ellen Gold, "Privacy,
Confidentiality, and the Use of Medical Records in Research," Science 207 (1980) p. 154.
13. Ibid.

4

On Whether a Misuse of Computer Technology Is a Violation of Personal Privacy

John W. Snapper

There has been considerable discussion in recent years of new potentials for "invasions of personal privacy" due to misuse of computer technology. Unfortunately, much of the discussion confuses invasions of privacy with other sorts of misconduct. This error has resulted in needlessly convoluted analyses of misconduct in terms of personal privacy, when the misconduct is easily understood in terms of other moral ideals. Moreover, the significance of the "right to privacy" argument has been obscured even in those cases when it is properly used.

I will begin with two examples of computer misuse that have been needlessly viewed as invasions of personal privacy: the unauthorized dissemination of medical records and government use of broad personal data files. These practices can be condemned without any appeal to a right to privacy. I will then look at references to "privacy" in three contexts. First, I will examine how the word has been used in certain "privacy laws" and "privacy commission" studies. Some of these include discussions that are only marginally related to privacy issues, and foster confusions over when privacy is an issue. Second, I will consider discussions of a "basic right" to privacy, including some appeals to such a right in controversial constitutional decisions. Here I argue that even though these "right to privacy" arguments may be important

to condemning a certain practice, other sorts
of arguments in both legal and ethical analysis should generally be preferred. Third, I
will consider an ordinary "right" to privacy
that is recognized in common law. The danger
with this notion is that it tends to get
"blown out of proportion" and is often given
more significance than it really has. Finally,
I will describe some of the rare situations in
which computer misconduct should indeed be
condemned as an invasion of privacy.

Although this chapter describes
conditions under which misconduct might be
viewed as an invasion of privacy, no explicit
definition of privacy is offered. I've taken
this approach, in part, because privacy is
best left as a tenuous notion with broad
application to as yet unsuspected forms of
activity; in part because I shall attempt to
draw conclusions about privacy that are independent of the diverse definitions found in
the literature. Depending, then, upon an
intuitive sense of personal privacy, I
initially assume that no use of information
can violate personal privacy if the information is either impersonal or public knowledge.

Dissemination of Medical Records

The improper dissemination of medical
records is a special problem in our new world
of computer networks and communication
systems. In past years, a doctor who received
a reasonable request for a medical record
would pull the relevant piece of information
from the medical files. With computerized
files, however, it has become easier to send
the whole medical record than to send a single
piece of information taken from the record.
Thus, an employer authorized to know some part
of an employee's medical record, might receive a complete medical file from a lazy
file-keeper. If the medical records become
part of the employment files, then those files
in turn become a source for further dissemination of medical information. In an environment

where all files are disseminated with ease, medical records can be seriously compromised by casual neglect.

The dissemination of a medical record is contrary to a patient's reasonable expectation of confidentiality. The confidentiality of the patient-doctor relationship was well established in medical ethics and the law long before the recent interest in privacy as a special human right. A violation of confidentiality is akin to breaking a promise (a promise to keep information secret) and is independent of the private nature of the information.[1] A corporate marketing strategy, for instance, may be viewed as a trade secret and its dissemination viewed as a breach of confidentiality, even though there is no question of personal or private information. Although medical files often contain information of a personal or private nature, I see no reason to point this out when accusing a doctor of a breach of medical confidence. If my doctor were to divulge information about me (to someone with no need to know), I would be injured even if I did not see my privacy threatened by the publication of the information (e.g., I really do not care if the world knows that my appendix was removed in 1950).

Government Use of Broad Personal Data Files

Although computers are an excellent tool for maintaining and accessing large data files, many people fear that the state will use this tool to keep extensive data files on each citizen. Those files could include data on incomes, religious practices, voting records, buying preferences, education, and so on. For some purposes, governments need to keep at least some of these records. To administer the voting process, the city of Chicago, for instance, needs to keep records on who votes in which primaries. The problem is not that the data is kept but that computerized file systems make it possible for a "Big Brother" government with easy access to those files to concern itself with all the minutiae of our lives.

The underlying concern is not whether the information contained in personal data files is private, but over the appropriate use of such information by the government. Consider, for instance, information on religious affiliation. I may be proud of my church activities, be prominent at major church functions, and be pleased to see my picture in the paper as a church representative. I would not consider publication of my church affiliation as an invasion of privacy. Yet, I might be injured if the state were to keep a file on my church activity, and I would certainly be injured if that file were consulted when I applied for civil service employment.

The injury is akin to a violation of my civil rights assured under the First and Fourteenth Amendments. The "equal protection" clause of the Fourteenth Amendment is usually interpreted as entailing that the state ought not to classify applicants on the basis of religion (and hence accord unequal treatment to followers of different religions) when hiring civil servants. More generally, equal protection entails that any classification of a person must be relevant to state actions based on that classification. To consult data is to classify the individual on the basis of the data; thus, it seems that broad data files should neither be consulted nor maintained by state agencies. (A legal challenge to state recordkeeping on the basis of the Fourteenth Amendment would probably not go far in the courts. I do not propose this legal challenge but simply point out that we recognize the principle that state decisions should be based on relevant information.)[2]

A central issue in government filekeeping involves when it is appropriate for state agencies to keep personal data files. Again, whether the files invade privacy is not the main issue. In fact, those very files that, if kept by the state, seem to violate a civil right, may be properly kept and made public by other institutions. For instance, we all have

access through NEXIS to newspaper files that
include broad personal profiles and often
church affiliations. If we have no objection
to the open maintenance of these files by
newspapers, we ought not accuse the state of
an invasion of privacy if it were to keep the
same files. If we accuse the state of violating a right, it is some other right we are
concerned about, not the right to privacy.

Recent Uses of the Term "Privacy"

Although we need not view the above examples as invasions of privacy, there may
still be reason for so viewing them. Perhaps
they should be condemned as invasions of privacy as well as violations of confidences and
of equal protection.

One reason for viewing the above cases as
involving privacy issues is simply the fact
that similar matters are often discussed under
the "privacy" rubric. They are the sorts of
activities that are discussed by the Privacy
Protection Study Commission and the Privacy
Act of 1974, as well as by other commissions
and statutes with the word "privacy" in their
titles.[3] The California Information Practices
Act, for instance, declares that "the right to
privacy is being threatened by the indiscriminate collection, maintenance, and dissemination of personal information" and finds that
"the increasing use of computers . . . has
greatly magnified the potential risk to individual privacy." The act then goes on to discuss the sorts of examples that are presented
above.

One must look with care into the details
of the commission reports and statutes to see
whether the "privacy" rubric is a misnomer. I
believe that it is often a misnomer but not
always. The California Information Practices
Act is an interesting example. The main pro-
visions of the act establish a reasonable
expectation of confidentiality for state-held
records, such as parole and probation records,
government health care records, and records of

informants giving evidence for criminal investigations. That is, the person who provides
such data (or about whom such data is collected) has a right to protection against the
indiscriminate use or disclosure of the data.
As a consequence, an individual may claim harm
when such data is disclosed by the state, just
as one may claim harm when medical records are
disclosed by a doctor. This is a new area,
then, in which confidentiality is guaranteed.

Whether the California Information Practices Act is truly directed at the issue of
privacy is a complex question. On one hand, a
breach of confidentiality typically is not a
matter of privacy. With regard to medical
records, a breach of confidentiality is wrong
because it violates a tacit (or sometimes explicit) patient-doctor agreement. On the other
hand, an individual's relation to state agencies is different in kind from his or her relation to doctors. The sorts of confidentiality established by the act do not always
stem from agreements that were entered into
openly and freely. In fact, some of the files
that the act treats as confidential may have
been created without the knowledge of the concerned individuals. The confidentiality violations defined by the act may be of the sort
that cannot be viewed as a breach of a promise. In such cases, when the act provides
protections that have no alternative basis in
law and ethics, perhaps we must introduce new
protections justified by a right to privacy.

It remains unclear, however, whether the
protections set by the act are indeed justified by a right to privacy or by some other
concern. In some clauses, the act refers to
disclosure that may be "psychologically detrimental to the individual," which seems to
indicate a concern for a person's sense of
privacy. In other clauses, the act refers to
files that have little bearing on personal
privacy; for example, it protects keys for
scoring licensing examinations. In general,
the act seems to vacillate between concerns
for privacy and other sorts of concerns, such
as state security. A close reading of other

privacy statutes and commission reports often leads to a similar conclusion. In fact, these statutes and reports illustrate the central concern of this paper: They confuse privacy issues with other sorts of issues.

A Basic Right to Privacy

In these examples, I condemn the dissemination of medical files and government use of broad data files as violations of confidences and of equal protection. Perhaps a sense of personal privacy underlies those condemnations. Perhaps we should view the moral duty to keep confidences as being justified in terms of a more basic duty to respect personal privacy. Then my preference for an analysis of the first example in terms of confidentiality amount to nothing more than a preference for the superficial.

This view is reflected in recent legal arguments that find a tacit concern for privacy underlying the civil rights that are explicitly guaranteed by the U.S. Constitution. In the extreme, a number of decisions have been based on the claim that the right to privacy lies within the penumbra of specific rights guaranteed by the Constitution. The most famous cases are Griswold v. Connecticut (a married couple may use contraceptives); In Re Quinlan (a moribund person may refuse extraordinary life support); and Roe v. Wade (a woman may terminate early pregnancy). Most of these cases involve a finding that state laws (e.g., against the promotion of birth control) are government intrusions into the private affairs of the citizenry. The courts have prohibited those intrusions on the basis of intuitions about what constitutes a private matter, supported by a sense of what the writers of the Constitution were trying to "get at" in particular amendments. This line of reasoning would lead to the assertion that even though the above discussion of government data files makes no appeal to privacy, it does appeal to civil rights that involve privacy on a more profound level.

In response, I will simply argue for leaving our analyses of computer misuse as much as possible on the "superficial" level. Even if the right to privacy underlies the above analysis of misuse of data, we would do well to ignore this basic right when studying actual cases. (This is not to say that we should never appeal to a right to privacy in law and ethics, but that the appeal is properly a last resort when no other principles apply.) In part we avoid those underlying arguments to avoid legal controversy. The legal decisions listed above are very controversial; the courts would certainly not have entered into that controversy if they could have found some more standard basis for their decisions. Beyond the desire to avoid controversy, there are at least two justifications for passing over a privacy analysis if at all possible.

First, the notion of a right to privacy is necessarily tenuous and hard to apply to specific cases. We all have some intuition about what constitutes an invasion of privacy. In recent years, a large number of books and articles that propose definitions for the notion of a right to privacy have appeared.[4] However defined, if the general notion of a right to privacy is to remain useful, its scope must be broad enough to apply to a wide variety of unforeseen cases. On this view, the principle that we should respect privacy is a basic ethical principle, like Jeremy Bentham's utilitarian principle (maximize pleasure and minimize pain) and Immanuel Kant's categorical imperative (treat all people as independent moral agents). Such principles typically have great intuitive appeal but are notoriously difficult to apply in actual cases. In the analysis of particular cases, an analysis on "superficial" ethical and legal grounds is more powerful simply because it is more direct.

The second reason to avoid discussion of privacy is to preserve a sense of why privacy is an important right. Were the U.S. Supreme

Court to make frequent appeals to a right to privacy, we would lose a sense of the fact that it is a basic right that supersedes lesser legal principles. The Court appeals to constitutional rights only when there are no lesser legal principles to guide it or when those lesser legal principles seem to violate a more basic right. And for those same reasons, ethicists should avoid the notion of privacy when at all possible. If we constantly cry "invasion of privacy," then when we do have a case that requires an analysis in terms of privacy, no one will see its significance.

The present argument contradicts an ethical intuition; namely, that one ought never ignore any ethical concerns, particularly such a serious matter as privacy. The argument only makes sense when privacy is treated as a broad right or a deep-level, ethical principle. In most situations, we are willing to reinforce ethical decisions with multiple ethical concerns. We may point out, for instance, that participation in a brawl involves hurting others, risk of property damage, lack of personal control, and so on. But we rarely push the argument to the level of civil rights and deep-level principles. We do not usually show how the duty to avoid hurt involves a civil right, or how respect for property rests on utilitarian principles. The notion of a basic right to privacy is, if anything, even more tenuously defined than the better-established civil rights of free speech and equal representation. It is used in extraordinary circumstances when we feel we must appeal to basic ethical concerns.

A Mundane Right to Privacy

Perhaps there is another sort of "right to privacy" that condemns peeping Toms and overly aggressive salespeople. This more mundane notion, however, is not the same as the basic right underlying arguments for a woman's right to terminate early pregnancy. It cannot in itself be used to condemn government misuse of computer data files. All the same, we may be able to identify this simpler notion and use it to condemn some misuses of data files.

The modern notion of a right to privacy has its roots in a famous 1890 <u>Harvard</u> <u>Law</u> <u>Review</u> article by Warren and Brandeis.[5] In no small degree, the present argument is an adaptation of that paper to a modern issue. The issue in 1890 involved the unauthorized publication of portrait photographs in newspapers. Warren and Brandeis intuitively felt that this was wrong and sought a principle on which to base a legal action for tort damages. Although no recognized legal principle applied directly to their concerns, they argued that several existing principles suggested a right to privacy and thus justified an extension of the law to cover the new cases.

It is important to be precise about the sort of right for which Warren and Brandeis argued, as their study has had a huge influence on the development of a common law right to privacy. In traditional legal theory, these common law rights are at the bottom of a legal hierarchy where statutory law overrides common law and constitutional rights override statutory law. A right to privacy, justified along the lines argued by Warren and Brandeis, is a very much weaker right than the basic right to privacy considered above. And a much stronger argument is needed to justify the basic right. At issue here are peeping Toms and aggressive salespeople.

The form of Warren and Brandeis's argument is particularly interesting in the context of the recent concern that computer technology threatens privacy. They argued that legal protections must be extended in the face of new technologies with new potentials for harm. (The new technology in 1890 enabled the publication of photographs.) Although valid when properly qualified, such arguments for new ethical or legal principles to cover new concerns must be used with care, as they can easily get out of hand. The scope of the right to privacy can grow beyond reasonable bounds. Prosser has noted that it already threatens to

engulf the whole law of defamation and libel.[6]
I have even heard rape and burglary seriously
condemned as invasions of privacy. Somehow, I
suspect that if one cannot think of more
direct grounds for condemning rape, then one's
sense of moral outrage is out of kilter. An
argument following that of Warren and Brandeis
to establish a challenge to the use of computers cannot be used to justify a criminal
prosecution or a basic civil right.

Warren and Brandeis carefully qualified
their new notion of privacy. First, they made
no appeal to a right to privacy when there is
a prior basis for a tort action. They did not
appeal to a right to privacy when, as in the
medical file case, there is an implied contract or a prior legal principle. (Their
example was the implied contract that exists
when a person hires a photographer to make a
portrait). Second, they excluded considerations of privacy when, as in the government
files discussed above, the information is not
of a private nature. In the common law influenced by their work, there are generally three
conditions that determine when a disclosure of
facts violates privacy: (1) The facts are not
public knowledge and not easily available to
public inspection; (2) there is public disclosure or publication; (3) the information made
public is such that a person of ordinary sen-
sibilities would object to its publication. I
have argued on the basis of both (1) and (3)
that at least some incidents of government
misuse of data files ought not to be seen as
privacy violations.

Once all the qualifications are recognized, we may still be able to identify certain ways in which computer technology creates
a potential for invasion of privacy in the
mundane sense. Consider, for instance, the
hacker who accesses your home computer over
the telephone in order to see what you have
been working on. Even if access is not guarded
by any password or key system, this might be
considered an invasion of privacy. (If access
is guarded and keys are needed to break in to
the system, we may be able to condemn the in-

vasion on other grounds.) This example may
indeed be one of a harm that would best be
viewed as an invasion of privacy. But now we
must be very careful not to fall prey to confusions with other senses of privacy.

We must be particularly leery of confusing the basic right to privacy with this
mundane right just because both are limited by
these same conditions. I believe that any
basic right to privacy will also be so qualified. But we cannot conclude that an act is
an invasion of privacy in any sense just because it is not excluded by limits set on the
scope of a right to privacy. In Whalen v. Roe,
429 US 589 (1977), the Supreme Court dismissed
a privacy plea on the basis of an argument
that looks like an extension of criterion (2)
above (involving public disclosure). This
case challenged a New York law setting up a
database on the use of drugs. Physicians were
required to report patients who received pre-
scriptions for drugs classified as potentially
abusive. The Court upheld the New York law,
finding that the state files were sufficiently
guarded to prevent any general access to the
data. The fact that this criterion was used
to dismiss the case does not show that there
would be a relevant right to privacy if the
condition did hold. All the range of rights
called "privacy" need their distinctive justifications and have their distinctive applications.

Above I argued that privacy should not be
the basis of an ethical analysis if a simpler,
more direct analysis is possible. It is worth
noting that this argument does not apply to
the discussion of the mundane sense of privacy. In such cases, we may wish to condemn
an act as an invasion of privacy as well as in
several other ways. As a legal principle, however, it is still preferable to appeal to
other, stronger legal arguments when they are
available.

Proper Appeals to a Right to Privacy

We may now wonder what sorts of misuse of computer files ought to be seen as violations of privacy. My answer is that there are very few. On the level of a common law intrusion, we may object to a system operator in a time-sharing system who out of curiosity watches the activity of his clients. Of more interest, however, are appeals to a right to privacy on a higher level. In this matter, Whalen v. Roe is suggestive.

The Court indicates that if the data maintained by the state of New York were to become public, privacy would be violated. A right to privacy then demands that the state set suitable safeguards on its files. When files are computerized and easily transportable, this requirement may entail special consideration for the manner in which those files are stored. In the extreme, if encryption codes and access codes can generally be broken, privacy may demand that no access be permitted to sensitive databanks over telecommunication lines of any sort. Thus, privacy may have a number of far-reaching consequences for the issue of how and when data may be placed in files that can be reached through computer networks. But we should not confuse this conclusion with other similar limits on the use of computer networks. If the data in question is sensitive for reasons other than privacy (e.g., trade secrecy agreements or national security), then discussing the limits in terms of privacy would only confuse matters.

This chapter has concentrated on issues relating to the disclosure of private information. I should note before concluding that there are many other sorts of privacy violations. Computer misuse may, for instance, seem to involve an intrusion on privacy. An example is computerized telephone advertising that intrudes on the privacy and peace of the home but involves no collection of private data. In

our discussions of these cases, as in the discussions of private information, we should be
wary of confusing privacy with other concerns.
   Decisions such as in the <u>Griswold</u> case
show more concern over intrusive methods of
gathering information than over the disclosure
of information, however gathered. There are a
wide range of unresolved issues relating to
computer use in this area. Consider, for instance, the computerized "bulletin boards"
kept by various organizations. A bird-watching
group might keep a list of recent sightings of
rare birds that can be accessed by all interested persons from their home computers. A
brokerage firm might keep a list of stock projections that is only accessible to select
customers. We may wonder whether it can be an
intrusion to access a bulletin board without
authorization. The issues are as complex as
the varieties of bulletin boards, mail services, and databanks that are appearing on
computer networks. In some cases, we may be
well served to view unauthorized access as an
intrusion on the privacy of the service operator. Sometimes, however, unauthorized access
is more simply seen as a theft of information
than as an invasion of privacy.

Notes

   1. Doctor-patient confidentiality cannot
always be seen as following from an agreement
between the doctor and the patient. An
accident victim who arrives unconscious at a
hospital can expect that the attending doctor
will keep confidences, even though they cannot
be said to enter into an agreement in the normal sense. One reason, of course, that doctors
prefer to avoid such anomalous situations is
just precisely because the usual
doctor-patient agreement cannot be established. This extension of doctor-patient

confidentiality, however, was recognized in
the law before the recent discussions of privacy became popular and does not depend on the
notion of privacy.

2. In present law, classifications of
individuals in a government program may be
challenged on the basis of the Fourteenth
Amendment. Programs that classify by race
(e.g., affirmative action programs) are said
to be "suspect," and the classification must
be shown to be necessary to a compelling state
interest. So a data file that includes racial
classifications may be challenged on the
Fourteenth Amendment with some expectation of
success. Most classifications, however, are
held up to a much lower level of scrutiny. The
courts have accepted almost any justification
as a "rational basis" for a government classification, and there is little basis for a
constitutional challenge of the sort discussed
here. Still, the principle is well established
that the government must, when classifying
individuals, have a "valid state interest" in
the classification. This chapter relates this
principle to the general claim that state-held
files must include only information that clas-
sifies individuals in ways relevant to the
decisions for which the files are consulted.
An argument to establish this claim as a
constitutional principle goes far beyond the
scope of this chapter.

3. In addition to a number of federal
statutes, many states now have at least one
statute that establishes protections for privacy. The central federal statutes are the
Privacy Act of 1974 (5 U.S.C. #552a), the
financial Privacy Act (12 U.S.C. #3401-3422,
1980), and the Fair Credit e taken of
the Massachusetts Fair Information Practices
Act (Gen. Laws Ann., Ch. 66A).

4. The classic starting point for most
modern discussions is John Stuart Mill, On
Liberty, Chapter 4. Mill is more concerned

with acts of the sort sometimes called "victimless crimes" than with information that is "personal and private." In "Privacy, Morality, and the Law" (Philosophy and Public Affairs 12, no. 4, 1983), William A. Parent suggests a definition that lies within the limits suggested here and seems very appropriate for the present discussion. Parent's definition, however, strikes me as too narrow to provide for broad constitutional applications.

5. Samuel D. Warren and Louis D. Brandeis, "The Right to Privacy," Harvard Law Review 4 (1890), p. 193. Referring to this article, William L. Prosser in Handbook of the Law of Torts (St. Paul, MN: West Publishing, 1955), p. 802, said that "The recognition and development of the so-called right to privacy is perhaps the outstanding illustration of the influence of legal periodicals upon the courts."

6. Prosser, Handbook of the Law of Torts, p. 813.

5

Carts, Horses, and Consent: An Ethical Dilemma for Computer Networking Policy

Robert J. Baum

Ethical questions arise when individuals make decisions that affect in some way the general well-being of other individuals. With regard to the currently evolving technology of computer networking, there are many individuals who regularly must make decisions affecting other individuals, and most, if not all, of these decisions raise ethical questions of one sort or another. In this chapter I will focus on a group of questions that arise in a relatively limited context, although my basic approach to these specific questions can be applied more or less directly to many of the questions in the various other contexts related to computer networking technology.

The specific ethical questions to be examined here are those encountered by <u>public policymakers</u> (usually legislators) who must make decisions as to what kinds of restrictions, if any, governmental units (local, state, or federal) ought to impose on <u>nongovernmental for-profit groups</u> (not individuals) that want to use computer networking technologies primarily for income-generating purposes. I will <u>not</u> directly address problems of computer networking unique to other areas, such as not-for-profit activities in the private sector (e.g., charitable projects or basic scientific research) or in governmental agencies.

There are at least two levels of moral consideration relevant to policymakers. The first is procedural, namely, <u>how</u> should they proceed to arrive at their decisions? In simplest terms, policymakers have a moral responsibility to study the relevant aspects of a topic in as thorough and open-minded a way as possible and to make every effort to avoid being influenced unduly by either personal or outside special interests. Governmental policymakers also have a responsibility not to increase the power of government beyond what is rationally justifiable. The second level of moral consideration for the policymaker is substantive, namely, <u>what</u> is the most ethically justifiable policy to enact? The morally correct policy is precisely the policy that would be arrived at if the policymakers were to follow the morally correct procedure. In this chapter the primary focus will be on the second (substantive) level of moral consideration, although some procedural issues will inevitably need to be addressed.

The question of governmental regulation of corporate for-profit use of computer networking technologies arises mainly because these technologies have <u>possible</u> negative effects. Corporations are creatures of the state. Their existence is (theoretically) justified on the grounds that under certain circumstances the state should protect the personal property of individuals in order to encourage the undertaking of risky economic activity that will be to the overall benefit of the society as a whole. Thus, whenever a corporate activity could produce more overall harm to society than benefit, the government that grants the privileges of incorporation also has the power to regulate or even prohibit that activity. It is normally the task of the policymakers to determine whether the risk of net harm is sufficiently great to justify government regulation and, if it is, to determine what kind of regulation is most appropriate.

With regard to the risks associated with for-profit uses of computer networking technology, it is generally agreed that governmental policymakers have at least four basic options available:

1. Allow private corporations to develop computer networks with <u>no</u> governmental restriction or controls.
2. Impose certain restrictions on corporate activities in this area.
3. Prohibit corporate development of computer networks.
4. Pass the responsibility for making such a decision on to other governmental units (e.g., regulatory agencies).

Although at first glance this list may appear to exhaust the range of possible choices open to the policymaker, it is in fact both oversimplified and incomplete. It is particularly oversimplified in option 2, which actually includes a large number of alternative suboptions, each of which would be a specific restriction or a conjunction of a number of different restrictions. More importantly, there is also at least one major option that is not included in this list; this fifth option will be the focus of the remainder of this chapter.

At the most abstract level, there are many different ethical theories, including egoism, a variety of forms of utilitarianism, Kantianism, and contractarianism. Despite this diversity at the theoretical level, in recent years there has been a striking degree of agreement at the more concrete levels of individual decision-making and public policy-making on at least one principle, namely, the <u>principle of informed consent</u>. This principle assumes that the affected parties, whoever they may be, are in fact most capable of understanding whatever is necessary and of making their own decisions as to which courses of action are in their own best interest. Although developed to a great extent in the context of medicine, the principle of informed consent has been carried over into an increasing number of different contexts in recent years, including engineering (which of course is closely related to the topic of computer networking). In simplest form, the principle asserts that no one has a moral right to do something that affects the well-being of any competent person without obtaining the fully informed, noncoerced consent of that individual.

The principle of informed consent, when applied at the governmental decision-making level, has two forms--indirect and direct. In the indirect form of the informed consent principle, elected policymakers have a responsibility to do everything possible to collect all relevant information and to communicate it to their constituents; the legislators then must determine the preferences of their constituents and subsequently act in accordance with the expressed preferences of their constituents.

In the direct form of the informed consent principle, policymakers have a responsibility to use the power of government to guarantee that their constituents themselves are able to obtain all reasonably available relevant information and that they are then in a position to make uncoerced choices based on this information. In other words, the responsibility of the policymaker is to create a social and institutional structure that will maximize the opportunities for individuals to have control over decisions affecting their own well-being. The proposal that I will be making shortly applies the direct form of the informed consent principle to the formulation of policies governing computer networking.

There is an extensive literature giving arguments in support of the principle of informed consent, presenting refinements of it, and applying it to specific situations. I will not attempt even to summarize these arguments and refinements here; instead, I shall limit my discussion to the problems that arise when one attempts to apply the principle of informed consent to the setting of public policy related to for-profit implementation of computer networking technologies.

One frequently cited problem in discussions of applying the Principle of Informed Consent to situations that involve technologically sophisticated elements is that in such situations the average member of society (such as the doctor's patient or the lawyer's client) is unable to understand and evaluate adequately the various risks and benefits associated with alternative courses of action, and that some other person may actually know better which of the alternatives would be in the best interest of the individual.

Critics of the Principle of Informed Consent argue, especially when sophisticated technologies are involved, that laypersons must waive their right to give informed consent and must tacitly or explicitly, voluntarily or involuntarily, delegate responsibility to others (legislators, physicians, or other "experts") who are entrusted with the responsibility of becoming as well informed as possible and then making the decisions as to what would be in the individuals' best interests. Proponents of this view go on to assert that elected officials have a moral responsibility to become fully informed, or to accept the judgments of fully informed experts, and then to vote on issues according to their own (or the experts') judgments--rather than their constituents' judgments--of what would be in the best interests of the parties affected by any new policy.

Although this objection--that the issues are too complicated for most of the potentially affected parties to understand--appears to hold for the case of computer networking, a more careful consideration shows it to be less than compelling. The issue here determining what it means for an individual to be "fully informed" about the potential effects of a technology (or medical treatment, etc.). What it does not mean is that the potentially affected parties must have the same understanding of all of the technical aspects of the situation as those considered to be experts. A person being informed of the alternative medical procedures for treating an ailment does not have to understand everything published about the ailment in medical texts and journals. The general nature of the procedures as well as the risks and the probabilities of success associated with each of the alternatives can be expressed in lay terms so that the patient adequately understands. It is the physician's responsibility to communicate this information in a way that the patient can understand. There is no clear evidence that the nature of computer networking technologies, their risks and their benefits, cannot be adequately explained in lay terms to the members of the general public who will be affected by them. And the burden of proof is on the persons who wish to claim that the experts' knowledge of the risks and benefits of computer networking cannot be adequately explained to the potentially affected parties.

The second problem with applying the Principle of Informed Consent to computer networking policy is tied to the fact that certain critical information is not available at the present time, namely, information about the unforeseen consequences (positive and/or negative) of implementing the technology. All major technological developments--including computer networking--bring with them many uncertainties and unknowns. The introduction of a major new technology to a society inevitably produces unforeseen and unanticipated effects throughout the society. To illustrate this point with one simple analogy, no one in 1900 envisioned the possibility that the development of the automobile would result in large areas of the surface of the earth being paved over for roads and parking lots. It is thus quite reasonable to assume that there are a number of significant benefits and harms associated with computer networking that have not yet even been conceptualized. In other words, reasonable persons are well justified in assuming that they are completely ignorant of some of the consequences of implementing computer networking technology.

It is precisely this reasonable assumption of a significant degree of ignorance that is the basis of the second problem confronting the application of the Principle of Informed Consent. In simplest terms, the problem is that truly informed consent cannot be obtained because no one can be fully informed. (As in our discussion of the first problem, it can be allowed that if complete information were available, it could be adequately communicated to the potentially affected parties.)

This problem has a two-part solution. The first part is relatively simple; the second will require the remainder of this chapter merely to provide an outline of it. The first part of the solution requires only that we recognize that insofar as this is a problem at all, it is also a problem for most of the alternatives to the informed consent approach as well. In other words, turning the decision over to "experts," however this term may be defined (with the possible exception of expert prophets!), is of no help because the experts would not be any more fully informed than lay-persons about the unknown future consequences of computer networking.

The second part of the solution requires addressing the fact that because of this lack of complete knowledge of the consequences of different policies, it is not even possible to determine who will be most affected or from whom consent must be obtained. The problem is one of getting the horse (information about the consequences) in front of the cart (the decisions of the affected parties). This problem seems to support a neo-Luddite argument against any and all development and implementation of computer networking technology.

In brief, this neo-Luddite argument would go as follows. In obtaining informed consent, it is necessary to provide the affected parties with as much information as possible both about what is happening in the present and about what the probable short-, medium-, and long-term consequences will be. The lack of anything that could plausibly be considered knowledge--even among the "experts"--about some of the medium- to long-term consequences of widespread implementation of a specific technology would seem to limit significantly the extent to which truly informed consent could be obtained. Some of the most important consequences—both beneficial and harmful—and the identities of the individuals affected, will quite possibly be discovered only after the technology has been implemented to the extent that particularly harmful, and possibly irreversible, effects occur. This harm could be compounded if a very large investment of resources has been made that would be costly (i.e., harmful to the investors and possibly to the entire economy), if not economically impossible, to write off. Thus, the neo-Luddite would conclude that no rational individual would freely consent to the implementation of computer networking (or any other large-scale, complex technology). From this perspective, if someone were to consent to its implementation, it would be good evidence that he or she was not rational and thus not competent to give consent.

The neo-Luddite's argument is similar to Pascal's famous "wager." Rather than Pascal's choice between the certainty of a few years of earthly pleasures or the slight possibility of an eternity of the horrors of Hell, the neo-Luddite offers the choice of (let us assume for the sake of the argument) the high probability of significant short-term benefits or the relatively small possibility of extremely negative (and irreversible) long-term consequences. Thus formulated, the choice would hinge on whether there is any way of effectively eliminating the risks of irreversible and strongly negative long-term consequences.

In its most positive form, the cart-horse problem is this: The policymaker cannot obtain informed consent from potentially affected parties to authorize the implementation of a technology (e.g., computer networking) that might have substantial net positive value without first providing information about the consequences. But such information cannot be obtained without actually implementing the technology, which apparently involves taking the risk of suffering extremely harmful and irreversible consequences.

The problem of getting the cart before the horse is grounded on the assumption that at least one system would be _fully_ implemented or else nothing at all would be done. But this assumption ignores the fact that any computer networking technology must be developed and implemented over a period of time, and (theoretically, at least) the decisions can be made at any moment to stop the project completely, reverse it, or go in an entirely new direction. The failure to make any of these decisions at any given moment is essentially the same as making a decision to continue according to the original plan. This observation suggests an alternative method for getting the horse (a rational decision about implementing a technology with some unknown consequences) in front of the cart (the occurrence of serious and irreversible consequences that could not have been anticipated). Specifically, this method involves implementing the technology in an incremental way so as to keep the economic loss as small as possible if the system has to be shut down (or even dismantled) at any given point.

This incremental approach avoids some of the more serious problems of the decision-theoretic approach, and it is fully consistent with the Principle of Informed Consent. It has not been fully developed at the theoretical level, nor to my knowledge has it been explicitly applied to the ethical analysis of any large-scale technology such as computer networking. I shall briefly outline some of the features of this mode of implementation as applied to the single case of computer networking.

The first step in the incremental application of the informed consent model is to disseminate as fully as possible the _already_ _available_ information to the potentially affected parties. For example, there is an immediate need for a large-scale education program to inform the public of the currently known benefits and risks of existing computer networking systems. It would seem that the responsibility for such an educational program should rest on the organizations operating the computer networks, just as it rests on physicians and experimenters in the medical context.

It is also important that individuals be informed in a timely manner of all inputs and outputs of information in existing computer networks that directly concern them. The reality today is that individuals have a legal right to request such information, but current laws and policies in most constituencies require that the individuals take the initiative and often require that they pay a fee. Insofar as the for-profit organizations seeking to establish computer networks presumably believe that these systems will be of benefit to them, these organizations should be assigned the responsibility of providing this information to potentially affected individuals; according to this plan, no initiative on the part of these individuals should be required. (Many of the affected individuals today have no idea that information pertaining to them is in a particular network.) It is clearly within the domain of legislators to require that steps be taken that would provide individual citizens with knowledge of what information about themselves is being entered into or drawn from a computer network.

It is also possible to provide full information about known possible risks and benefits of new networking systems to potentially affected parties well in advance of their implementation. There are many ways in which this task might be carried out by either the government or the private sector and by which it might be financed. Legislators need not decide either of these questions; they would be fulfilling their moral responsibility (under the direct informed consent model) if they simply mandated that the corporate users of computer networks and the individuals affected by them present proposals to each

other and try to work out a mutually acceptable plan. If an agreement cannot be worked
out among these parties, then some governmental body might play the role of mediator or
arbitrator. The leverage for obtaining the
cooperation of the the corporate interests
could involve a governmentally enforced prohibition (with either civil or criminal penalties) on the implementation of any technology without having provided all available
information to potentially affected parties.
The leverage for getting potentially affected
individuals to cooperate would be the threat
that they would not receive the benefits of
the technology (which would presumably be well
publicized by the corporate interests as they
already are through commercial advertising)
unless such an agreement was reached.

The incremental method of implementing
new computer networking systems should ideally
use a form of active rather than passive consent. That is, the potentially affected
individuals should be required to take some
action to indicate their willingness to allow
a specific network to be established, rather
than to require them to do something to indicate that they do not want it to be implemented.

A new concept of "tentative" or limited
consent must be developed and refined so that
implementation can be authorized with the
understanding that, as more information becomes available, the affected parties can
withdraw their consent. This approach is
really not radically different from what goes
on theoretically in a true "free market"
system. The existing reality is an elaborate
system of laws and policies that protect
corporate interests on the assumption that
such a system is really in the best interests
of individual citizens. To allow individuals
to give true informed consent to new technologies, it may be necessary to remove some
or all of the existing governmental protections of corporate interests and other coercive factors that act against a truly "free"
market.

Given the existence of "tentative" or limited consent, the corporate interests (at least those which are rationally grounded) would carefully plan the stages of the incremental implementation process so that there would be minimal economic loss associated with the stopping and dismantling of a specific new stage, when and if substantial numbers of individuals register dissatisfaction by withdrawing their consent. Each increment would be kept as small as possible. Insofar as there is such a thing as "tyranny by the corporation" or "corporate domination," it is usually tied to a sufficiently massive commitment of economic and human resources to create a degree of inertia that cannot be overcome without serious dislocations throughout the society. If the implementation of a complex large-scale technology could be managed as a collection of relatively independent small commitments, individuals or small groups would be able to exert effective control over each of the small units as they come on line.

There are, of course, also many ways (most of which have been in use for decades) whereby companies can protect themselves against large losses on new products being introduced for direct purchase by consumers, methods which include surveys and test marketing in limited areas. Maintaining a capital "buffer" to protect themselves in the event of a market failure is also a standard practice (although legislation may be necessary to prevent such an accumulation of funds from acting as bait to attract corporate raiders). Ford did not go out of business when the Edsel failed, and Coca-Cola was not seriously hurt when its marketing analysis for a new formula proved faulty.

Because at least some networks would involve only the portion of the population that chose to be part of it, attention must be paid to what might be called the "hit-and-run victims" (in contrast to what is referred to in the literature as "free-riders"). These are individuals who have chosen not to be part of a particular network but whose interests may still be harmed by that network. Furthermore, insofar as at least some of the potential harms of computer networking technology (including those yet unknown) would affect society as a whole, it is necessary to consider ways of making its benefits accessible to everyone (i.e., giving everyone the option of utilizing the computer networks). One of the ironies of the development of the automobile is that the people who have suffered the most from its negative effects (inner-city residents whose homes were torn down and neighborhoods destroyed for expressways, etc.) have been those who have not been able to afford cars.

Computer networks may enable individuals who are able to make the most use of them to have some kind of an advantage over other individuals who do not have equal access to the networks. This problem is not necessarily one of protecting a minority against the majority; it is conceivable that computer networks could give the advantage to the minority that has access to them. In this case, governmental intervention may be justifiable to protect the interests of the majority. It is here that governmental policymakers have to face the very difficult problem of weighing the interests of different segments of the overall society. This specific problem deserves more attention, but it can only be noted here that it is as much of a problem for opponents as it is for proponents of the informed consent principle.

Many other questions exist that cannot be explored here, such as the following. The concept of informed consent carries with it the requirement that the consent not be coerced. But it is sometimes quite unclear whether coercion is present in a specific circumstance and whether it is avoidable. For example, is it coercive for a bank or store to say that they will not give credit to persons who do not consent to having a complete financial record in a centralized computer file?

As the preceding discussion demonstrates, there are many problems associated with apply-

ing the Principle of Informed Consent to the
implementation of computer networking technology, including many that are distinct from
the cart-horse problem. The immediate response
of many readers will undoubtedly be that there
are just too many problems with the notion of
informed consent and with its application to
make it worth trying to apply it to a large-
scale complex technology like computer networking. It should be sufficient to note in
response that there have been difficult problems with applying the Principle of Informed
Consent in most fields, including medicine.
But difficulties do not imply invalidity. The
principle expresses an _ideal_, and like any
ideal, it will never be fully and perfectly
actualized. But it <u>can</u> and should be striven
for.

6

What Is a Computer Program in a Network Environment?

M. Peter Jurkat

In this chapter, I will suggest that certain types of computer programs should be accorded the full protection of the law as private property. I will then suggest a way to characterize computer programs so that the algorithms and data structures they embody can be specified and thereby protected. As not all computer programs are to be thus protected, criteria will be suggested for the types of computer programs for which it may be appropriate to restrict protection and ownership.

Definition of Computer Programs

The question of the title is based on a more basic question: What is a computer program? This question must be answered before one can go on to consider the application of property law as one method of protecting and rewarding an individual's effort and ingenuity in the creation of a computer program. The answer, however, is not obvious, particularly in a computer network environment, and I maintain that it has not been obvious since the very first stored program computers were invented.

That a program, whatever it is, should be considered property has been questioned[1] and argued.[2] Some have discussed this question in the context of information and have included programs under the word "information" and/or

"software."[3]   Throughout these discussions
there is usually at least a tacit definition
of what a computer program is.

Although the distinction is not hard and
fast, in this chapter I wish to distinguish
between computer data, information, and computer programs; I will focus primarily on
computer programs. I consider computer data
to be symbolic representations of whatever is
being represented; information can be defined
as interpreted data; and computer programs are
<u>specifications for data structures and proce-
dures to manipulate symbols (data) by a
computer</u>. For this chapter I would like to
restrict the term "computer program" to programs that actually can be executed on some
computer. To relax this condition would imply
that almost any text or symbolic representation could be considered a program, and I am
not ready to deal with such a generality at
this time. I will offer thoughts concerning
an operational definition below. Note that
computer programs can be data to other computer programs and, as procedural knowledge,
can be considered information.

Under this definition of a computer program, the manipulation of symbols is a primary
consideration. When people read or write programs, the symbols used are letters, numbers,
and other such marks; when the computer exe-
cutes a program, the symbols are voltages,
currents, the state of switches, and other
such physically describable entities. I inter-
pret the statement that a computer "solves a
problem" to mean that:

1. There is an interpretation of part of
    the environment that results in the
    identification of a problem and the
    symbolic representation of at least
    part of that problem.
2. This symbolic representation (part of
    which includes the data) is then
    manipulated by one or more computer
    programs on one or more intercon-
    nected computers.
3. The resulting symbols (the output of

the programs) are then interpreted to be part or the whole of the solution to the problem.

The network environment requires that programs must contain the ability to execute over a computer network or in parallel; that is, to have portions of the program executing independently on interconnected, autonomous, or semiautonomous machines, with synchronization as needed. Symbol manipulation in a computer network consists of all the forms mentioned above plus the exchange of messages from one computer, or semiautonomous component of a network, to another. One form of what has been considered "a computer" is actually a collection of semiautonomous devices (e.g., CPU, memory, disk controller), each of which may be considered a special purpose computer, interconnected with devices sometimes called "buses." One way of viewing the operation of such a computer is to think of each of the devices placing messages onto the bus; then these messages are received by all other devices on the bus and are accepted and acted upon by the devices for which they were intended. The other devices ignore the messages beyond their starting codes and addresses. This common architectural feature of computers is analogous to the manner in which some computer networks, for instance the Ethernets and their variants, actually operate.

Computer Program Protection

That it may take considerable human effort and ingenuity to produce a program that is useful, and therefore valuable to others, has been demonstrated to my satisfaction. The person who spent the effort creating such a program should be rewarded, if that person so wishes. Protection as private property is one of the most common methods of rewarding people in similar cases.

The roots of the notion that people should be rewarded for their efforts go back a

long time; today's discussions usually start
with Locke's labor theory. A modern development of the labor theory of property acquisition may be found in Becker.[4] Although Becker
expressed reservations about the overall
theory, he stated the following labor-desert
argument for property:

> (1) When it is beyond what morality
> requires them to do for others, people
> deserve some benefit for the value their
> . . . labor produces. . . .
> (2) The benefits . . . deserved are those
> proportional to the values . . . pro-
> duced. . . .
> (3) When, in terms of the purposes of the
> labor, nothing but property rights in the
> thing produced can be considered a fit-
> ting benefit for the labor . . . the pro-
> perty rights are deserved. . . .

Becker further argued that (1) meets the
standards for a fundamental principle in the
sense that it is the best choice among the
alternatives available for a justificatory
starting point; that is, a principle that is
not proved but acts as an indisputable axiom.
Further, Becker states:

> (4) Any diminution of value produced by
> labor must be assessed against the labor-
> er as a penalty deserved for the loss
> thus produced.

Becker calls (4) the no-loss requirement; it
will be referenced as such later in this
chapter.
    The standard protection devices in place
for the type of property that includes computer programs include trade secret, copyright, and patent protection. The uses and
problems with these devices for protection and
reward of programming efforts have been often
examined; my knowledge of this question comes
primarily from Graham[5] and Johnson[6] who have
reviewed and summarized the history of applicability and the use of these legal and

social devices in the protection of computer programs. More detailed discussions may be found in Gemignani,[7] Novick and Wallenstein,[8] Abel,[9] Rose,[10] and Beckett.[11]

Each of these three forms of protection has its applicability, advantages, and disadvantages. None has emerged as the preferred and universally applicable method to protect computer programs. I accept that conclusion and will suggest an approach to a form of protection unique for computer programs and examine how such a form might be further specified. No claim for immediate applicability is made; indeed much more work in areas studied by logicians, computer scientists, and lawyers will need to be done before this approach could be seriously proposed as a method to protect the rewards of computer program developers.

According to Graham in the paper mentioned above, the advantages and disadvantages of each of the traditional methods of protecting computer programs may be summarized as follows:

Trade Secret Laws. One of the major advantages of trade secret laws is that they "address the underlying concepts in software--they protect the ideas rather than their manifestation."[12] In this regard they protect what is often the object, namely the algorithm, to which most of the effort in the development of the program was devoted and which makes it valuable and unique. The disadvantages are that a trade secret can be lost, is considered irretrievable, and its protection is based on case law. Such laws vary from state to state and from country to country, which is a major disadvantage to developers in today's international economy. A practical problem for the developers is how much to disclose to potential customers and users.

Copyright Laws. Since 1980, the 1976 Copyright Act explicitly covers computer programs, regardless of whether

they are embodied in source or object
code. This development is a major benefit
to copyright protection; in addition,
statutory, special damages, and injunc-
tive relief are available once it is
established that the copyrighted program
is an original work that has been copied
by another. The major disadvantage is
that the protection only covers copying
the expression of the underlying concepts. Thus, there is "no protection in
cases where a third party analyzes the
program, discovers the basic method of
operation, and independently develops a
program in accordance with these concepts."[13]

Patent Protection. Patent protection is the method preferred by software
developers; it protects the "underlying
concepts embodied in a program, and . . .
cannot be destroyed by accidental disclosure of the central idea."[14] It requires
that the patented idea be novel, not obvious in light of prior art, and be
directed to statutory matter. This last
requirement limits its applicability in
that the U. S. Supreme Court has consistently denied the patentability of computer programs themselves[15] while allowing protection for devices that include
computer programs. The operational phrase
that indicated what the Court meant by an
unpatentable program in one case is: "an
algorithm, or mathematical formula . . .
like a law of nature, . . . cannot be the
subject of a patent."[16]

Based on this statement, Johnson concluded that "a program that merely allowed a
computer to take input of a certain kind, process it, and produce output would be ineli-
gible."[17] I suggest that if an automatic e-
quivalence between laws of nature and computer
programs is made, and the ruling that laws of
nature are not patentable stands, then many,
if not most, computer programs are not patentable. Novick and Wallenstein, in an extensive
review of the various cases concerning com-

puter programs that have come before the
Supreme Court and the Court of Customs and
Patent Appeals before 1980, concluded:

> The courts have exhibited a lack of
> understanding and expertise in recent
> cases dealing with computer software
> patentability. This lack of under-
> standing is reflected in the initial pre-
> mises upon which the decisions were made.
> If the Supreme Court were to reevaluate
> this area, precedent may be overruled as
> having been decided incorrectly . . . or
> it may be severely limited. Either out-
> come would allow for computer software
> patentability.[18]

I believe, however, that little has changed to
date.

This review supports the conclusion that
the current forms of protection for computer
programs are not adequate to provide the rewards many of us believe ought to be available
to program developers for their effort. It is
possible, and maybe even likely, that the
courts will, in future cases, be able to
refine these methods and make them satisfactory. In fact, Johnson, writing about the
apparent ambivalence of the Supreme Court
concerning the patentability of computer programs (protecting devices with programs but
not the programs themselves), offered the
judgment that "the Court has not done poorly
with its case by case analysis"[19] and
suggested that "the Court has been trying to
walk a tightrope of preventing mathematical
algorithms from becoming private property, and
yet granting patent protection where it can,
in order to give program creators protection."[20]

Restrictions on Protection
of Computer Networks

Johnson went on to suggest that different
sorts of protection could be granted to pro-

grams depending on their type, without making explicit type distinctions. I will make at least one type distinction based on some characteristics of a concept that has been called "laws of nature," regardless whether such entities really exist. These "laws" are used to describe theories and relationships that their discoverers and authors claim about our universe; they are subsequently supported by what may be considered evidence and are then found useful in realized applications. It may be claimed that mathematical formulas and algorithms that have these characteristics should not be owned.

A justification for excluding algorithms that implement laws of nature can be based on the no-loss principle quoted from Becker above.[21] In his analysis of this principle he stated that, as in the case of certain problems for which there is a unique solution, to have such an invention or discovery owned by one person significantly diminishes the opportunities of others and thereby causes loss to those others. This loss, as Becker stated, provides the grounds on which patents are taxed or sharply limited both in time and content. I suggest that statements of laws of nature are like unique solutions to problems in that, if "proven true" and found useful, they are unique--to the extent that there is only one reality--and are like a scarce resource--in that if owned by one individual, they are not available to others. Becker also invoked an argument from social disutility when he stated:

> (1) Any system of property rights which permits private ownership (in the full, liberal sense) of land or the means of production which are scarce, or are non-renewable, or are capable of monopolization, inevitably produces inequality in wealth of a sort which increases over generations, hardens the social order into a class structure, and (a) yields an unjustifiable amount of poverty, and (b) yields an unjustifiable amount of social

> instability. . . .
> (4) Since the social stability people
> need is impossible given a system which
> permits private ownership of those things
> (from (1) above) . . . it follows that
> private ownership of those things ought
> not to be permitted.[22]

Many useful computer programs, however, do not
fit these descriptions of property for which
ownership should be restricted. They do not
proclaim or describe general truths about our
universe and therefore cannot, necessarily, be
said to be like laws of nature. The activity
they perform is not scarce nor can it be monopolized.

Two examples of computer programs that
are not like laws of nature are sorting algorithms and database management systems. There
are many algorithms for sorting (e.g., bin
sort, trickle sort) any list of symbols that
come from a set on which an ordinal relationship can be defined; no one of them is "true"
or in any way natural. Similarly with database management systems, there are at least
three basic approaches to their architecture
and many different implementations.

An example of a computer program that
should not be protected as private property
might be an algorithm that implements the
series definition of the Fourier Transform of
a mathematical function for which the Transform exists. By this I mean that the program
calculates the values of the coefficients of
the series by evaluating the integrals that
define these coefficients. The integrals
would be calculated by evaluating the limit of
the upper or lower sums to the precision of
the computer. (An arbitrary limit would be
set if infinite precision arithmetic is used.)

Alternately, a computer program that
implements the so-called Fast Fourier Transform (FFT) algorithm for the calculation of
the Fourier coefficients of a function is an
example of a program for which protection
should be granted. There is nothing "natural"
or definitional about the algorithm; on first

appearance is bears little relationship to the series definition. It is a very clever way to calculate the values of the coefficients by ordering the calculations in a certain way, using some trigonometric identities and using values of calculations repeatedly to reduce the time and steps required.

If distinctions like these can success-fully be made, then patent protection may be applied to some types of computer programs.

Characterization of Computer Programs

If the courts, Congress, or other insti-tutions make distinctions like those mentioned and the protection desired by some becomes practice, the rest of this chapter will become irrelevant; but in case further details are desired and because the topic is inherently interesting, I offer the following comments.

Many people seek property right protec-tion as a reward for their effort in discover-ing and developing the data structures and al-gorithms of computer programs. Computer pro-grams, then, should be protected at the data structure and algorithm level, as a statutory category of their own. This protection should not be by copyright, which does not protect the ideas inherent in the program, but by patents or a new category. The criteria for when something is patentable should also ap-ply; namely, that the algorithm be novel and not obvious in the light of prior art.

Both of these criteria are difficult to judge, but such judgments are made routinely by patent examiners and doctoral committees. The rest of this chapter addresses the ques-tion of how computer programs can be charac-terized so that they can be specified unam-biguously and so that novelty and obviousness may be judged in somewhat objective ways.

To decide whether something is novel, it is necessary to compare it with existing items of a similar nature and to judge whether the differences are significant enough to warrant the conclusion of novelty. In order to make such a judgment, one should have some notion of what the entity is and some understanding of all the possible ways it can be what it is. Most people have some notion of what a computer program is, but the number of ways that it can be what it is are numerous, and judging when two of these are significantly different is a difficult matter.

Binary Representation

One approach to deciding if two programs are different is based on the observation, made by Johnson[23] and others, that there is a representation of programs in terms of 1's and 0's that in effect maps a program into one long binary number. The mapping is accomplished with an algorithm similar to the one that transforms the written version of a program, the so-called source code, into the executable version, the so-called object code, which is made readable to people as a sequence of binary numbers. These binary numbers are then concatenated to form the one long binary number mentioned above, and two programs are then identical if the two binary numbers they are mapped into are identical.

I have three objections to this technique as a way to characterize a program and to decide whether a program is novel; that is, if it is unlike all other programs so far developed. The first objection is that the binary representation of programs is arbitrary and is machine dependent, in that the binary representation of a particular component instruction, such as "add" or "move," has different binary representations on two different machines even when these two machines are executing algorithms that most would judge are the same. The objective of using so-called high level languages, such as FORTRAN and Pascal, is, in fact, to embody the data structures and algorithms of the program without making the data structures and algorithms depend on the particular machine on which the program will be executed, and it is the ideas in the FORTRAN or Pascal version of a computer program for which protection if often sought.

My second objection is that it is highly likely that in any such representation, one or more bits could be changed, and the program represented by these bits would execute in a manner not significantly different than it did before these bits were changed. Thus, two different binary representations of a program could really be the same program, even on a single machine.

A third objection concerns the supposed reality of programs in binary form as opposed to their nonreality in some other form. This assumption seems to underlie some of the discussions about the applicability of copyright procedures to the protection of programs. There are not really 1's and 0's anywhere in a computer while it is executing a program, other than those printed on components for identification purposes, which has little to do with the program being executed. Computers, while executing programs, consist of tangible, mechanical devices, some in motion, and voltages, currents, light rays, and other phenomena classified as physical or electrical--not many 1's or 0's anywhere.

Concerning the Algorithmic Constructs
of Computer Programs

Programmers speak of high- and low-level language representation of computer programs, the binary representation mentioned above being low level and programming languages similar to natural language being considered high level. It is at the high level that data structures and algorithms are most easily understood and specified, and it is at this level that I believe computer programs, and the data structures and algorithms they embody, should be defined, specified, and tested for novelty.

I suggest that a computer program representation based on high-level statements be considered as the definitive declaration of

the data structures and algorithm used by the
program, and that this representation be used
to define a program and to judge the novelty
of the program when compared to similar representations of other programs. My experience
indicates that five basic high-level constructs are sufficient to characterize a rich
variety of computer programs; they can serve
as a starting set of constructs with which to
build a high-level representation scheme for
computer programs. More formal work currently
under way and to come may modify the set
and/or the individual constructs themselves.

One of these five should be a simple
command, based on the natural language con-
struct of an imperative or declarative
sentence and specified with constructs such as
those used by Searle in his specification of
the speech acts that he calls "request" and
"assert."[24] Guided by this work, the specification of the syntax and semantics of a simple
command could include some or all of the following:

1. The proposition being asserted or
   requested.
2. The intention of the programmer.
3. The meaning of the assertion or
   request.
4. The understanding of the various
   compilers and computers that will
   process the assertion or the request.
5. The syntax and semantics of the
   words used to state the assertion or
   request.

The use of speech acts in the specification of computer programs is not as farfetched
as it might first appear in that it is de-
finitely within the realm of possibility;
soon, a computer will be able to be programmed
by speaking the algorithm to it. Where and
what, in this case, is the source code, the
object code, and any other representation between the spoken words and the execution of
the program? Obvious adjustments to the work

of Searle may have to be made, in that the
listener of the speech act is not a person,
but I suspect that these adjustments would not
have to be very extensive to allow their
applicability.

Some of the simple commands and structures might be the following:

>Declare (items that could be declared
>include atomic symbols such as bits,
>characters, and bytes as well as
>higher-level data structures such as
>words, lists, records, arrays, and
>files).

>Move data while maintaining its infor-
>mation, with or without transforming
>data representation (includes input
>and output command such as INPUT,
>PRINT, etc.).

>Production function or rule, such as "IF
>condition THEN action" or "IF ante-
>cedent THEN consequent."

>Send message.

>Wait until receipt of message.

each with the appropriate type and number of
arguments.

It may be argued that there are only
three really distinct commands here, namely
"declare," "move," and "wait." Indeed the
"move" command is quite basic as one acceptable method of developing language compilers
and interpreters is to develop a fundamental
move command and define all others in terms of
it.

The presence of the "send message" and
its counterpart "wait until receipt of message" in this list reflects the requirement
that programs must contain the ability to
execute over a computer network or in parallel; that is, to have portions of the program
executing on interconnected, autonomous or
semiautonomous machines. These two commands
are used to synchronize the execution of the
various distributed and/or parallel portions
of a program in the network and concurrent
program execution environment.

Although this list is not complete, given the objective to characterize programs, it seems at least possible that the computer science community, in conjunction with others, could develop a sufficiently complete list of simple commands and command constructs to be used in the characterization of computer programs. Limited conversations with some of my colleagues (Ralph Tindell for one, who sparked some of these ideas in my mind) have indicated that work along these lines is being done and may be quite advanced, although the problem is difficult and may yet prove intractable in the near future.

Four additional basic constructs, which I will call command structure sequence types, with which to characterize computer programs might be:

Sequences of simple commands without iteration or branching.

Iterations of sequences with initiation and termination tests.

Compare data and transfer (branching) to one of several sequences of primitive commands.

Procedure modules.

Again, this list may have to be modified and augmented upon further consideration. From my experience these commands and command sequence types are sufficiently complete to be useful, in that many useful programs could be constructed using programming constructs based on these two lists.

These constructs could be used by having the developers of program development tools, such as programming languages and their compilers and interpreters, map the commands and features of the language into the currently accepted list of simple commands and command sequence types. Program developers using these programming tools would then be able to characterize their programs by a unique sequence of simple commands and command sequence types.

Summary and Conclusion

The intent of this chapter was to devise useful methods to protect inventiveness and procedures embodied in computer programs at the level where much labor is expended in their creation. One method is to bring some computer programs under the statutory protection of the law, either under patent protection or some new form. In order to achieve this goal, computer programs must be defined with sufficient specificity to allow their unambiguous characterization. I suggest that programs characterized by simple command structures and command structure sequence types, such as those listed above, might be specified and protected at the level where the effort to produce them was actually made, thereby allowing assignments of deserved rewards for people's efforts.

Notes

The research reported in this chapter was supported by a grant from the Ethical Values in Science and Technology Program of the National Science Foundation. The author wishes to thank the Foundation and the study's principal investigator, Carol C. Gould, for their support and encouragement.

1. "Prosecution of computer crime has been hindered because much of the property involved does not fit into statutory definitions of property." H. Rep. No. 894, 98th Cong., 2nd Sess. 9, reprinted in 1984 U.S. Code Cong. & Ad. News 3689, 3694.
2. Deborah Johnson, "Should Computer

Programs Be Owned?" Lecture at Stevens Institute of Technology, 29 April 1985.

3. John Ladd, "Ethics and the Computer Revolution," Lecture at Stevens Institute of Technology, 5 February 1985.

4. Lawrence Becker, Property Rights: Philosophic Foundations (Boston: Routledge and Kegan Paul, 1977).

5. Robert L. Graham, "The Legal Protection of Computer Software," Communications of the ACM 27, no. 5 (May 1984).

6. Deborah G. Johnson, Computer Ethics (Englewood Cliffs, NJ: Prentice-Hall, 1985), Chapter 6.

7. Michael C. Gemignani, "Legal Protection for Computer Software: The View from '79," Rutgers Journal of Computers, Technology and the Law 7 (1980), pp. 269-312.

8. Mitchell P. Novick and Helene Wallenstein, "The Algorithm and Computer Software: A Scientific View of a Legal Problem," Rutgers Journal of Computers, Technology and the Law 7 (1980), pp. 313-.

9. Ira R. Abel, "World-Wide Protection of Computer Software: An Analysis of the WIPO Draft Proposal," New York Journal of International and Computer Law.

10. Alan C. Rose, "Protection of Intellectual Property Rights in Computer and Computer Programs: Recent Developments," Pepperdine Law Review 9 (1980), pp. 547-567.

11. J. Thomas Beckett, "Computer Law," Annual Survey of American Law, Issue 4 (1984).

12. Graham, "The Legal Protection of Computer Software," p. 423.

13. Ibid., p. 424.

14. Ibid., pp. 424-425.

15. Rose, "Protection of Intellectual Property Rights," p. 552.

16. Diamond v. Diehr, 101 S. Ct. 1048 (1981).

17. Johnson, Computer Ethics, p. 101.

18. Novick and Wallenstein, "The Algorithm and Computer Software," p. 341.

19. Johnson, Computer Ethics, p. 101.

20. Ibid., p. 101.

118

21. Becker, _Property Rights_, p. 54.
22. Ibid., p. 89.
23. Johnson, _Computer Ethics_, p. 100.
24. John R. Searle, _Speech Acts: An Essay in the Philosophy of Language_ (London: Cambridge University Press, 1969).

7

Ethics and the Practice of Science in a Computer Networked Environment

I. Richard Lapidus

In this chapter I will explore future scenarios in which the practice of science is carried out in a completely networked computer environment. This development could occur in the early part of the twenty-first century, and some of the readers of this book may be participants in such a scenario.

The development of these scenarios is dependent on a number of simplifying assumptions. These assumptions may actually prove to be much too conservative in view of the rapid changes taking place in computer and telecommunications technology at the present time. I have restricted my considerations to technological capabilities that are either presently available or may reasonably be expected to become available in the near future. I have not attempted to extrapolate into new technological areas that may or may not exist for the next generation of scientists. But if the technological changes in the next twenty or thirty years are no greater than they have been during the comparable period that has just passed, the actual networked computer environment in which the practice of science will take place may go beyond the most outrageous speculations we make today.

I assume that:

1. The cost of the computer and the communication technology will continue to decrease dramatically, thereby

accelerating the use of computer and communications technology, particularly in the field of science. The most sophisticated facilities will be available to scientists throughout the world.

2. The computer work station, which will be part of the worldwide network, will have capabilities for high-speed computation; facsimile printing of documents, including fine details of photographs; real-time video transmission and receiving capabilities of live and filmed materials; and remote control of instrumentation located at distant points.

3. Government and industrial funding will continue to be the primary source of support for scientific activities, with a significant fraction of such activity taking place in universities and university-type research institutions. These agencies will exert legal and ethical controls over the use of the network facilities. Alternatively, I shall consider the possibility that a significant component of scientific activity throughout the world will take place in a "marketplace" environment, and I will examine some of the ethical and practical implications of such a commercially controlled computer networked environment for the practice of science.

4. Communication of scientific results will continue to be an important aspect of scientific endeavor. A new set of legal and ethical considerations will be developed to deal with questions of privacy, priority, recognition, responsibility, and compensation. And to the extent that science becomes a "commodity" in a worldwide market, such communication may be restricted by economic considerations.

Jennings et al.[1] have summarized the status of national networking facilities available to scientists at the present time. These include NSFnet, which will probably have the most significant impact on scientific practice in the United States because it is directly linked to the NSF Supercomputer Initiative. Other wide-area networks in use today are ARPANET (Defense Advanced Research Projects Agency), which has been functioning for the past fifteen years and will be a component of NSFnet; CSNET (Computer Science Network), which is used by 165 university, government, and industrial research groups; BITNET, a noncommercial university-based network; MFENET (Magnetic Fusion Energy Network); and USENET, a UNIX-based network. In addition, there are a variety of networks not primarily designed for scientific usage but which are used by scientists to transfer information from one computer to another. Finally, there are many state, multicampus, and campus-wide university networks used for linking local laboratories and mainframe computer facilities.

Denning[2] has also discussed the impact of networks and supernetworks on scientific activity and has addressed some of the technical problems that may arise in attempting to make extremely large systems "user friendly."

In the primary scenario that I consider, the practice of science remains very traditional. The motivations of individual scientists and even scientific "organizations," such as universities and research laboratories, do not change significantly. But the computer networked environment dramatically alters the "style" in which science is carried out on a daily basis by individual scientists and scientific groups. In the alternate marketplace scenario, some aspects of the practice of science as we have known it in the past are significantly changed.

The traditional stereotype of the scientist working alone and making great discoveries has already been destroyed by the advent of "big science" in the fields of chemistry, physics, biology, and computer mathematics. Part of this change is the result of the dependence on funding from government agencies and industry. But perhaps more important, it must be recognized that there are very few opportunities for the lone scientist to compete against highly financed research groups. And the lone scientist cannot keep up with the flood of information necessary for scientific competition. One must be aware of the latest work of other scientists in one's immediate field as well as that of others who have developed new techniques that may enhance one's own research efforts. And one must be sure that one's efforts over a period of years have not already been completed by someone else. In the "open" future scenario, scientific information will be available to everyone. In the alternative scenario, in which information is a marketplace economic item, the lone scientist will be essentially extinct.

Despite the trend toward big science, a significant contribution to the scientific establishment presently is made by many scientists working in small university or commercial laboratories. The advent of the computer networked environment may facilitate the work of such scientists by making the same resources available, such as access to information and facilities, that are available at larger institutions.

Consider the manner in which big science experiments in high energy physics are now carried out. The use of a major particle accelerator may require a two-year lead time for application, approval, funding (at a level of hundreds of thousands of dollars for a single experiment), building of apparatus, and so on. Such experiments are carried out by a small number of scientists with the assistance of many members of the permanent accelerator facility technical staff at a government or large university laboratory. These experiments may produce hundreds of thousands of photographs, which must be analyzed in a reasonably short period of time. In order to do this task, the primary investigator develops a number of collaborative arrangements with scientists at other institutions (usually universities). The film is distributed to other laboratories, where it is analyzed. The total database is then pooled in order to obtain the final results. In this way small laboratories with limited funding may participate in "big" experiments, and scientists who would not otherwise be able to participate in this type of "frontier" research effort can now play a significant role.

The networked scientific environment will be ideally suited for this type of collaboration. Data will be transferred very easily from one laboratory to another almost instantaneously. The analysis effort of many laboratories will be online constantly so that results of the data analysis will be pooled continuously. Even the physical film need not be transported to the cooperating laboratories; video images will be sufficient.

Such large-scale cooperative efforts will raise new ethical issues with regard to the sharing of credit, priority, responsibility, and the like. Some of these issues are discussed below.

The Practice of Science

The practice of science in a networked environment will be considerably different from the practice as we know it today. The worldwide scientific community will be directly linked, almost as closely as groups of scientists now working at the same institution. In addition, the immediate availability of the world's scientific literature, enormous databanks, and the accessibility of computer and instrumental resources located thousands of miles from the individual scientist will complement the high-speed communication capabilities among scientists in different locations. In this section I will explore a few of the aspects of the manner in which science is likely to be carried out in such an environment.

Sidney Fernbach[3] has suggested a number of developments in computer technology that may become part of scientific practice in the near future. He notes that we may expect to see the keyboard, tape, and disk supplemented by direct oral and optical input into computers. This development will enable scientists to interact with computer systems in a much more rapid and flexible manner. However, these developments are only in their most primitive stages at the present time.

Just as in business and other fields of endeavor, the whole scientific community will have immediate access to large-scale databanks containing the entire scientific literature. In fact, the assembling and maintenance of such databanks will become an occupational field in itself. People trained in science as well as library skills will be required to update the numerous files in many fields that will be available on the network. The problem of efficient searching will become a serious one, and the network will employ information and routing operators who will assist network users in locating the specific databanks they require.

For example, every molecular biologist will have immediate access to all the known sequences of proteins, DNA, and RNA, as well as other biopolymers. Genetic linkage maps for microorganisms and higher organisms will be readily available, as will be cell lineage maps of numerous organisms, three-dimensional molecular structures, metabolic pathways, and taxonomic charts. Similarly, physicists and chemists will have immediate access to data about the physical properties of elements, compounds, crystals, and so on. Mathematicians will have access to mathematical functions and their properties and even a compendium of proven theorems and outstanding problems. Demographic and test data will be available for workers in the social, political, and behavioral sciences. And the properties of all the known drugs will be available to medical researchers.

All users will have access to supercom-
puting facilities. However, it will be
necessary to establish a priority scheme for
access as well as a scheme for payment for the
use of such facilities. Users will have access
to computer-controlled instrumentation at distant locations, which may be used directly for
experimental measurement or in conjunction
with on site collaborators. In our primary
scenario, these facilities will be available
to all, although a scheme for use priority
will be developed to queue the users.

I will not discuss here possible schemes
for the detailed allocation of these resources. However, it will be necessary to address
some of the ethical issues involved in such
schemes because they will have a significant
impact on the manner in which the daily practice of science will take place in a computer
networked environment. The resolution of these
ethical issues in terms of their practical impact may involve public policy through law or
marketplace pressures.

Consider the manner in which scientific
collaboration takes place today. In a formal
setting, research groups may join together to
carry out an experiment or its analysis when
the magnitude of the task is too great for a
single group. But more common is the situation
in which two or more scientists working in the
same field may decide to spend time together
for a short period--perhaps a year on a sab-
batical leave--in order to join their experience. The scientist who wishes to
collaborate with one or more of his or her
colleagues does so by physically traveling to
another laboratory or, if the collaboration
primarily involves a writing project, by
sending a manuscript back and forth through
the mail and by using the telephone.

In the networked environment, the scientist will have immediate access to all other
workers in his or her particular field. Furthermore, the use of remote-controlled
computer-directed instrumentation will eliminate much of the need for scientists to have
meetings in person. As a result there will be

considerably more collaboration among scientists at distant locations. This new "social interaction" among scientists also will be motivated by the necessity of small laboratories to share their resources, human as well as financial, in order to compete with the great research establishments, which will be supported by private industry.

Even such mundane tasks as job hunting will be facilitated by the networked environment. The "old boy" network will no longer be a suitable vehicle for obtaining a job. Interested job seekers will file applications on the worldwide network, which will match them up with requests for applications. The first round of selection will be done automatically by the network itself, and there will be a sequence of steps eventually leading to direct communication between the applicant and the potential employer. Interviews often will be conducted via the network using real-time video displays.

Although competition will continue to be an important motivation for scientists, secrecy will be extremely difficult. Government agencies, through the control of funding, will make available on the network results of all research supported by the agency. These agencies will also "advertise" on the network for scientists to study problems of interest to the agency. An important feature of the networked environment will be the immediate access by numerous scientific workers to "work in progress." These factors will lead to a closer "community of science."

However, in the alternate scenario of the marketplace of science, in which control of resources and results is in the hands of large industrial corporations, the computer networked environment will almost eliminate individuals and small groups from the scientific mainstream. Data and other forms of information will be "industrial secrets," which will be sold to other commercial groups if such a step is deemed to be profitable. Collaboration between scientists will be limited to "in-house" collaboration unless a commercial

contract has been signed between two companies. Scientific results, as well as the
applications derived from them, will be
treated as commercial "products."

The use of government authority to control the availability of information raises an
important ethical issue. Traditionally government agencies have been able to exert extensive control over the type of research carried
out within the scientific community; the agencies control the funding and therefore the
ability to make the research possible. As a
result, certain fields of study are supported
strongly--for example, areas that may have
military applications. Fortunately, the control is not strictly bureaucratic--proposals
for support of research are "peer reviewed"
and the distribution of funds to different
fields is ultimately subject to congressional
or state legislative approval. Universities
and groups of scientists have effectively
exerted pressure on government agencies to
support research that might not have been
supported otherwise. (Of course, this type of
pressure also has a negative impact because it
may bypass the peer review system.)

However, despite the control that the
government exerts over the type of research
funded, once a grant is made to a scientist,
the government control over the actual practice is usually very limited, except to assure
that the terms of the grant are actually carried out. For example, at the present time
there is no requirement that government-
supported scientists make available, in a
fully public manner, the raw data that forms
the basis of the results, which may be published in a professional journal. I shall
discuss below some of the professional
implications of making such data available;
here we are concerned only with the ethical
issue of whether the government should exert
this authority.

The issue is closely related to the
question of ownership of scientific knowledge.
At the present time the government may claim
patent rights to any discoveries that result

from work done under a contract or grant. However, in practice this right normally has not been exercised. But if the government insisted that public disclosure of data was a condition of financial support, this condition would become a part of the scientific practice.

The authority of the government to restrict the flow of scientific information has been exercised many times in cases of "classified" information, and such restrictions have been deemed necessary because of national security interests. I believe that if the National Science Foundation, the National Institutes of Health, the Department of Defense, the Department of Energy, and so on demanded as a condition of support that data be made available to the public in a networked environment, this demand would be enforceable.

Dissemination of Scientific Results

An essential, integral part of scientific activity is the dissemination of scientific results to the scientific community and the general public. Although the history of science is replete with numerous examples of the withholding of results by individuals for many years, it is usually expected that new discoveries or other developments will be reported promptly at professional meetings or in the professional literature. In fact, the "need to know" quickly has become so strong that many authors distribute "preprints" of their results before their papers are published.

The networked scientific environment will facilitate this trend and at the same time exacerbate the problems of premature dissemination of scientific results. A number of ethical issues will then be raised, which will be resolved by the development of new practices in the dissemination of scientific results.

In discussing the networked environment, it is important to distinguish between the computer-assisted environment and the truly networked environment. In a computer-assisted environment many of the daily activities associated with the dissemination of scientific results will be carried out in essentially the same manner as they are today, except that computers will increase the efficiency of operations and decrease the communication time.

For example, consider the submission of scientific papers for publication in professional journals. In a computer-assisted environment, an author prepares a manuscript for publication using a word processor. The finished manuscript is transferred as a file directly to the computer at the office of the journal via a communications system (such as a telephone line). The editor selects reviewers and transfers the file to the reviewers' computers. The reviewers comment on the manuscript and submit their comments to the editor by computer. These comments are then transferred to the author, who revises the manuscript and repeats the process. When the manuscript is accepted for publication, it is forwarded to the publication staff who prepare it in its "typeset" form and return it to the author for proofreading. Nothing has really changed in this scenario, except that the manuscript is not printed on paper and mailed around the country (or the world). But the essential interaction among author, editor, reviewer, and publisher remains on a one-to-one basis.

Now consider the networked environment. In the extreme case of the completely open network, every user of the network has complete access to every file on the network. The preliminary manuscript will become available immediately to all users. Presumably there will be a "disclaimer" notice attached to such files indicating that they have not been reviewed and may be revised before publication.

Nonetheless, the cat is out of the bag. As most of the results will survive the review process, other investigators will take such manuscripts fairly seriously. This development will place additional obligations on the authors to ensure the validity of any results given in the manuscript. On one hand, the open network may deprive the author of the benefit of the reviewers' comments. Such comments could enhance the final manuscript, but reviewers may be reluctant to suggest significant changes in a manuscript that has already been widely disseminated. On the other hand, the open network will provide an opportunity for any network user to offer his or her comments to the author before publication, which could enhance the final manuscript.

In the more general case of limited access, there are significant ethical issues that must be resolved. These include fairness, protection of privacy, who has the authority to determine access right, and so on. Of course these issues are not restricted to the scientific community. They are discussed briefly below.

And what about the nature of the journals themselves? We may anticipate that printed magazines mailed regularly to subscribers will disappear. Perhaps "archive" copies will be sent to libraries, universities, and research laboratories. But the individual subscriber will subscribe to a computer version of the journal. The journal will have an extensive indexing system, which will allow the user to search for articles of interest. Then the user may copy those articles of interest or immediately make a hard copy of the article on a local printer. The era of the reprint will have ended. In addition to saving shelf space, which is often a serious problem today, the cost of such journals will be much less than they are today because the cost of layout work be greatly reduced. Consequently, it will be possible for an individual subscriber to subscribe to many more journals. I have no suggestions, however, regarding how to find the additional time to read these journals.

The index, abstract, and reprint service industries will grow significantly. Individual scientists who do not wish to "browse" through the literature will subscribe to such services rather than subscribe to journals themselves. Depending on the financial resources of an individual, only titles, abstracts, or complete articles on specific topics will be ordered on a standing basis. Of course, they will be delivered through the local computer facility. The individual subscriber will establish his or her own reprint library and indexing system for rapid retrieval of articles on specific topics. The networked environment also will give the researcher and scholar access, upon request, to all journals on the network. Presumably this service will include every journal published. In addition, books will be available in toto, thereby avoiding the necessity of searching in libraries for hard copy versions. The impact of the networked environment on the book publishing industry will be very dramatic. For individuals wishing to read books while they are not at their terminals, all books will be available on microdisks that may be read using a portable, hand-held micro-microcomputer.

In addition to the type of information available today, including journals and books, the network user will have access to video films and extensive databases containing research results submitted by other authors and compiled by the network. The problem of lack of access to information will be replaced by the problem of overabundance.

What will be the responsibilities of the scientist in this environment? For example, it is now expected that an author will review the literature and conduct a reasonable search. It is expected that credit will be given to previous relevant work. In the networked environment, the scientist may be responsible for providing references for anything that can be accessed through the network, even the most "obscure" sources. But it may not be necessary to give a reference in the standard form, such as "Lapidus, I. R., J. Comp. Phys. 78, 1289 (2024)." One might simply give the reference in the databank as "PHYS-WW-S=23JC58/SV265F.635A6." The interested reader will then access the article directly. The author may include a search protocol as part of an article, which will enable the reader to conduct his or her own search and make it unnecessary for the author to give any references at all! Thus, instead of being scrupulous about giving credit, it may be sufficient for the author to reference only the key articles that are directly relevant, both in the field and in other research areas.

Another important vehicle for the dissemination of scientific information is the scientific meeting. Although the need for such meetings will decrease, they do provide an isolated, informal (often very enjoyable) setting for person-to-person interactions. Meetings also provide an opportunity for scientists to become acquainted with work outside their narrow specialty, an activity they may consider as an intellectual "luxury" for which they do not have time in their normal work setting. Therefore, meetings and special conferences will continue in the era of computer networking.

But the format of these meetings will change significantly. Papers will be presented "by computer"--the ultimate in poster sessions. Authors need not even be present if they cannot attend the meeting. Contributed and invited "stand up" papers will be presented as video films that will be submitted to the conference organizers (by computer network, of course). A presentation at a poster session will merely consist of being available for direct communication at certain times, or else answers will be provided to questions through a "post office" system.

As I shall discuss below, receiving credit is one of the rewards of scientific endeavor. The flood of data and other information available on the network system will create an imposing task for the "ethical" researcher. The solution to this problem may be a revision of the ethical requirements of authors, because it will be so easy for readers to access the same information base used by the author.

But the problem of plagiarism may become a severe one. Authors with direct access to the writings of everyone else may steal words, paragraphs, pages, and chapters and use them in their own writing. In fact, it will be so easy that the author will not even have to retype such stolen words. Detection of this type of theft may not be difficult if the theft is from another scientist working in a closely allied field, as both writings would be seen by the same group of readers. But one cannot expect that anyone will be able to monitor all fields of publication to protect one's own writings. This would be more than a full-time job in itself.

A few comments about the proliferation of journals are in order. At the present time it is impossible for any individual to keep up with the literature in even a "broad" specialized field. New journals come into existence on a daily basis and the flood of publications is overwhelming. One may anticipate that this trend will continue. However, the supposed benefits of such a plethora of autonomous publications may be obscured when all are avail-able via computer networks. The network also will allow an automatic "marketplace" evaluation to take place. Every time a journal article is accessed, cited, or copied, a record will be made. Thus, the impact of a particular paper on the scientific community as a whole can be assessed directly in evaluating the quality of authors' publications. This procedure may eventually restrict the growth in the number of new journals by leading to the demise of those which are unsuccessful in this marketplace.

Even more significant changes associated with the dissemination of scientific information will result from the use of alternative methods of presentation, forms that go beyond the printed word--even if the printing is via computer. The networked environment will permit "publication" of scientific and educational results using both still and moving pictures, including direct video transcription of live presentations by authors. Animation, image enhancement, playback, and all the techniques available to the video industry will be used to present scientific results.

A few examples will illustrate the possibilities: (1) A team of surgeons will "write up" their new techniques for brain transplants by showing live films of actual surgical procedures; (2) animal behaviorists will include films of the mating behavior of the giant condor; (3) sociologists will include actual live conversations of astronauts on the first Saturn mission. The use of these new techniques in scientific "publications" will necessitate the development of new review procedures. Authors will employ public relations and media personnel to enhance their presentations. Will the efforts of these people be invisible, or will publications close with screen after screen of media credits?

Verification of New Scientific Results

When we teach students about the "scientific method," one of the essential elements is "verification." Scientific results are considered to have validity because they can be obtained independently by different investigators. Or so goes the myth. The notion that a scientist would literally repeat the work of another scientist arose in an era of small-scale experiments carried out with home-made equipment. In actual practice today, it is not at all common to repeat literally another investigator's experiments. Many factors make such repetitions difficult or impossible: (1) One cannot obtain financial support for this type of work; (2) one is unwilling to stop one's own work to do it unless there is doubt about the correctness of the result; (3) the original experiment may have been so costly that it is not possible to repeat it; and (4) the experiment may have required special techniques or kinds of equipment not available to other workers. Verification of results is usually accomplished by testing the same idea using different methods. If two different experiments yield the same conclusions, one builds confidence in the ideas used to explain both experiments.

There is another means of verification that is rarely used today but will be an integral part of the networked scientific environment: One may examine in detail the original data obtained by the primary investigator. Such an examination may provide the basis for a set of independent conclusions based on the original data, or it may provide the basis for criticism of the published results. There are numerous examples of experiments that were carried out correctly but interpreted incorrectly due to faulty analysis of the data. Conclusions based on such faulty analyses will rarely escape the scrutiny of other scientists in the networked environment because the original data as well as the published manuscript will be available on the network.

Verification by examination of original data assumes that there will be open access to the scientific computer network. But in the marketplace environment of our alternate scenario, there will be unequal access to the network. Two questions must then be asked: (1) What will be the hierarchies of access? (2) Who will decide where one is placed in the hierarchy? These questions may be resolved directly in a marketplace environment by making use of a general principle: "To each according to his ability to pay."

What other considerations, in addition to money, will be invoked in establishing priorities for network usage? And what general principles should be used in an open networked environment? These are issues that must be resolved as the networked environment becomes a reality. It is reasonable to assume that some form of generalized copyright system will be developed to protect authors from direct plagiarism of their written words. But in the scientific context, the printing of raw data is not an end in itself. It is for the interpretation of that data that one obtains fame and glory (and maybe even money). One can imagine a situation in which a scientist will publish a set of data with an interpretation that is either invalid or incomplete. Or perhaps the scientist missed a very significant result that actually was contained in the data. As the raw data will be available, another scientist may use that data to develop a completely different interpretation, which may be "better" or more "correct."

But who owns the data? Dorothy Nelkin[4] has examined the question of ownership of scientific information. Many of the issues raised by her are exacerbated in the context of the computer networked environment. Does the original scientist get any credit for the new discovery beyond an acknowledgment regarding the source of the data? These ethical issues do not arise in our present closed environment because the original investigator usually maintains complete control of the raw data and releases it to other investigators under strictly limited conditions. There have been remarkably few legal disputes over this issue in the past. But in a networked environment where investigators will be required to make their raw data available to other investigators, such disputes will become commonplace and a set of rules will have to be developed to resolve them.

Science and Education

In the networked scientific environment, seminars, just as papers at meetings, will be given via the network. The speaker will be on live, interactive, large-screen video and will make his or her presentation to many locations at the same time. Questions from the audience and responses from the speaker will be networked to all participants in the seminar at all locations. The seminar will become a permanent part of the network information base and could be accessed at any time.

The education of scientists by scientists will be dramatically enhanced. It will be possible to access a wide variety of talks by scientists working in many fields. Individuals will select which seminars they wish to "attend" (via computer) and will allocate

their time accordingly. If they do not wish
to participate in the discussion they may
access the seminar at a later time. Seminars
and lectures will be available to all. Thus,
it will be possible to "keep up" with recent
developments even though one is located in an
out-of-the-way place, such as a small college
or commercial laboratory. As a result, it will
be possible for many more persons to participate actively in the scientific community.

The same technology will be used in the
classroom. In this way, education will be
available for all. However, in this case
there are pedagogical issues that must be
resolved. These issues include, for example,
an assessment of the importance of
person-to-person interactions in the educational environment. This area needs much
study; however, it will not be discussed here.
The use of prerecorded lectures and demonstra-
tions for classroom use is already a common
practice. The use of these techniques for
presentation of current scientific activity
will bring the scientific community closer
together and make these presentations available to scientists working in small colleges,
laboratories, and other countries.

The Rewards of Science

Despite numerous studies by psycholo-
gists, sociologists, and other investigators
of human behavior and motivation, we still do
not know why certain people enter the field of
science. Certainly scientists share a group
of characteristics, including curiosity, de-
light in solving puzzles, an organized view of
their existence, and so on, and of course the
usual needs for economic success, personal
adulation, and satisfaction. In our society
the scientist is almost unique as an economic
player. The intellectual requirements and
long period of training exceed those for law
and medicine, to pick two examples. Yet, although the time commitment of the scientist to
his work may even exceed those of the lawyer

or physician, the financial rewards are usually considerably less. (To some extent these comments apply to college and university faculty in general.)

Clearly there are other professional benefits to the scientist. Among the most important is recognition or credit for discoveries and other scientific achievements. How will this reward system be affected by the networked environment?

The impact of big science has already changed the perceptions of the public and the scientific profession with regard to recognition. Recent Nobel Prizes in physics have been awarded for experiments that required external funding of hundreds of thousands of dollars, usually from government sources. Dozens of scientists have been involved in such projects, with perhaps hundreds of others assisting with design and manufacturing of necessary specialized equipment and even the administration of such a large project. Yet all these workers remain anonymous while one or two project "leaders" are credited with the "discovery" that may have been in the planning stage for five years. Furthermore, the media have treated these scientists as "entertainers" (although they do not command the financial rewards of even mediocre rock singers!). In a recent issue of Science 85, a lay magazine published by the American Association for the Advancement of Science, a number of "leading" scientists were interviewed about twenty-five great discoveries in science that could be expected to change our lives in the near future. Many of the interviewees were shown in familiar slick magazine poses--a mathematician standing on a stone wall in front of a waterfall, neuroscientists leaning against walls and window sills, a paleontologist wearing a torn "Indiana Jones" hat.

In our future scenario, scientists will engage in an intensified worldwide competition that will bear a striking resemblance to MTV and the "Top 40." The essential ingredient required for this change will be the rapid worldwide communication network, which will make scientific "breakthroughs" known to the entire world almost immediately. Institutions and agencies will compete for scientific "stars." Even if the network itself is not run in a marketplace environment, commercial companies and industries will market science as they do soap. A scientific achievement by General Science Industries will help to sell its new line of see-through jeans.

The superstar mentality will be encouraged by another development. As the time scale between scientific "landmarks" shrinks, the ability of most individual scientists to make dramatic "breakthroughs" will decrease. In the rush to compete, these scientists will necessarily publish only small pieces of the solutions to timely scientific questions. It will be very difficult for the nonsuperstars or losing competitors to obtain recognition for their efforts. Thus, a larger proportion of the scientific community will be team players who will serve as resources for the stars. Industrial corporations will compete for the superstars in science as they now compete for athletes. Unfortunately, these superstars will not command the million dollar salaries of athletic superstars.

We have already witnessed the first stages of this development. Drug companies have long maintained copyright and patent rights to molecules. Scientists at General Electric recently have developed a mutant bacterium that has interesting biological properties (it digests oil). General Electric has claimed copyright and patent rights on this organism. The entire field of biotechnology, especially gene-splicing technology, which will develop rapidly in the next few years, will be deeply involved in legal disputes between companies claiming the rights to certain enzymes, plasmids, viruses, microbial cells, and eventually larger organisms including grains that grow faster and bigger, livestock that has less fat, or new breeds of race horses. The computer networked environment will accelerate this process because of the dramatic changes in data acquisition and communication.

Dangers of a Networked
Scientific Environment

I next turn to some of the problems and dangers of the computer networked environment. The changes in the scientific subsociety and the society as a whole that result from the technological impact of the networked environment will raise a number of ethical issues that will be resolved by law or marketplace dynamics.

The dangers to society from increased reliance on computerized information systems has been discussed by David Burnham in his book The Rise of the Computer State.[5] These dangers, which include invasion of privacy, control of individual behavior, and control of access to information, are important within the limited context of scientific activity. They will become even more important in the context of the computer networked environment.

In his book The Network Revolution, Jacques Vallee discusses the changes that take place in workers and the mode of their working behavior in a computer environment.[6] These same considerations apply to the computer networked environment. Although we may look forward to a time in the future when computers may be able to respond directly to a wide variety of direct human inputs by voice or other means, in the near future the communication with computers will still be via a restricted set of operations using a highly structured format, even if it is "user friendly." Thus, to a certain extent the activities of the humans will be determined by the limitations and structure of the computers and the networks. Vallee also discusses the hypothetical scenario in which an error on one computer is propagated throughout a worldwide business network leading to the collapse of the stock market. Although such a scenario is unlikely to lead to the collapse of the scientific establishment, one can certainly imagine that there will be numerous system errors that could lead to the propagation of misinformation and could have a significant professional and financial effect on many scientists using the network.

Who will own the network? In our primary scenario, the scientific network is a public facility available to all. It may be run as an international utility company or an intergovernmental agency. This organization will establish a set of rules for the operation of the network. The rules will reflect decisions that will have been made with regard to efficiency, expediency, and fairness. The opposing demands between these factors will require some set of criteria for decision-making, and the formulation and application of these criteria, of necessity, will involve ethical considerations.

In our alternate scenario, the network will be privately owned. There will be a number of competing networks, similar to the competing telephone companies as they will exist in the very near future. Such companies will offer a variety of services to their customers, including those mentioned earlier (e.g., information operators, larger databases, faster access, priorities). Network customers will pay for the use of the network on the basis of the time for access and the level of access. Files will not be available to all users; instead there will be a priority system based on commercial interests.

The network industry will develop an elaborate set of measures to protect the privacy of the customer, including files and records of access. Such materials will be considered "trade secrets" and will not be available to other users. This procedure will be accomplished through the development of elaborate schemes for encrypting the files and access to them. The control of this security will be in the hands of the user, rather than the network operators. In this scenario information will be a commodity with an economic value. It will be traded and sold like wheat on the Information Exchange with its formal headquarters in Boston.

Within the context of the level of knowledge at the time, individual scientific productivity has not significantly changed during the past few hundred years, despite the rapid increase in the available factual database. But the increased flood of data that will be available in the networked environment may alter the relationship between scientists and the knowledge that will now be readily available to every individual.

Scientists today are trained to master a fundamental body of knowledge and to be familiar with a set of facts of reasonable size. The almost instant availability of enormous quantities of factual material will require that scientists develop new skills in retrieval of information. In fact, there will be specialists who are highly expert in finding information and who don't actually know anything! Such people are being trained today, although not in a formal manner. Many of us are familiar with student "computerniks" who know all the details about how a number of software or hardware systems work but have no interest in or understanding of the content areas that make the computer system a useful tool for carrying out some other activity. The overspecialized scientific professional of today may appear as a generalist in comparison with his colleagues of the next generation. Although this development may accelerate "progress" in certain restricted fields, the probability of obtaining really new deep insights into basic scientific questions may be diminished. It was Andy Warhol who once said, "In the future everyone will be world-famous for fifteen minutes." In this context we might add, "In the future everyone will know only one thing."

The Scientist as an Ethical Being

The practice of science and the activities of scientists necessarily involve ethical considerations, some of which are common to a number of professions and some of which are uniquely appropriate to this field of endeavor. All the ethical issues that face the computer industry today will be magnified in the international scientific networked environment. These issues include protection of privacy, fairness of access, protection of property, and the like. How will these considerations be altered by the networked environment?

In her book <u>Computer</u> <u>Ethics</u>, Deborah Johnson considered ethical issues in relation to general computer usage.[7] But she did not address ethical issues that may be unique to computer networked systems. Although many of her general comments may be extended to the computer networked environment, there are a number of new problems that must be addressed.

We have already alluded to a number of areas in which ethical considerations will play a significant role--for example, in the area of dissemination of knowledge. The responsibilities of the scientist in assuring the accuracy of the data entered into the network will be very great. Furthermore, in the event that data or other information must be corrected, the scientist must ensure that this is done so that other workers will not base their efforts on erroneous information.

In the marketplace networked environment, one can expect to find commercial sabotage taking place. Commercial theft will be a goal pursued by whole departments in major industries, while other departments will make efforts at countermeasures, including the development of the art of disinformation. Such activities may or may not be illegal. If the networks are regulated by governments, then one may expect that there will be laws regarding such activities. But if the networks are controlled by commercial interests, it will be the responsibility of the International Network Corporation and its rivals to establish their own means of restricting such behavior.

Scientists will be expected to be honest in their investigations and their reporting of

results.   They will be expected to give adequate credit to other workers who contributed
to their efforts. But how is such credit to
be allocated?   And how is even unintentional
plagiarism to be avoided when all the literature of the world is literally at one's
fingertips?   The large number of people involved in many scientific projects mitigates
against the listing of all the involved people
as "authors" of publications. Perhaps scientific papers will be formally "authored" by
superstars but will actually be produced like
"handbooks" or "instruction manuals," created
by anonymous scientific writers sitting in
cubicles in the publications offices of major
industrial corporations.
     We have already noted the major role that
"media" considerations may play in scientific
presentations as well as the marketing of
scientific results.   Will scientists invoke
their usual caution with regard to the significance of their scientific discoveries, or
will this reticence be subverted in favor of
the "hype" needed to establish priority and
obtain funding?   Despite good intentions,
scientists may find themselves caught in the
flow of company economic interests that must
supersede their own professional interests,
just as "national interests" have superseded
ethical considerations of individuals who have
carried out government research programs in
the past. These considerations, already relevant in today's scientific activity, will
become more important in the computer networked environment in which questions of
priority, credit, and ownership will become
more difficult to resolve.

Conclusion

     I have considered two variations on a
scenario for science in a networked environment as it may be in the not too distant
future. Obviously, any attempt to predict the
nature of even one aspect of society in the
future is a risky business. Nonetheless, the

models I have presented may be useful at the present time as the necessity for dealing with the ethical issues involved in networking of the whole society becomes apparent to lawmakers and businesses as well as the few academics who have thus far made these matters an area of concern.

In the present state of society, in the United States and the other industrial states that will be using networks in the immediate future, it will be necessary to rely on the rule of law in order to have the assurance that the network environment will be such that it will allow for the "ethical" use of its facilities. But actions based on ethical considerations are not the usual activities of lawmakers. Thus, it will be the responsibility of scientists, and perhaps even of philosophers, to develop a strategy for lobbying the decision-makers so that the laws, rules, and regulations that are enunciated will be based on considerations other than expediency, power brokering, and privilege.

I do not look forward to a society in which science is a commercial item under the control of major industrial corporations. In such a scenario the potentially great breakthroughs in knowledge will be difficult to achieve in the face of pressure for financial profit. The notion is not outrageous. A few years ago there was a motion picture called "Rollerball" in which rollerball teams were owned by competing international industrial corporations, which had replaced national governments as the political organizational units of the near future. Not surprisingly, the rollerball game was high tech and characterized by high violence.

The computer networked environment can provide new opportunities for significant intellectual advances in science. We can only hope that such advances will take place in a setting that will improve the lives of all people who will be able to benefit from new discoveries and a deeper understanding of our world and ourselves.

Notes

1.   Dennis M. Jennings et al., "Computer Networking for Scientists," Science 231 (28 February 1986), pp. 943-950.

2.   Peter J. Denning, "The Science of Computing: Computer Networks," American Science 73 (1985), p. 127; and "The Science of Computing: Supernetworks," American Science, 73 (1985), p. 225.

3.   Sidney Fernbach, "Scientific Use of Computers," in The Computer Age: A Twenty Year View, Michael L. Dertouzos and Joel Moses, eds. (Cambridge, MA: MIT Press, 1983).

4.   Dorothy Nelkin, "Intellectual Property: The Control of Scientific Information," Science 216 (1982), p. 704; and Science as Intellectual Property (New York: Macmillan Publishing, 1984).

5.   David Burnham, The Rise of the Computer State (New York: Vintage Books, 1984).

6.   Jacques Vallee, The Network Revolution (Berkeley, CA: And/Or Press, 1982).

7.   Deborah G. Johnson, Computer Ethics (Englewood Cliffs, NJ: Prentice-Hall, 1985).

8

Ethics in Scientific Research via Networking

Frank T. Boesch

The impact of computer networks on scientific research has only begun. The use of such networks in scientific research, however, is not new. For example, ARPANET, the scientific network managed by the Defense Advanced Research Projects Agency of the United States, has been in existence for almost two decades.

In order to explore some of the ethical issues related to computer networks in scientific research, one needs a clear understanding of the term "computer network." In this chapter, a computer network is considered to be an interconnection of computers where the computers are capable of "stand-alone" operation but are also interconnected to exchange information or utilization. This definition seems sufficiently general to include all cases of interest. However, there are some exclusions. For example, this definition does not include the case where one merely has a terminal in a remote location connected to a central computer. For an extensive discussion of the technical details of those computer networks defined here, see Tanenbaum.[1]

ARPANET is an excellent example of such a computer network. Computing facilities at more that 300 universities, government facilities, and industrial laboratories are interconnected to form a network that spans the entire United States. Individual locations share resources ("compute power") as well as data. The tech-

nological sophistication of such networks far
surpasses that of electronic mail systems.
Furthermore, ARPANET is currently undergoing
an extremely powerful expansion to form
NSFnet, the new National Science Foundation
Network of supercomputers.

Perhaps one of the first issues to be
considered in discussing the ethics involved
in using these networks for scientific research is what Ladd called the
Replacement-Improvement-Extension (RIE) principle.[2] Namely, this principle states
that the advent of computer networks does not
change the basic ethical issues, but merely
expands the speed and magnitude of previous
mechanistic processes. Ladd has presented
many cases to argue that the computer alone,
without a network, creates situations that are
not merely examples of the RIE principle.
Namely, Ladd showed that entirely new ethical
issues were created by the advent of computers. In the case of computer networks,
Ladd's conclusion is even more strongly supported, as we shall demonstrate in this
chapter.

In a work devoted specifically to the
ethical issues of scientific research in a
computer network environment, Lapidus presented many new ideas demonstrating that
networks lead to new questions regarding the
practices and principles involved in scientific research.[3] This hypothesis that networks
lead to new ethical issues is further supported by the work of Johnson and Nelkin.
Johnson[4] considered the ethical issues that
arise from the use of computers in a general
setting. Nelkin[5] considered the ethical
issues that arise from private and government
direct funding of scientific research.
Nelkin's ideas are clearly pertinent here, as
current scientific computer research networks
are funded this way and future networks will
no doubt be similarly funded. Most of the
work cited above is concerned with normative
theories and meta-ethical questions. In
addition, some descriptive theories have been
advanced that support the hypothesis that new

ethical practices are evolving with the use of this new technology. A discussion of this point can be found in Mowshowitz.[6]

A recent informal study also gives credence to this hypothesis. A vice president of a major industrial research laboratory recently authorized the installation of an electronic mail system involving thousands of employees. He was particularly interested in the sociological impact it would have on the work habits and attitudes of the scientists. He initiated a private study that involved hundreds of scientists. Much to his surprise, he found that the major impact was on the personal code of conduct among the scientists. Namely, people who would never open a mail envelope addressed to someone else began to consistently break codes to read other people's electronic mail. Extensive interviews and surveys revealed that the scientists had developed a different moral code with respect to electronic mail. They saw it as a puzzle, a challenge, a test of skill to break the code. They thought of themselves as acting similarly to Richard Feynman, who picked the locks of military officers' top secret files during the Manhattan project.[7] (One might note that this analogy is rather weak, as Feynman was a member of the Manhattan project and thus entitled to see the contents anyway.)

Based on the above discussion, it is reasonable to presume that new ethical questions will emerge with the accelerated use of networks. Most of the works cited above are concerned with ethical issues that have already arisen in today's world. There have been many projections of future computerized environments and their related ethical issues; for example, see Licklider[8] and Mowshowitz. However, they do not consider scientific research. Lapidus has considered most of the ethical issues related specifically to scientific research in a computer network environment. He considered:

1. accessibility of results
2. accessibility of data

3. ownership of results
4. dissemination of results
5. verification of results
6. security of data
7. rewards to individuals

An important area that deserves greater attention is that of dissemination and retrieval of scientific information. This subject is intimately involved with the basic issue of motivation for performing scientific research and for disseminating the results. In this chapter, these specific issues will be considered in more detail. First, I will review the classical motivation and dissemination issues. I will then consider issues arising from future scenarios of extensive networking.

In both the classical and future settings, the research being considered is performed by professional scientists whose work is disseminated in scientific books and periodicals. In the classical case, a scientific research ethic has evolved. I will review this ethic and consider possible issues that may evolve in the future.

Classical Motivation for
Scientific Research Performance
and Dissemination

In the temple of science are many mansions, and various indeed are they that dwell therein and the motives that have led them thither. Many take to science out of a joyful sense of superior intellectual power; science is their own special sport to which they look for vivid experience and the satisfaction of ambition; many others are to be found in the temple who have offered the products of their brains on this altar for purely utilitarian purposes. Were an angel of the Lord to come and drive all the people belonging to these two categories out of

the temple, the assemblage would be
seriously depleted, but there would still
be some men, of both present and past
times, left inside.   --<u>Albert Einstein</u>[9]

Certainly there are many intangible
motives for individuals to perform and document scientific research; however, there are
also tangible motives.   The famous slogan
"publish or perish" captures these motives,
which include raises, promotions, funding,
awards, tenure, new employment offers, and
travel opportunities. These motives apply to
both university and industrial laboratory
scientists. However, scientific administrators
and colleagues feel that it is necessary to
further refine the evaluation of research;
mere publication does not demonstrate research
success.   The importance of specific publications and the prestige of a scientist are also
subject to scrutiny. It has been noted many
times that the most famous scientist who ever
lived was Einstein Here the concept of famous
(or perhaps infamous) is related to the number
of people who know the scientist's name. Of
course, Einstein's fame is attributed to the
media, and most researchers have no delusions
of acquiring that level of prestige. But
prestige of some form plays an important role
in every scientist's career. Consider, for
example, the typical questions that arise when
reviewing a scientist's resume: How significant are his or her publications? Are the
journals prestigious? How important is his or
her role in creating the results contained in
a multi-authored publication?
It is typically held true that the
prestige of a researcher is directly related
to the impact of his or her work on that of
others.   Seminal theories and results find
their way into textbooks. Important work is
referenced in publications by other researchers. Indeed some scientists have attempted to
demonstrate their prestige by using library
abstracting and indexing services to generate
a forward citation index (a list of publications by other people who reference their

work).

The customs and accepted ethics involved
in scientific publication are intimately related to these motivations. A brief review of
these customs and ethics for classical scientific research is given in the next section.

Classical Customs and Ethics
in Scientific Research Performance
and Dissemination

Currently the majority of dissemination
is accomplished via periodicals, journals, and
books. A typical scenario is that someone or
some group becomes interested in a specific
field of science. They try to learn what has
been done by others (literature search); they
assimilate the ideas; they obtain and verify a
new result; they document it in writing; they
present it at a conference or discuss it with
other people in the field; they submit a carefully edited document to a scholarly journal;
they obtain a report from the editor regarding
its acceptability; they rewrite the manuscript; they submit the revised version to the
publishers "backlog." Then the article finally
appears (often two or three years subsequent
to the original verification), and people read
their work.

An ethic, or accepted code of conduct,
for scientific research and publication has
evolved. It is difficult to document this
code of conduct. For example, the Association
for Computing Machinery, a major professional
society for computer scientists, has a code of
ethics that never mentions research or publication. However, there is an ethic accepted
by most scientists and enforced by most journal editors. The details of this research and
publication ethic are many and varied. A few
examples are as follows:

It is the obligation of the scientist to
disseminate his or her results.
It is the obligation of journals to maintain standards for originality, cor-

rectness, and importance (in this context, a result is not important if it is trivial; i.e., the solution is original and correct but follows obviously from the application of well-known principles).

It is the obligation of the author to make every reasonable attempt to credit prior work.

It is the obligation of the author to show the relevance of his or her work to that of others.

It is the obligation of the scientist to give due credit to all contributors. (It is often the case that one of the authors is only responsible for having identified the problem.)

It is the obligation of the scientist not to announce premature results.

Notice that the concept of crediting prior work is clearly based on being able to retrieve the information. It is often the case that two scientists obtain the same result independently. Even if the discoveries are not simultaneous, the scientific community will often credit both people when it can be assumed that they had no reasonable chance to learn of the other's work. Examples of this phenomenon are principles and theorems named after two people who did not obtain similar results by working together; for example, Bose-Einstein, Fermi-Dirac, and Cauchy-Schwarz-Buniakovski.

A Future Scenario for Scientific Research

Certainly the main function of scientific journals and periodicals is to disseminate results to other interested people. It is not unreasonable to presume that in the future all such dissemination will be via computer networks. Subnetworks of some major scientific network, such as NSFnet will be available for each field of interest. As a result, the procedure for production and dissemination will

change.   Clearly, instant literature searches
and publication will be possible and likely to
occur.   Such a publication may bear some nota-
tion indicating that it has not yet been subject to peer review.   However, each scientist,
in effect, will be able to publish his or her
own "journal," and everyone in the field will
automatically have a subscription.   Perhaps
this scenario is similar to an inexpensive
"vanity press."
     Notice that in this scenario, individual
journals disappear.   The hard copy of a journal is not merely replaced by an electronic
mail system.   Indeed there would be no need to
have many individual journals, each with its
own editorial board, in a completely networked
environment.   Furthermore, it is unlikely that
scientists would allow all dissemination to be
controlled by a small group.[10]   Hence, one
should not postulate that access and announcements will be controlled by some benevolent
oracle.   It is more likely that "free" access
and announcements will be the normal process.
In a sense, this scenario is not unlike the
situation that existed before journals were
established.
     Such a networked environment will also
provide for new methods of producing research
results.   Large collaborations will probably
be common in theoretical as well as experimental work.   Indeed it seems likely that a
network inquiry about a particular problem
will stimulate many people to collaborate in
its solution.
     Furthermore, it is quite likely that the
computer network itself will generate new
problems.   One does not have to postulate the
existence of a highly sophisticated artificial
intelligence to assume that computers can
generate new propositions that have not been
previously entered into the database.   But if
the computer can be used to generate new problems, can it not also solve them?
     This possibility will most likely have
its major impact on theoretical work, where
examples already exist.   In mathematics there
have always been famous unsolved problems.   An

example is the four-color problem, which can be described as follows. One might observe that maps are usually printed in color and that the colors are chosen such that countries or territories sharing a common border have different colors. A natural question is, How many different colors are required to ensure that adjacent countries have different colors? Of course, the question pertains to any possible map with any number of divisions. For example, the United States has been divided into an arbitrary set of territories in Figure 8.1. If one tries to solve the coloring problem for this particular map, one might discover that four colors are sufficient. One possible solution is given in Figure 8.2. An example of a map that requires more than four colors has never been produced. However, for more than 100 years, mathematicians were not able to prove that four colors suffice for any possible map.

In 1977, Appel and Hakeny, having used an awesome amount of computer power, announced that they had produced a computer proof of the

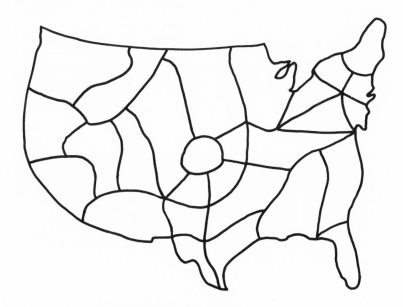

Fig. 8.1 A Hypothetical Map

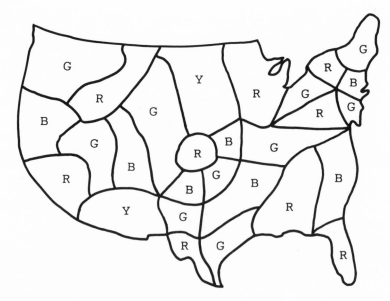

Fig. 8.2 A Valid Coloring
R-Red   G-Green   Y-Yellow   B-Blue

old conjecture that four colors always suffice.[11]   Hence, the four-color theorem was
established by computer. This computer proof
is regarded by mathematicians as a dramatic
change from the classical methods of proving
theorems. In this regard, one should note
that the computer was not merely used to
examine all possible colorings by an exhaus-
tive search. Indeed, there are an infinite
number of possible maps. To prove the theorem,
one must show that four colors suffice for all
maps. Obviously, the computer did not examine
an infinite number of maps; rather, the computer was used as an integral part of determining the method of proof.[12] Furthermore,
this particular computer proof has not led to
any new "classical" proofs. Clearly, this
fact supports the contention that the computer
was used to create a new method of proof.
Surely the advent of supercomputer networks
will enable many more computer proofs of complex problems.
        This future scenario gives rise to many
new issues related to scientific research.

Some of the obvious issues are discussed
below.

New Issues Related to Research
in the Future Networked Environment

One of the obvious results that arises
from the future environment for research pos-
tulated above is the elimination, via immediate literature searches, of duplication of
effort. But the independent discovery of results is not necessarily a negative aspect of
the classical approach. Different individuals
bring different insights and distinct approaches to the same problem. Will this situation actually discourage work?

The possible impacts of immediate an-
nouncement of results are numerous. Certainly
the prestige associated with publication in
high caliber journals will be affected. It is
not clear what, if anything, will replace the
classical list of publications and journals
that is now included in a scientist's resume.
If everyone could "publish his or her own
journal," approval by a group of peer referees
would not be required before dissemination.
Of course, the result of such an environment
might be the same as if each scientist oper-
ated his or her own publishing company. Reviews of published works would appear, but
what would be the impact of such reviews?
Would they be used to determine some method of
purging the database at regular intervals?
Many unpredictable issues arise from such a
purging assumption. The analogy to the variant
of the classical system, where each person
operates his or her own publishing company,
does not seem to predict the situation of a
completely networked environment. There remains the question of what, if anything, will
replace the referee process that exists today.

Furthermore, the network environment scenario described here allows for many abuses.
For example, consider the case of announcing a
result before it has been proven or verified.
Certainly there is a great temptation to cap-

ture   a conjectured result for oneself so that others will not receive credit by verifying it first.   Such preannouncement is prevented in the   classical journal scheme by the referees, who   demand   all the details before they allow publication.   Although this classical process can often lead to long delays, it does produce the   benefit   of   the natural improvement that comes   from   age; namely, scientific works are generally   of   higher quality when authors and editors   have   time   to   reflect   and   improve style, method of presentation, motivation, and so on.

As noted above, this new scenario will no doubt   lead   to   large   collaborations,   the obvious   result   of   which   is   the diminished prestige   associated   with the individual.   It will   perhaps   become   necessary to invent new methods of allocating prestige to researchers. Furthermore,   it may also be the case that the network   itself   will   generate   the problems. Very often it is the senior scientist who gen-erates the problems in the classical scenario, as   he   or   she has acquired the wisdom to see the forest and not merely the trees. What will be   the   role   of the senior researcher if the computer network fills that role?

One   of   the   most interesting aspects of the   supercomputer network for theoretical re-search   is the possibility of computer proofs. As   indicated   in   the discussion of the four-color   problem, this scenario has already come to pass; however, the full impact of this pos-sibility   is   yet to arrive.   Many issues will have   to be resolved in the near future regar-ding   computer   proofs.   If   the computer is capable of generating proofs, what will be the role   of the theoretical scientist?   If a com-puter   can   prove   the four-color theorem, why not suppose that a supercomputer network could generate   such   monumental   works   as   that of Bertrand Russell and Alfred N. Whitehead? In a sense,   the results contained in the _Principia_ follow   directly   from   the axiomatic ideas of Frege,   Cantor,   and   Peano.   Should the same level   of   prestige be afforded to someone who merely asks the computer to generate all valid

conclusions that follow from some known postu-
lates?

But how does one know if a computer proof
is correct? Perhaps it can be verified independently with another computer running a different program. Of course, the question of
correctness of proof arises in the classical
scientific approach also. Indeed, in theoretical areas the result must follow the axioms
by application of the rules of deductive
logic. How does one know that there are no
mistakes? Actually, there have indeed been
mistakes in classical proofs. For example, in
the case of the four-color problem, a proof
appeared in a very prestigious journal in
1879.[13] Eleven years after this refereed
paper appeared, it was found to contain an
error in logic.

Notes

1. A. S. Tanenbaum, Computer Networks
(Englewood Cliffs, NJ: Prentice-Hall, 1981).

2. John Ladd, "Ethics and the Computer
Revolution".

3. I. Richard Lapidus, "Ethics and the
Practice of Science in a Computer Networked
Environment" (Chapter 7, this book).

4. Deborah G. Johnson, Computer Ethhics
(Englewood Cliffs, NJ: Prentice-Hall, 1985).

5. D. Nelkin, Science as Intellectual
Property (New York: Macmillan, 1984).

6. Abbe Mowshowitz, "The Bias of
Computer Technology," in Ethics and the
Management of Computer Technology, M. Hoffman
and J. Moore, eds. (Cambridge, MA:
Oelgeschlager, Gunn and Hain, 1983), pp.
28-114.

7. R. P. Feynman, Surely You're Joking
Mr. Feynman (New York: W. W. Norton, 1985).

8. J.C.R. Licklider, "Computer and
Government," in The Computer Age: A 20 Year

160

View, M. Dertousos and J. Moses, eds. (Cambridge, MA: MIT Press, 1979), pp. 87-128.

9. Albert Einstein, Ideas and Opinions (New York: Crown Publishers, 1954).

10. Such control exists in some cases, such as in the publications of the National Academy of Sciences, which only allows submission via a member of the Academy. However, their publications are only a small fraction of the total scientific literature.

11. K. Appel and W. Haken, "The Solution of the Four-Color Map Problem," Scientific American 237 (1977), pp. 108-121.

12. Herein we avoid discussion of the complexities of what constitutes a proof in mathematics. See B. Russell and A. N. Whitehead, Principia Mathematica (Cambridge: Cambridge University Press, 1910). Suffice it to say that the majority of the mathematical community has accepted the approach of Appel and Haken.

13. A. B. Kemp, "On the Geometrical Problem of the Four Colors," American Journal of Mathematics 2 (1879), pp. 193-200.

9

Computer Networks and Normative Change

James W. Nickel

It is widely held that new technology is one of the major causes of changes in our values and norms. In this chapter I will present a framework for analyzing normative change and use it to discuss the possible impacts of computer networking on our conceptions of privacy and democracy. My approach here is more analytical than prescriptive. Overall, my contention is that the impacts of implementing this technology on our conceptions of privacy and democracy are likely to be small. Here, as elsewhere in the computer field, hype has often outrun genuine prospects.

Normative Changes in Response to New Technology

Technological innovation produces new sorts of entities and relations calling for implementation, regulation, and protection. When a promising new invention appears, people try to envisage what social and institutional changes will be required for its effective use, what regulations will be needed to ensure that it is more help than hazard, and what protections will be needed to guard it against familiar sorts of threats (e.g., thefts, floods, or patent violations). In the past few decades, these questions have been posed, and partially answered, for computer hardware

161

and software.

Norms, as I use the term here, may be moral, institutional, or legal--or all three of these at once. Examples of norms are: "don't open other people's letters without permission" (a moral obligation); "the department chair has the authority to schedule meetings of the department" (an institutional power); "in the United States we have a constitutional right against unreasonable searches and seizures" (a legal right).

As we apply and adapt norms to new technologies, the normative changes produced may range from minor to major, from small extensions of existing norms to the wholesale creation of new ones. There are many types and degrees of change along this continuum, but for our purposes it will suffice to discuss a case at each end.

Minor Normative Changes

Some new technologies fit easily into previously established normative patterns and require little normative change as they come into widespread use. The phonograph seems to be an example of this type. Although bringing phonographs into millions of homes may have contributed to social changes, it did not cause much normative change. The hazards posed by phonographs were small and similar to those of other household appliances. In regard to protections for this technology, phonographs needed to be protected against theft and had to be made insurable along with other household goods, but these protections required no significant innovation. It was not hard to figure out that the phonograph was a small appliance and that the protections generally conferred on small appliances would make good sense for phonographs. Even an uneducated thief could reason: "The phonograph is a small appliance; the unauthorized taking of small appliances is illegal; hence, the unauthorized taking of phonographs is illegal." The introduction of phonographs meant that the extension or denotation of "theft" would change, but not its connotation or meaning.

One area in which phonographs required a small amount of normative change was payment for musical compositions and performances. The creation of a recording industry meant that the system of rewarding musical composers and performers for their work had to be modified to apply to the new medium.

Major Normative Change

At the other end of the continuum of normative change we find cases where putting a new technology into use requires substantial changes in the normative structure of society. In such cases, the hazards posed by the technology cannot be adequately treated through established regulatory patterns, and the protections required by the technology go far beyond familiar protections of property against theft, accident, and natural disasters.

Clear cases of this sort are hard to identify. Marx seems to have thought that the technologies of the industrial revolution had this effect, that these new industrial technologies undermined feudalism by requiring for their effective implementation a system of large-scale production, labor mobility, and labor markets that could not exist within the feudal system. The capitalist political and economic system that emerged as a replacement granted greater freedom of movement and greater freedom to enter into labor contracts on an individual basis. If this historical analysis is correct, then we have a case where a change in technology led to a fundamental reconstruction of the normative structure of society, where new roles and norms had to be created to accommodate new technology.[1] Many important aspects of personal and economic relationships were totally changed. Notice, however, that Marx's claim is about a large set of new industrial technologies, not merely a particular item, such as the steam engine or the stamping press.

Computers and Privacy

The framework just presented suggests some questions to ask about computer networks. Will the normative changes brought about by widespread computer networking be minor or major, and will they concern implementation, regulation, or protection?

Concerns about privacy focus on what regulations will be required to protect privacy against threats posed by computer networking. One way to proceed here involves identifying the elements of privacy norms and then asking what changes in these elements might be motivated by the new technology. To understand the right to privacy, four questions are relevant: (1) Who has the right to privacy? (2) What information and actions does it cover? (3) What invasions by whom are covered? (4) How are these protected, and by whom?

It is obvious that computer networking can change the kinds of invasions that are possible and thus the sorts of protections that are needed. These changes, in turn, may affect the scope of the right. Something like this process has, in fact, happened, although the extent of change turns out not to be very large.

The idea of privacy has traditionally involved keeping other people from seeing or knowing things about oneself that one doesn't want them to see or know.[2] A person may wish to control other people's knowledge about the appearance and functioning of one's body, the details of one's personal relationships, the state of one's finances, and one's political sympathies. Of course, some of these things will be known by one's doctor, employer, banker, accountant, pastor, or best friends, but these people are bound by moral restraints to keep this information to themselves or reveal it only under appropriate circumstances. To protect our privacy we may lock our doors, curtain our windows, hide our private papers, refuse interviews with the press, and reasonably expect associates and friends to refrain from revealing facts about us to others.

The introduction and use of computerized databanks linked by telephone lines has not changed this traditional conception of privacy very much. The focus of privacy remains control over the same sorts of information. One change, however, involves the number of parties holding detailed information about a person. There are now computerized records of one's telephone calls, credit card purchases, political contributions (as represented in shared mailing lists), the ups and downs of one's checking and savings accounts, as well as one's traffic tickets, arrests, and convictions.[3]

Computer networks create new ways of getting information about people that those people cannot control. Others may be able to gain electronic access to several databases and then use programs that map data from these sources onto a single data form for each individual. In this way one can paint a composite picture of a person that reveals far more than any one of these sources alone. Several sources of "public" information, legitimately obtained, may, after sophisticated processing and analysis, reveal far more about people than they wish to have known. The total content, after combination and analysis, may be far greater than the mere sum of the parts.

A case of this sort recently occurred in Sweden, where for twenty years a team of sociologists had been combining data from computerized official records. Using personal identification numbers as a guide, this team assembled data from a variety of sources, including health and criminal records. The result, in one person's words, is that "They know more about these people than these people remember about themselves."[4]

The locks, curtains, and restrictions on friends and associates that have traditionally protected people's privacy will not prevent this sort of invasion. We need new sorts of protections, such as restrictions on access to databases, on giving out information to third parties, and on how long one can keep the information. A committee appointed by the Japanese government to study this problem recommended five governing principles: "that limits be put on the collection of personal information; that limits be put on its use; that the individual be given the right of access to the information held about himself or herself; that the data be kept up-to-date and safe from tampering; and that those in charge be held accountable."[5]

If we provide protections in accordance with these principles, the powers that people can use in controlling information about themselves will be expanded. Thus, a central part of the right to privacy will have been expanded in response to some new threats. Using the continuum of normative change sketched earlier, these fall somewhere between the middle and the "minor changes" end of the continuum. The changes here are not so radical as to qualify as creating a new norm. This result is interesting but far from earthshaking.

Computers and Democracy

It has often been thought, or hoped, that the introduction of large computer networks would revolutionize American democratic practices. If voting, lobbying, or participating in debates could be done using television and a computerized telephone set, perhaps declining participation in American democracy could be reversed and democratic procedures made more meaningful.

The technology for electronic democracy would include: (1) a home computer; (2) a telephone link for this computer; (3) a television set; and (4) universally accessible phone and television channels. The first three requirements could be met by using what the French call a minitel, a small video display, computer terminal, and telephone. Simple models of such a machine will soon be available for as little as $100.[6] To avoid disenfranchising people who do not own their own machines, electronic democracy would require that banks of these machines be made available at regular polling places or in other easily available public areas.

One way of discerning the potential impact of computer networking on American democracy is to ask what has happened thus far. To answer this question, we need to identify the moral or legal rights involved in effective practices of democracy and ask whether the computer networks already in use have had much impact on the activities protected by these rights. I will treat democratic rights under three categories:

<u>Rights</u> <u>to</u> <u>a</u> <u>Democratic</u> <u>System</u>. This category involves having the right to choose political leaders in regular, fair, and meaningful elections.

<u>Office</u> <u>Seeking</u> <u>and</u> <u>Holding</u>. The relevant rights are to run for and serve in political offices; conduct a campaign involving advertising and public appearances; and solicit contributions of money and time. This category also includes fair electoral procedures and freedom from violence directed against one as a candidate or official.

<u>Popular</u> <u>Political</u> <u>Activity</u>. This category relates to being able to engage effectively in political action to elect officials or to influence decisions. The relevant rights include the right to present grievances to officials; to communicate by mail and telephone without restrictions; to organize parties and pressure groups; to work on behalf of candidates and causes; to vote in elections; and to have one's vote count as much as other people's. It also includes freedom of speech, press, and assembly and freedom from violence directed against one's campaign, party, or pressure group.

If one goes through this list and tries to identify areas in which computers and computer networks have already had a substantial impact, one finds four main areas of change. These are:

1. How campaigns are conducted: New techniques include systematic polling and the strategic targeting of advertising and appearances in accordance with the results.

2. How contributions are solicited: Mailing lists can now classify people in accordance with their contributions and affiliations, and computer-generated mailings to generate contributions now routinely take place.

3. How election results are tabulated: Here we have electronic voting and vote-counting systems.

4. How people petition government: Here we have the use of computer-generated letters to petition representatives and massive mailings to generate letter writing by political sympathizers.

Reflection on this list suggests that computers have mainly been used for clerical purposes: to keep lists, store and process data; tabulate results; and combine form letters and address lists into "personalized" letters. None of these techniques seem to require new rights or duties, or the revision of old ones. So far, the impact of computers on American democracy has not been a very interesting story. By comparison to the impact of television, the impact of computers has been tiny. Experiments using telephone voting and polling to increase citizen participation have been conducted, but these have been small in scale and primitive in methods.[7]
This is only the story up to now, however. An enthusiast of computerized democracy might hold that we are only beginning to understand the potential of computer networks for improving democracy. It might also be suggested that, for this purpose, computer networking cannot be separated from television and video technology. Here, it might be

argued, we need a conception of <u>electronic democracy</u> that integrates the technologies involved in telecommunications, computers, television and video, and electronic voting.[8]

If some system of electronic democracy were implemented, would it require changes in any of the key democratic rights that we have identified? Rights to choose political leaders in regular, fair, and meaningful elections would not be affected. These rights might be implemented in different ways, but their substance has to remain unchanged if we are to have democracy at all.

We have already seen that computers and computer networks are being used to assist with the clerical aspects of office seeking and holding. It seems unlikely, however, that the fundamental roles and rights involved here will be changed. I doubt that electronic democracy will give us a fundamentally different conception of what it is to be a candidate for public office, to campaign for office, or to serve as an elected representative. Similarly, I doubt that electronic democracy will change the basic rights that people in these roles ought to have. It is quite possible, however, that electronic democracy will pose new, additional threats--and hence generate a need for new rights and protections.

Rights protecting popular political activity are concerned with people's efforts to elect officials and influence decisions. Electronic democracy will certainly involve different modes of engaging in these activities, but it seems unlikely that their goals will be much changed. Roles such as voter, concerned citizen, political speaker, and lobbyist will still be in use, and protections for these roles and the activities they involve will still be needed.

One reason why the political use of computer networks does not require many changes in the normative structure of democracy is that these networks can be effectively used in a wide variety of forms of democracy. For example, if referenda are thought important parts of democracy, computer networks can be

used to make these easier and less expensive.
If televised debates and subsequent opinion
polling are thought useful to democracy, computer networks will make it easier to conduct
opinion polls. But nothing in the technology
itself requires or promotes the use of referenda or televised debates followed by opinion
polls. If I am right in thinking that computer networking is largely neutral between
different forms of democracy, then implementation of this technology by itself cannot be
expected to bring about large political trans-
formations.

Perhaps we should shift the focus from
what is inevitable to what is possible. For
this task, we might ask whether computer networks will give us technological means for
improving democracy, for overcoming some of
the problems that currently afflict democratic
institutions in the United States. To consider
this possibility, we can identify some of
these problems and try to determine whether
computer networks are likely to contribute
substantially to their resolution. I will
discuss three trends that I take to be current
problems: (1) low levels of meaningful participation in political decisions; (2) the
disproportionate influence of the wealthy
through large contributions to political campaigns; and (3) the inability of Congress and
other representative bodies to make the polit-
ically unpopular decisions needed to control
budget deficits, military spending, and
health-care costs.

Limited Participation

Nonparticipation in politics and elections is very widespread in the United States
today. Less than 60 percent of eligible voters
have voted in recent presidential elections,
and less than 40 percent voted in the 1982
off-year congressional elections. Participation by working-class people and blacks is
substantially lower than average.[9] To make
the problem worse, the quality of participation by many of those who do vote is not very

high.   Many voters receive most of their information about politics from television and
do not participate in politics at the local or
state level.

Given this unattractive picture of
American democracy, it is obvious that some
means of improvement are needed. And technological means, which do not require a prior
transformation in attitudes, are especially
attractive. If the technology for electronic
democracy can be made widely available, perhaps political participation can be made
easier and more interesting. This development
may then lead to greater popular participation
in politics at a variety of levels.

The hope that electronic democracy would
increase levels of participation might be
based on the idea that lowering the "cost" of
voting--by making it as easy as using one's
telephone--would lead to increased willingness
to participate.   This may be true, as many
people have difficulty finding time on election days to go to a polling place and often
wait in line in order to vote. But if nonparticipation is due instead to a deeper dis-
interest in or disaffection from electoral
politics, merely making participation somewhat
easier will not have much effect. Further,
the people that currently have the lowest
participation rates (e.g., working-class
people or blacks) are the people who are least
likely to be able to afford their own mini-
tels.   They will still have to vote by going
to the polls; thus, their participation rate
is unlikely to be changed.

Disproportionate Influence of the Wealthy

Few theories of democracy suggest that
having much more money than most, or owning or
managing a large business, should give one
greater political influence than other people.
Yet it is apparent that business interests in
the United States do in fact have a disproportionate share of political influence.
Through large campaign contributions to sympathetic candidates, corporations and trade

associations can help to elect politicians who
will defend their interests and take their
suggestions seriously.[10] Measures introduced
in the post-Watergate era to counteract influence peddling seem to have been largely
ineffective.

One might hope that expanded political
participation made possible by electronic
democracy will reduce the influence of business interests and increase the influence of
other groups. I doubt that this will happen.
As we have just seen, electronic democracy is
unlikely to change anything for those who cannot afford their own phone lines and minitel
machines. Further, the well-funded groups are
likely to be able to use or influence the system in ways that perpetuate their influence.
Making use of a system involving television
and computers is something that corporations
and trade associations are likely to be good
at and to have experience with. The same may
not be true of a local labor union, black
church, or parent-teacher association.

Inability to Make Hard Choices

Congress has had a hard time dealing with
key budgetary issues in the past few decades.
It has been unable to avoid substantial deficit spending and to keep a lid on health-care
costs, social security costs, and military
spending. It is not surprising that decisions
on these matters are difficult to make, as
expenditures in these areas are motivated by
important values, supported by powerful interest groups, affect nearly everyone in the
country, and provoke strong responses from
both ends of the political spectrum. But these
factors, although they may make meaningful decisions difficult, should not make them impossible. Yet they seem mostly to have done so
in recent years.

Electronic democracy might change this
situation if it were used for direct referenda
on particular issues. Procedures might be
developed whereby direct votes on key national
issues could be put on the electoral agenda,

publicly debated, and decided by national vote. As we saw earlier, however, making greater use of referenda is not at all required by electronic democracy; at most, the use of such referenda would be made easier if electronic voting were widely available. At present, referenda systems are mainly used in the western part of the United States. It is far from clear that referenda would find support elsewhere, particularly as many people believe that a stable democracy requires decision-making by what Henry Kissinger calls a "political aristocracy."

If electronic democracy led to much greater use of referenda on difficult and controversial issues, the result would be to change slightly our conception of democracy. I doubt that this will happen; but even if it did, referenda are already recognized as a mainstream democratic procedure, and hence, the normative changes involved would be relatively minor.

Conclusion

Computer networks and related technology will have some impact on our conceptions of privacy and democracy. But this impact will mainly be confined to the protections needed for our privacy and the ways in which we debate and vote on political decisions. If electronic democracy led to the greater use of referenda, this development would be a significant change for the United States. But the implementation of electronic democracy does not require use of referenda; it merely makes it easier. Overall, computer networks are likely to produce small rather than major normative changes in our conceptions of privacy and democracy. Here, at least, the idea that new technologies drive normative change finds only modest support.

174

Notes

1. For an account of Marx along roughly
these lines, see Gerald Cohen, Karl Marx's
Theory of History (Princeton: Princeton
University Press, 1978).
2. For a good account of privacy see
Hyman Gross, "Privacy and Autonomy," in Nomos
XIII, Privacy, John Chapman and Roland
Pennock, eds. (New York: Lieber-Atherton,
1971, pp. 169-182).
3. On databanks see David Burnham, The
Rise of the Computer State (New York: Random
House, 1980), pp. 49-87; and Robert Ellis
Smith, Privacy: How to Protect What's Left of
It (Garden City, NY: Anchor Press/Doubleday,
1979).
4. "Worried Swedes Questioning Wide Reach
of Researchers," The New York Times (11 March
1986), pp. 1, 6.
5. Robert Rice, "Report of the Aspen
Institute International Symposium,
Communications, Technology and Human Values,"
1-2 July 1985, Tokyo, Aspen Institute
Communications and Society Forum Report, 1985,
p. 15.
6. See "Et Voila! Le Minitel," The New
York Sunday Times Magazine (9 March 1986), pp.
46, 48-49, 69.
7. For reports on these by an enthusiast,
see Ted Becker, "Teledemocracy: Bringing
Power Back to People," The Futurist (December
1981), pp. 6-9; and Ted Becker and Christa
Slaton, "Hawaii Televote: Measuring Public
Opinion on Complex Policy Issues," Political
Science 33 (1981), pp. 52-65. For a critique
of the political promise of the QUBE system,
see Jean Bethke Elshtain, "Democracy and the
QUBE Tube," The Nation (7-14 August 1982), pp.
108-110.
8. For a conception of democracy that
uses television and computer networks to make
participation more meaningful, see Benjamin R.

Barber, <u>Strong</u> <u>Democracy</u> (Berkeley: University of California Press, 1984), pp. 261-311. On ways of using computer technology in group deliberations and choice see, Thomas B. Sheridan, "Technology for Group Dialogue and Social Choice," in <u>Talking</u> <u>Back:</u> <u>Citizen</u> <u>Feedback</u> <u>and</u> <u>Cable</u> <u>Technology</u> Ithiel De Sola Pool, ed. (Cambridge, MA: MIT Press, 1973), pp. 223-236.

　　9. See Joshua Cohen and Joel Rogers, <u>On</u> <u>Democracy</u> (New York: Penguin Books, 1983), pp. 32-35.

　　10. See Cohen and Rogers, <u>On</u> <u>Democracy</u>, pp. 34-35; and Charles Lindblom, <u>Politics</u> <u>and</u> <u>Markets</u> (New York: Basic Books, 1977), pp. 170-188.

10

Voting in a Computer Networking Environment

Arnold B. Urken

Using a computer network to vote may seem futuristic, but computers have been used for nearly two decades as part of the voting process in public elections. If we define a network as a set of autonomous actors who communicate with each other to produce outcomes, we can identify the normal and potential use of computers as a connecting device that facilitates communication. Normally, computers are used to record the votes of citizens in elections and tally these records on a particular machine or to aggregate the results of election outcomes from electronic (or mechanical) voting machines within a region.

Because the potential for using computers as more than adding machines is not well defined, there are many questions about how and if they should be used. When computers were first developed to facilitate group decision-making, one of the primary objectives was to promote broader participation in group decisions to draw on the "collective intelligence" of technological problem-solvers.[1] Even though pioneers in computer-based group decision-making shared an interest in using computers in public affairs, they were diverted from the goal of improving citizen access by the development of another primary objective: management of information via computer. Access to computers will not help citizens to participate if they do not have the information needed to make informed de-

177

cisions. But it became apparent that there
are different ways of sending and receiving
computer messages. The creators of synchronous
and asynchronous "conferences" or "meetings,"
elaborations of the idea of "computer mail,"
have been preoccupied with file management
rather than with tailoring their systems to
increase citizen participation in government.[2]
Although political theorists interested in
"teledemocracy" agree that computerized voting
could increase citizen control in public
affairs,[3] there is no clear conception of the
relative normative importance of the goals of
maximizing citizen access to computers and to
information. In a computer networking environment, these goals are not necessarily comple-
mentary, so one must take account of technical
and social feasibility in resolving normative
questions.

Political theorists often end their
analysis of "teledemocracy" without considering the implications of what they seem to
regard as purely instrumental issues.[4] In
this chapter, I will attempt to counterbalance
this mode of analysis by describing the effect
of computer networking on the voting process
and highlighting and clarifying normative
questions. There may be voting norms that
should exist in some or all social contexts,
but it is important to understand the feasibility of creating such norms in order to make
a rational assessment of policy choices. For
this reason, I have adopted a conditionally
normative approach to deciding if and how
voting should be computerized. Because the
medium affects the message, I focus on what
happens (or could happen) if individuals voted
under different constraints or norms. By
focusing on the conditioning effects of norms
on individual and group behavior, I do not
intend to argue that any norms are "infea-
sible" and therefore undesirable. Instead, my
objective is to describe theoretical and
empirical limits on voting in computer networking environments. These limits must be
understood in order to create conditions that
make our conceptions of what ought to be part

of reality.

In the next section, I begin by defining a voting process in network terminology and drawing an analogy between a computer network and a voting network. This analogy helps us to appreciate the difference between voting _in_ and voting _through_ a computer networking environment and to understand the effects of alternative voting rules on the process of communication in different social contexts. In the following sections, I will describe three qualitative effects of computer conferencing on the voting process: speed, organizational culture, and the quality of representation. In the last section, I will discuss the effects of different forms of computer network voting on our traditional concepts of positive and negative liberty, pointing out ways in which computer conferencing can help us make rational choices about normative questions.

Voting as a Network Phenomenon

Traditionally, most of us associate voting with the process of allocating a single vote to one of two or more alternatives. This vote is aggregated with the votes of other members of a group according to a rule--typically majority or plurality--that specifies the requirement for reaching a consensus. If no alternative satisfies this requirement, the group may vote again with the original agenda or modify the agenda (for example, by eliminating all alternatives except the two most popular) for another collective decision.

This familiar concept of voting is related to the following definition: A voting process is an activity that occurs when autonomous actors express their preferences for agenda alternatives by casting votes. Communication of information is constrained by rules that govern the allocation of votes to achieve social objectives. This definition suggests that voter constraints and objectives will vary according to the organizational context.

The Social Context of Voting

In most public elections, the basic objective is to form a group preference. However, depending on the circumstances, individuals may pursue selfish objectives that may lead them to throw their support to a protocoalition[5] that promises to maximize their private benefits or to cast their vote to prevent a (privately) undesirable protocoalition from winning. Moreover, if the agenda includes candidates running for office, the voting process may be perceived as a competition in which a candidate markets himself or herself in order to attract enough votes to win.[6] An underlying similarity in all of these situations is that the decision-making environment involves a "political disagreement," a divergence of opinion about values or objectives.

In contrast, an environment in which there is a consensus on basic values or objectives may entail an "administrative disagreement," where a social choice must be made between alternative means of pursuing common interests. In this type of situation, voting becomes a method for carrying out the "cognitive" task of identifying the optimal or best solutions.[7]

In some situations, the nature of the group decision task is not an issue. For instance, in experimental situations, problems or puzzles that have optimal answers may be presented. In nonexperimental environments, however, decisions may be viewed as political or administrative tasks. For example, it is often assumed that the goal of jurors is to reach a fair or correct verdict; but juror decision-making is also analyzed as if the collective outcome were completely noncognitive, simply a playing out of individual biases.[8] Conversely, in collective decision-making, such as in presidential elections, the decision task is normally consi- dered to be a political concern, but an analytical tradition

interprets these group choices as cognitive
problems.[9]

Voting Networks

Regardless of one's perspective on a particular decision task, the act of voting can
be seen as part of a network in which autonomous actors (voters) allocate resources
(votes) to communicate with each other and
form a consensus. The communication process
may involve group deliberation and interpersonal pressure, and these factors may affect
the collective outcome. If voters are engaged
in making a political decision, the outcome
may be a victory for one alternative, a tie
among two or more alternatives, or a result
that does not satisfy the consensus requirement. Under some circumstances, outcomes may
have "paradoxical" characteristics that prevent the most preferred alternative from being
adopted as the collective choice.[10] In administrative decisions, the issues may be qualita-
tively different, but the voting process operates in the same way.

Although one can imagine computers programmed to make rule-based or random decisions
like human beings in a voting network, an
analogy between computer and voting networks
does not depend on this perspective. For
networked computers are an "interconnected
collection of autonomous computers . . .
capable of exchanging information."[11] Copper
wire may be the communications link, or
lasers, microwaves, and earth satellites may
be used.[12] In either case, computers cannot be
related to each other in a clear master-slave
relationship in which one machine could uni-
laterally start, stop, or control the other.
Remote card readers, printers, and terminals
tied to a large computer do not a network
make.

If this definition is accepted, then it
may seem that my introductory remark about the
use of computer networks in public elections
is mistaken. However, this conclusion depends
on the electoral process one has in mind. If

individuals vote via a terminal connected to a large computer,[13] then the voting process is not part of a network because the voters cannot communicate with each other without working through the controlling influence of a central machine. But if individual computers are used to aggregate precinct voting information and transmit it to a regional computer to be further aggregated, then the process can be seen as part of network in which raw data is transmitted and aggregated into an electoral outcome, which is communicated down to the regions. Obviously, this example shows only a rudimentary computer networking environment in which networked computers are used simply to transmit information about the voting outcome, but it does put us in a position to appreciate the difference between voting in and voting through a computer network.

Voting in a computerized network means that the process involves the use of computers to at least collect and tabulate the results. Voting through such a network signifies that the computer is used in as much of the voting process as possible. To appreciate the implications of computerizing the voting process, it is important to understand the options for representing information about voting preferences.

Alternative Voting Networks

In the academic study of voting systems, it is normally assumed that a voting process satisfies (or should satisfy) certain conditions. In the context of our discussion, these conditions can be interpreted as specific requirements related to the issues of access, security, and censorship. These requirements include the following ideas: (1) nondistortion of the voting process, which means that no rule or action should be allowed to change individual vote allocations, count them unequally, or produce a collective outcome that does not accurately represent the preferences of a majority of the voters; and (2) nonmanipulability of the voting process, or no strategic individual vote allocation decisions.

These allocations allow one individual (or a coalition) to change the collective outcome. No system is immune to manipulation, but theorists disagree about the characteristics of different systems.[14] Clearly, these ideals are not shared by everyone who uses voting and are not appropriate under all social circumstances. For example, if we were using voting to make a correct or optimal choice, manipulation might be considered desirable if it improved our ability to achieve our objective. In fact, the ideals of nondistortion and nonmanipulability describe norms associated with a conception of voting in public elections.

As different ideals are appropriate to different social conditions, it is reasonable to explore the impact of new forms of computerized voting on these standards. Although the type of computer network will affect the voting process, the ability to vote using different voting networks can occur in either hierarchichal or distributed networks. A voting network includes the following elements:

• Number of voters: Access (equal voting rights) and participation rates may affect this number.

• Voting endowment: The number of votes each person has to communicate preference information in a collective choice process. In the traditional one-person, one-vote system, each individual is endowed with one vote. Under approval voting,[15] individuals are endowed with n votes where n equals the number of alternatives or candidates. Under "weighted voting," n may be larger or smaller than the number of alternatives in the agenda.

• Vote allocation rule: This parameter controls the number of votes a person can allocate in a collective choice process. In a one-person, one-vote system, an individual must make a categorical decision; votes cannot be saved, traded, or divided.[16] Under approval voting, a person must decide which alternatives should be approved by casting one vote

184

in favor of those alternatives. And under weighted voting, individuals can allocate from 1 to n votes for an alternative in proportion to their preferences.

    • Vote aggregation rule: This rule describes the number of votes required to stop a collective choice process. Examples of stopping rules include plurality, majority, and unanimity.

An Example

    Table 10.1 illustrates how these rules can affect the collective outcome produced by a voting network. It lists the cardinal preference ratings of three hypothetical voters (I, II, and III) for three alternatives (A, B, and C). These ratings provide a ratio scale measurement of individual preferences; they indicate that voter II prefers B six times as much as A and twice as much as C. Table 10.2 shows a dramatic difference between one-person, one-vote and approval voting (both using a plurality decision rule). In the former network, the outcome is a tie, while in the latter network, C is selected.

TABLE 10.1
Hypothetical Voting Situation: Cardinal Preference Ratings of Three Voters (I, II, and III) for Three Alternatives (A, B, and C)
==

Voting
Alternatives   Voters
-----------   ------------

	I	II	III
A	4	1	4
B	3	6	1
C	3	3	5

TABLE 10.2
Collective Outcomes Produced by One Person One Vote(OPOV) and Approval Voting(AV)[a] Using a Plurality Aggregation Rule
==
Votes Allocated Under Rules by Voters I, II, and III

Voting Alternatives	OPOV			AV		
	I	II	III	I	II	III
A	1	0	0	1	0	0
B	0	1	0	1	1	0
C	0	0	1	1	1	1

Totals: A=1   Totals: A=2
B=1   B=2
C=1   C=3
Outcome: Tie   Outcome: C Wins

[a]The rule governing the allocation of approval votes is based on the theoretical assumption that individuals cast a vote for each alternative which equals or exceeds their average utility (in this case, 3). See Samuel Merrill III, _Decision Analysis for Multicandidate Voting Systems,_ Boston: Birkhauser, 1980.

The "science" of voting deals with the effects of procedural rules on collective outcomes. How frequently do certain rules produce decisive outcomes, ties, or "correct choices"? Are some procedures more likely to select the most preferred alternative than other procedures? How manipulable are different procedures? And which sets of procedures satisfy axiomatic or normative rules?[17]

Other Voting Networks

Normally, the idea of a voting network is not associated with rules such as consensus or market exchange.[18] But these rules can be analyzed as if they applied to networks in which the constraints on vote endowment, vote allocation, and vote aggregation were changed. In consensus processes, individuals have preferences but articulate them according to tacit or explicit rules that structure the collective decision in a different way. For example, a leader may announce a choice, and the members of the group may not block adoption of the leader's selection unless enough of them decide that the proposed choice does not satisfy a minimum utility threshold. There are many variations on consensus rules, including the classic practice of "voting with one's feet."

In contrast, in a "fungible" voting network,[19] preferences are represented by vote allocation, but votes can be saved and traded like money. Under fungible rules, citizens would have an endowment of votes that could be saved or traded to produce desired collective outcomes. Depending on the organizational context, citizens might allocate their votes directly or give them to middlemen (e.g., legislators or interest group leaders).

Computers and Voting Speed

Computer networking has increased the speed of vote aggregation in the traditional voting process but has had little effect on the act of communicating by allocating votes. In public elections, computers have tallied votes at different levels of election administration. In some cases, if voters have used electronic rather than mechanical voting machines, computers have also improved the efficiency of conducting recounts and audits.

In a computer networking environment, speed will make it possible to approach the ideal of simultaneous allocation of votes and will thus minimize the effects of sequential voting that occur in elections (e.g., U.S. presidential elections) carried out across different time zones.[20] However, as voting becomes more asynchronous, networking will allow individuals to manipulate the process in

different ways. For instance, it will be possible to change one's vote in response to information about voting patterns. This information could be used to cast votes to maximize
the individual utility derived from collective
choices. For example, suppose that your preference ordering was A>B, B>C, A>C (A=first
choice, B=second choice, and C=third choice)
and that your network connection informed you
that with 50 percent of the votes tallied, A
had 10 percent of the vote, B received 40
percent, and C received 50 percent. In this
case, you could take a risk and--assuming that
you are casting one vote--bet your allocation
on B instead of voting for your sincere
choice, A, hoping to make B the collective
choice. As the constraints on voting change,
the process of betting would become more complex and the types of feedback from the network connection would become tailored to meet
the information needs of voters. The most extreme changes would occur under fungible voting; because votes could be saved and traded,
it would be necessary not only to keep track
of vote allocations but of vote saving and
trading as well. In some cases, this information could be exploited, not to create a win-
ner but to prevent another alternative from
being selected as the collective choice.

Speed will make it easier to process information derived from voting processes other
than the traditional one-person, one-vote
network. Although more complex voting networks
have been used, their effectiveness has been
limited owing to the costs associated with information processing and concerns about fraud.
Computer networking will make it possible to
cut costs and minimize fraudulent manipulation
of the system. The control of fraud will depend on available technology; at a simple
level, the ability to conduct an audit of the
number of votes cast by an individual (assigned a random identification number) will
make it possible to counteract computerized
ballot stuffing.[21] In a more sophisticated
technological environment, cryptographic techniques could provide security by making it

practically impossible to track voting processes without a computerized key.[22]

Organizational Culture

In computer networking environments, the
psychological and sociological aspects of voting processes will no longer be bound by tradition. Instead, artificial environments will
be developed in voting networks appropriate to
the political or administrative decision
tasks.

In computer conferencing networks, in
which groups make decisions online, users have
not developed explicit norms for voting. In
cultures that have not been computerized, the
homogeneity of social values is correlated
with the genesis of voting rules. Group size
is not necessarily a determinant of these
rules. In Switzerland, for example, citizens
used to announce their votes publicly in can-
ton elections. But in more heterogeneous
groups, regardless of size, an absence of
trust leads to the development of institutions
designed to protect the privacy of voters.
For example, reformers of the U.S. electoral
process in the early twentieth century viewed
the "secret ballot" as a means of protecting
immigrants from the effects of ethnic or class
particularism and creating nationalistic identification with the voting process.[23] In public affairs, the important role of voting in
legitimizing social action is well recognized.
But in collective decisions not connected with
the traditional relationship between individuals and the state, voting norms are more
fluid.

Online Voting Norms

Voting is not used very frequently in
nonexperimental computer conferencing environments, but there has been a concern with issues such as security and censorship in such
environments.[24] These issues are related to
voting in that they affect access to informa-

tion that may influence voting decisions. For example, in one of the major commercial conferencing systems, a system owner censored messages sent by members of a conference involved in making a collective choice. When the conferencers discovered the censorship, they had to threaten to cancel their subscriptions before management apologized and pledged not to censor their messages again.[25] In nongovernmental affairs, market pressures may provide a means of self-regulation not immediately apparent in collective decisions about government leaders or issues. Yet even in "private" conference systems open to the public, it is not clear whether system managers are abstaining from censorship (or abuse of security privileges) or simply conducting their activities with a speed and sophistication that defy detection.

Access is an important issue in governmental and nongovernmental voting in a computer network. In the latter, information exchange and voting normally take place on a commercially available, in-house conferencing system. Although little is known about how these systems are being used in corporate environments, a vendor of conferencing software reported that corporate purchasers normally require that the software be modified to prevent employees from gaining equal access to all the features of the network.[26] This practice seems to be aimed at limiting the formation of coalitions among lower organizational workers and does not involve voting per se. Yet if subordinates had access to the system, they might use voting to promote decentralization and legitimize the viewpoint of coalitions seeking administrative or political change.

In governmental organizations, control of access can also affect the balance between centralization and decentralization. In the QUBE experiment, for instance, in Columbus, Ohio, cable television lines were used to promote citizen participation in policymaking by enabling individuals to vote on issues presented on the cable network.[27] In this rudi-

mentary model of voting in a networking environment, citizens expressed their preferences
by voting "yes" or "no." Despite the fact that
the participants were mainly only the upper-
middle-class and middle-class citizens, QUBE
polls were sometimes treated as if they represented a democratic consensus. Moreover, even
those individuals who had access to QUBE voting had no control over the voting agenda.
In fact, the QUBE model is an example of a
hierarchical network in which the autonomy of
the actors is extremely limited. Commercial
conferencing systems are also hierarchical in
the sense that communication is controlled by
a single machine. Although the act of voting
is autonomous, the integrity of the voting
process is contingent on the absence of malicious or incompetent distortion. Some faith
is required even if encryption is used.

Some theorists have assumed that using
the traditional system of voting in a computer
networking environment would improve the process either because individuals would be better informed or the costs of participation
would be reduced.[28] Certainly, networking
makes it possible to gain information and to
participate by voting, sending messages to
politicians, or by taking part in debates, but
computers can also easily lead to information
overload and make it easier for poorly informed people to control the outcomes of collective decisions. In a hierarchical network,
it is reasonable to assume that decisions
about agendas will still be made out of the
public eye--perhaps in secret conferences--and
that citizens will have to depend on trust to
maintain the integrity of the system. Conferencing will make it possible to cut the costs
of forming coalitions and will increase the
amount of pressure on politicians who set
agendas. This pressure will make it more difficult to manipulate the agenda, but politicians will probably engage in tacit, rather
than explicit, accommodation.

Decentralization is not a necessary consequence of computer networking even in a
"distributed network," in which each user can

access all other users without being controlled by a central machine. Political theorists[29] have not been explicit about the type
of networking environment that could be operational, but distributed networking is clearly
the most favorable scenario for those who want
to "democratize" the political system. In this
environment, individuals could discuss their
preferences and voting decisions and use this
information to ensure the integrity of vote
reporting and aggregation. Of course, it would
still be possible for security to be breached
within different parts of the network.

In a hierarchical network in which access, security, and censorship are not problems, organizations could adapt computing
options to achieve their objectives. Sometimes
this may lead to decentralization, depending
on the functional basis of the organization.[30]
Consider the case of "administrative" organi-
zations--public or private--guided by commitment to common objectives (e.g., maximize
profit or maximize clientele).[31] In a stable
environment in which demands on the organization are predictable, computers would help
the organization change its structure to ad-
just to its environment. In a more unstable
environment, computerization will lead to
greater demands on the network hierarchy and
lead managers to increase constraints on
system use. These constraints may include
scheduling restrictions, reduced consultant
services, and regionalization of decision-
making. Computer-based voting is an unlikely
phenomenon in this type of situation.

In environments in which social conflict
is partially or totally "political," voting is
likely to be very important. Conversely, voting seems to be avoided as a means of making
group decisions when disagreements involve
primarily administrative matters. For example,
a laboratory of a large telecommunications
company used computers to enable designers of
microchips to communicate with others in order
to decide on chip designs. Decisions were
guided by an explicit agreement that certain
technical standards be satisfied by any de-

sign. Researchers used electronic mail to communicate their designs and gain the consensus of colleagues.[32] Typically, if the consensus was not unanimous, the group would not discard the design but instead would send asynchronous messages in order to create a consensus. This informal system seemed to work so well that when the idea of online voting was proposed to the manager of chip design, he reacted negatively because he believed that voting would create divisiveness and discord.[33] In contrast, Digital Equipment Corporation uses voting (via PARTICIPATE) to make decisions about product design but finds it difficult to induce designers to use computerized voting rather than voice (via phone) and face-to-face communication.[34]

This practical experience suggests that the cues associated with voice and face-to-face communication play an important role in group decision-making.[35] It is possible that equivalent cues may evolve that would facilitate the information exchange needed to make informed voting decisions on computer conferencing systems. In fact, among conferencing zealots, it is common to find messages that recreate verbal and other cues by using expressive words and "nonsense" symbols. As computer networks begin to provide voice, video, and data communication, online culture will come closer to recreating the trappings of face-to-face communication. But experienced users of existing messaging systems can manipulate the exchange of information to avoid acknowledging receipt of a message. In conferencing, receipt of private messages is normally confirmed to the sender, but if one knows how to "pre-read" messages, one can select the messages that are received and prevent a sender from finding out that his or her message was received and ignored.[36]

Anonymity

Experimental studies of computer conferencing have disclosed that users exploit the anonymous nature of online group decision-making to exhibit verbal behavior that would be neutralized in a face-to-face environment.[37] However, anonymity may serve a positive role in voting processes. First, computer-based group decision-making can filter out information that may lead to biases or prejudices that would affect the political viability of ideas or candidates.[38] And second, if a group's objective is to make an optimal decision, anonymity may be desirable if it minimizes social interaction and allows individual voting decisions to be statistically independent (i.e., one person's likelihood of voting for the optimal choice is not affected by another voter's pressure or persuasion). Under these conditions, it is theorized that the group would maximize its likelihood of selecting the optimal choice.[39]

Secret Balloting

As noted above, secret ballots seem to be associated with heterogeneous organizations in which anonymity neutralizes identification with ideological, class, ethnic, or other bases of particularism that threaten the legitimacy of the collective outcome. In homogeneous social situations, individuals declare their voting preferences in public as part of a celebration of the legitimation process.

In computer networking environments, voters can rely on anonymity to preserve their right to privacy in voting, but they must also grapple with new options for exercising this right. Let us assume that all citizens should be accorded maximum privacy in balloting; likewise, we must recognize that a computer makes it possible for an individual to be selective in distributing information about his or her preferences. In a face-to-face environment, where votes are made public, each person includes information about his or her identity and vote allocation indiscriminately. In a computer network, however, one can control the type of information about voting behavior that is sent to or read by others. For instance, suppose that a Republican wants to inform other party members about his voting behavior without revealing his identity. He might create a file that includes his vote allocations but not his name. Alternatively, he might omit his name but provide geographical location and/or socioeconomic status data, which might be valuable to party leaders monitoring the election, as they might use such information to maximize voter turnout in their favor.

The Quality of Representation

Computer networks will make it possible to analyze problems of group choice that have seemed intractable. Experiments with computer-based decision-making will enable us to study patterns of behavior in complex voting networks and improve the quality of representation by designing appropriate network rules.

Choosing a Voting Procedure

The choice of a voting procedure is an important theoretical issue[40] that goes beyond the scope of this discussion. There is no consensus about how to handle this problem in voting processes that are not computer-based. In fact, no procedure satisfies all of the normative criteria developed by social choice theorists for "political" choices, and some theorists have concluded that the choice is a matter of taste, not a decision involving an "optimal" answer. However, some characteristics of a computer networking environment are straightforward. First of all, if taste is not whimsical, it should be based on a knowledge of the consequences of using different voting procedures. Why? Simply because tastes cannot be satisfied if preferences are not feasible. For example, suppose I prefer using approval voting rather than the one-person, one-vote procedure. But if I knew that the former rule would produce a tie and the latter procedure would create a decisive outcome, I might change my taste if a decisive social choice were my objective. Of course, it would be simple to figure out the outcomes produced by different rules and display the results for voters. Then the choice of a procedure could become the subject of a computer conference. This possibility would not be desirable in all social environments. The information on the displays might overwhelm some users, and even if the information did not produce an over-load, the data would have to be organized to facilitate searching, so that individuals motivated to rationalize their tastes could do so.

In some organizational contexts, the choice of a voting rule may be considered an administrative rather than a political choice. For example, if groups were making decisions about questions with "optimal" answers, a con-ference or "meeting" moderator might select the procedure that would produce the greatest group probability of making a correct choice. This selection would distort individual pref-erences, but as the context is administra-tive, the sharing of common objectives (e.g., making accurate decisions to maximize profit) could legitimize the procedure.

Access

Voting via computer in a political or administrative context raises questions about access, security, and censorship. It is not necessary for all citizens to have powerful microcomputers to take part in the online voting process, for a mass-produced version of the cable television technology used in the QUBE system could provide universal access. But would citizens trust such a "tele-democracy"? Would they fear that "Big Brother" would be watching them? If citizens would not use such a system, then voting could become anonymous by using encryption in transmitting information. Still, each person's voting terminal would have a node address on the network and it would be possible to trace the source of the voting information and correlate it with the decrypted outcome. This problem could be alleviated by using public voting installations that would permit individuals to preserve the anonymity of their choice. In a hierarchical computer network, this type of installation might be located in a bank or post office to facilitate public access. In a distributed computer network, however, the same effect might be achieved by subaggregating vote allocations in random patterns to make it difficult to match vote allocations to their source. Ultimately, however, there is no guarantee that voting in a computer networking environment would be secure, even with more sophisticated technology.

If secure, physical access to the voting process is no obstacle, the classical problems of representation would still face us. For example, the control of agendas would affect online voting, but collection of data from computer decision-making environments would enable us to clarify the origins and implications of agenda structures.[41] Weighted voting would be criticized as unfair, and anything short of universal voter participation would be regarded as unacceptable. In a computer network, it would be possible to gather data to test theories about the relationship between weighted votes and control over collective outcomes.[42] Similarly, it would be possible to study theories about the optimal relationship between distributions of weighted votes and the group probability of making an optimal choice.[43] Finally, the relationship between universal voter participation and collective outcomes would be scrutinized based on data derived from political and administrative online choices. This type of study would enable us to understand the functional relationship between voter turnout and the characteristics of collective outcomes.

Understanding Complex Voting Networks

Networked-based voting would enable us to discover patterns in voting processes that cannot even be described without a computer.

For instance, the dynamics of consensus processes are poorly understood because the rules
governing collective decisions change and often operate on a tacit rather than an explicit
basis. The theoretical status of fungible voting systems would be modified as analysts
began to see that large corporations use consensus processes and rely on trading and
saving votes, the value of which changes frequently. Similarly, auction systems and markets would be better understood as processes
that mediate collective decision-making.

Computer networks themselves would be
seen in terms of social choice concepts. For
example, the problem of gaining access to
network resources is normally handled by
imposing the preferences and priorities of
systems managers on users or by relying on the
first-come, first-serve principle. Alternative
approaches could be developed by allowing
users to set policies that require that a user
gain sufficient access to the computer network
to inform online users about his or her needs
before any decision is made about limiting
their access to the network.

Indirect Representation

Critics of the traditional liberal
democracy have challenged indirect representation because it takes control out of the
hands of the individual.[44] These critics have
argued for decentralizing political decision-
making in order to maximize individual control. Under one scenario for the future, the
scope of individual control would make it
unnecessary for individuals to rely on the
state to provide goods or services,[45] and
private organizations would spring up to
provide the goods and services previously
monopolized by the state. In this situation,
teledemocracy would not use voting to create
authoritative allocations of values; the
market would be used to make these decisions.
Nevertheless, if voting were used to obtain
nonbinding poll information about group preferences, fungible voting might be used. In a

198

less radical scenario, a fungible procedure
could still be desirable to maximize the scope
of individual control in centralized decisions
(such as defense, monetary policy, etc.) and
decentralized choices (such as urban planning,
local taxes, and education policy). In this
setting, citizens who were constrained from
attending meetings might still use a network
to gather news about political developments
and allocate their votes indirectly to candidates, office holders, or interest groups
engaged in the competitive process of forming
winning or blocking coalitions. Security
would become a more serious problem because
fungible votes could be stolen or destroyed,
and these abuses would affect collective
outcomes significantly. At the same time, the
institutionalization of fungible voting would
create strong incentives to develop better
deterrents against corruption. Moreover,
censorship would become a more volatile issue,
and supporters and critics would allocate
their resources to respond to specific cases.

In some situations, voting decisions are
made by lot. Usually these choices involve no
special qualifications for office holders.[46]
Voting in a computer network could facilitate
the creation of stratified random sampling
procedures that provide valid statistical
bases for inference.

Election Administration

One of the obstacles to achieving maximum
voter participation is voter registration.
Ignorance about deadlines, registration locations, and voting rules disenfranchises many
citizens.[47] Computer networks make it possible
to create files that can easily be transferred
from one voting administrative unit to
another. At the same time, this data can be
used to subvert the tradition of privacy associated with liberal political culture. For
this reason, some analysts are pessimistic
about the consequences of developing such
data-bases.[48] But the problem is not the collection of or access to the data but use of

the information. Technology is not the problem; in fact, technology can be a positive
factor in preserving privacy. For instance,
if all citizens had access to a computer network, technology would now permit us to automatically notify an individual each time
someone read or wrote on his or her file
stored in the network's memory.

Computer networks also make it possible
to cut election costs, particularly those
associated with recounts or runoff elections.
Recounts would become feasible for collective
choices that were made using noncategorical
rules, such as approval voting and weighted
voting. One of the practical problems raised
in the evaluation of approval voting is verifying vote allocations in an audit.[49] In a
one-person, one-vote network, there should
always be a one-to-one relationship between
the number of voters and allocated votes.
Under approval voting, the number of allocated
votes per voter varies and must be recorded so
that recounts can be done in a systematic manner. The costs of runoff elections would be
cut drastically--if they were still used--for
voting in a computer networking environment
would change our thinking about runoff elections. In a future environment, a computer
might automatically choose a voting rule that
would minimize the probability that a tie or
indecisive outcome would occur, thereby obvi-
ating the need for another election. Social
choice theorists[50] have complained about the
distorting effects of runoff elections on
citizen preferences, so this development would
have significant normative implications. But
even if runoffs were not completely eliminated, the practice of limiting the number of
candidates in the election could be modified.

Computers, Voting, and Liberty

For some social theorists, voting is the
central act of democratic control;[51] for
others, it is a mechanism that deceives citizens into thinking they have control.[52] Re-

gardless of ideology, the prospect of using
computers to make collective decisions can be
considered as a separate issue that affects
liberty. Critics of computer technology usually forget that the liberal concept of liberty
is dualistic: It is positive as well as negative. This dualism recognizes the merits of
the ideal of keeping the government off our
backs in order to maximize individual control,
but it also appreciates the fact that collective action is a positive force that can be a
necessary condition for individual freedom and
dignity. The balance between these aspects of
liberty is dynamic, and there are no simple
solutions for preserving liberty.

The analogy between computer and voting
networks gives us a different perspective on
problems of voting by focusing on the implications of autonomy. In both types of networks, actors have independence and freedom,
but the structure of the network provides
responses that allow each node to be self-
regulating. As computer networking improves
our knowledge about the consequences of
structuring voting processes, it will challenge us to reconsider traditional philosophical conceptions of fairness. By highlighting the functional implications of rules,
the network analogy will enable us to understand the conditions under which procedural
fairness necessarily produces just outcomes.

Notes

1. Starr Roxanne Hiltz and Murray Turoff,
The Network Nation: Human Communication via
Computer (Reading, MA: Addison-Wesley, 1978),
Chapters 2 and 5; J.C.R. Licklider, "Computers
and Government," in The Computer Age: A
Twenty-Year View, M. L. Dertouzos and J.
Moses, eds. (Cambridge: MIT Press, 1979); I.
de Sola Pool, Talking Back: Citizen Feedback

and Cable Technology (Cambridge: MIT Press,
1983); and M. Shubik, "Information,
Rationality, and Free Choice in a Future
Democratic Society," Daedalus 96 (1977), pp.
771-778.
    2. One exception to this pattern is the
experimental work on group decision-making at
New Jersey Institute of Technology (NJIT) and
Carnegie Mellon University (CMU). Although
CMU's work has not dealt with computerized
voting, Murray Turoff of NJIT has developed
Delphi voting alternatives on the EIES
(Electronic Information Exchange System).
Commercial computer conferencing packages such
as PARTICIPATE have been designed to allow
voting to take place in different ways, but
these options are not widely used or adver-
tised because the developers have tailored
their systems to meet the needs of their
private-sector clientele.
    3. For example, Michael Margolis, Viable
Democracy (New York: Penguin Books, 1979), and
C. B. Macpherson, The Life and Times of
Liberal Democracy (New York: Oxford University
Press, 1977).
    4. Ted Becker, "Teledemocracy: Bringing
the Power to the People," The Futurist 15, no.
6 (December 1981). In "Let's Redesign
Democracy," Behavioral Science 23 (1978),
Merrill M. Flood advocates using computer
technology to experiment with "dynamic value
voting" but does not consider the implications
of computer networking developed in this
chapter.
    5. A protocoalition is a coalition of
voters that does not satisfy the defined
consensus requirement, e.g., majority rule.
    6. For examples of these perspectives,
see Steven J. Brams, The Presidential Election
Game (New Haven: Yale University Press, 1982),
and Anthony Downs, An Economic Theory of
Democracy (New York: Harper and Row, 1957).
    7. See Joseph E. McGrath, Groups:
Interaction and Performance (Englewood Cliffs,
NJ: Prentice-Hall, 1984).
    8. For a discussion of these perspec-
tives, see Arnold B. Urken, "Optimal Jury

Design," _Jurimetrics_ 24, no. 3 (Spring 1984).

9. The Marquis de Condorcet is the originator of this cognitive perspective. The philosophy is explained in Keith M. Baker, _Condorcet: From Natural Philosophy to Social Mathematics_ (Chicago: University of Chicago Press, 1975), and the mathematical exposition of ideas can be found in B. Grofman and G. Owen, "Thirteen Theorems in Search of Truth," _Theory and Decision_ 15 (1983).

10. For a general discussion of this problem, see William H. Riker, _Liberalism Against Populism_ (San Francisco: W. H. Freeman, 1982), Chapter 5.

11. This definition is drawn from Andrew S. Tanenbaum, _Computer Network_ (Englewood Cliffs, NJ: Prentice-Hall, 1981).

12. In the future, these links may integrate voice and video communication with computer conferencing. See R. Johansen, J. Vallee, and K. Spangler, _Electronic Meetings: Technical Alternatives and Social Choices_ (Reading, MA: Addison-Wesley, 1979).

13. In the U.S. House of Representatives, legislators vote electronically in a network, which expedites vote counting but does not augment the options that might be developed with online voting. The fact that this system has not changed in more than a decade indicates the importance of having computer-based voting pose no threat to the traditional face-to-face controls of congressional leaders. For a description of this system, see Frank B. Ryan, "The Electronic Voting System for the U.S. House of Representatives," _Proceedings of the IEEE-Computers_ (1972).

14. See Dennis C. Mueller, _Public Choice_ (Cambridge: Cambridge University Press, 1979), Chapter 10, for an exposition of these ideas.

15. Steven J. Brams and Peter C. Fishburn, _Approval Voting_ (Boston: Birkhauser, 1982).

16. These are normative rules. In practice, voters try to circumvent these constraints, but sometimes the manipulation backfires and leaves everyone worse off than they would have been if they had not traded at

all! For example, see the discussion of vote
trading in Arnold B. Urken, Markets for Votes
(Washington: American Political Science
Association, 1979), and "A Review and Critique
of Some Vote Trading Reform Plans," in
American Re-Evolution, Richard Auster, ed.
(Tucson: University of Arizona Press, 1977).
    17. Riker, Liberalism Against Populism.
    18. Gerald M. Phillips and Julia T. Wood,
Emergent Issues in Human Decision Making
(Carbondale, Il: Southern Illinois University
Press, 1984).
    19. A "fungible" resource can be substi-
tuted for other resources. For example, paper
currency and other instruments of economic
exchange are fungible. See Urken, Markets for
Votes, and "A Review and Critique of Some Vote
Trading Reform Plans"; and James S. Coleman,
"Political Money," American Political Science
Review (September 1973), and The Mathematics
of Collective Action (Chicago: Aldine, 1976).
The idea of "dynamic value voting" discussed
in Flood, "Let's Redesign Democracy," resem-
bles fungible voting.
    20. Max Power, "Logic and Legitimacy: On
Understanding the Electoral College
Controversy," in Perspectives on Presidential
Selection, D. R. Matthews, ed. (Washington,
D.C.: The Brookings Institution, 1973).
    21. This problem was raised by county
clerks in evaluating the use of approval
voting in New Jersey gubernatorial elections.
See A. B. Urken, "Two from Column A . . .,"
New Jersey Political Reporter (March 1981).
    22. David Chaum, "Security Without
Identification: Transaction Systems to Make
Big Brother Obselete," Communications of the
ACM 28, no. 10 (October 1985).
    23. For a contemporary criticism of the
role of the secret ballot in U.S. liberal
tradition, see Benjamin Barber, Strong
Democracy (Berkeley: University of California
Press, 1984).
    24. John Lockwood, "Computerized Decision
Making," Computer Decisions (November 1984).
    25. Matthew McClure, "At Risk: Your
On-Line Freedom," Popular Computing (June

1985).
26. Personal Communication from an anonymous technical manager of a computer conferencing company.
27. Pool, Talking Back.
28. Margolis, Viable Democracy.
29. See Herbert A. Simon, "The Consequences of Computers for Centralization and Decentralization," in The Computer Age: A Twenty-Year View, M. L. Dertouzos and Joel Moses eds. (Cambridge: MIT Press); and Margolis, Viable Democracy.
30. P. W. Keen and M. S. Morton, Decision Support Systems: An Organizational Perspective (Reading, MA: Addison-Wesley, 1978).
31. See Anthony Downs, Inside Bureaucracy (Boston: Little, Brown, 1970).
32. Electronic mail is only one part of computer conferencing, which includes file management options to enrich online communication.
33. This viewpoint is shared by some social scientists who view face-to-face consensus as more desirable than voting. See Julia T. Wood, "Alternative Methods of Decision Making: A Comparative Examination of Consensus, Negotiation, and Voting," in Phillips and Wood, Emergent Issues, pp. 3-18.
34. Lockwood, "Computerized Decision Making."
35. Johansen et al., Electronic Meetings, and Jacques Vallee, Computer Message Systems (New York: McGraw Hill, 1984).
36. Cf. D. K. Brotz, "Message System Mores: Etiquette in Laurel," ACM Transactions on Office Information Systems 1 (1983), pp. 179-192.
37. See Starr Roxanne Hiltz, Kenneth Johnson, Charles Aronovitch, and Murray Turoff, "Face-to-Face vs. Computerized Conferences: A Controlled Experiment" (Newark, NJ: Computerized Conferencing and Communications Center, 1980), and Sara Kiesler, Jane Siegel, and Timothy W. Mcguire, "Social Psychological Aspects of Computer-Mediated Communication," American Psychologist 39, no. 10 (1984), pp. 1123-1134.

38. For example, in a small Pennsylvania town with corrupt, male-dominated machine politics, the introduction of teleconferencing was a critical factor in making it possible for a woman to overthrow the political machine. See Christopher Arterton, Edward H. Lazarus, John Griffen, and Monica C. Andres, "Telecommunications Technologies and Political Participation" (Washington, D.C.: Roosevelt Center for American Policy Studies, 1984).

39. Even if interaction does occur, anonymity may create an environment in which one voter's pressure or persuasion is neutralized by the countervailing influence of another voter. In this type of situation, the symmetry of statistical independence is preserved. See Baker, Condorcet.

40. See Richard Niemi and William H. Riker, "The Choice of a Voting System," Scientific American (June 1976).

41. Cf. Herbert A. Simon, "Human Nature in Politics: The Dialogue of Psychology with Political Science," American Political Science Review 79, no. 2 (June 1985).

42. John Banzhaf, "Weighted Voting Doesn't Work: A Mathematical Analysis," Rutgers Law Review 19 (Winter 1965).

43. L. Shapley and B. Grofman, "Optimizing Group Judgmental Accuracy in the Presence of Interdependencies," Public Choice 43, no. 3 (1984).

44. Margolis, Viable Democracy; Barber, Strong Democracy; and MacPherson, The Life and Times of Liberal Democracy.

45. Robert Nozick, Anarchy, State, and Utopia (New York: Basic Books, 1974).

46. A good example of this practice is the use of a lottery to select leaders in ancient Athens. See William Shavely, Voting in Ancient Greece and Rome (New York: Oxford University Press, 1979).

47. The difficulties associated with noncomputer-based means for facilitating voter participation are described in David B. Magleby, "Mail Ballot Elections: A New Approach to Direct Democracy," paper presented at the annual meeting of the American

Political   Science   Association,   Washington,
D.C., 1984.
    48.   A.   F.   Westin   and   M.   A.   Baker,
Databanks   in   a   Free   Society   (New   York:
Quadrangle   Books,   1972);   and David Burnham,
The   Rise   of   the   Computer   State (New York:
Random House, 1983).
    49. See Urken, "Two from Column A . . .."
    50.   See   Riker,   Liberalism   Against
Populism.
    51. Riker, Ibid.
    52.   This   viewpoint   is   expounded   by
Marxist   and   Fascist   thinkers.   See   Urken,
Markets for Votes.

11

Computers and Moral Responsibility: A Framework for an Ethical Analysis

John Ladd

The Need for New Ethical Concepts

This chapter will deal with an issue that is as much a problem for moral philosophy as it is for the computer world. My basic theme is that high technology, and computer technology in particular, raises ethical problems of a new sort that require considerable restructuring of our traditional ethical categories. It follows that our job as philosophers is not, as it is often thought to be, simply to apply ready-made categories to new situations; rather, it is to find new categories, or new ways of interpreting old categories, in order to accommodate the challenges presented by new technologies.

Although I shall not directly address privacy issues here, they do provide a good illustration of the way that our traditional categories, such as the category of rights, are unable to provide needed direction in dealing with new realities. The traditional concept of privacy itself, involving, say, control over information about oneself of the sort that formerly was secured by pulling down curtains and locking drawers, has no application in the modern world of computer technology, where detrimental information about individuals can be easily collected without violating physical barriers. In view of new developments, the very definition of privacy needs to be revamped. In addition to problems of definition, there is the further problem of what might be called <u>complicity</u>--on the part of everyone with the system itself--through the use of inherently privacy-invading mechanisms such as credit cards. The concept of rights begins to lose its bite when we freely abandon the claim to privacy without a second thought whenever it is personally convenient for us to do so. The lapse into this kind of inconsistency deprives our complaints of their credibility and leaves us in a kind of ethical no-man's land.

Much the same sort of predicament about basic ethical categories is encountered in other issues coming under the rubric of computer ethics--issues relating to intrusion, piracy, and others that this chapter explores. Having used the concept of privacy to make a simple point, I leave that subject to others who are better equipped than I to deal with it and turn directly to my subject: computers and moral responsibility.

As its title indicates, my main concern in this chapter, is with what I call _moral responsibility,_ in particular, with moral responsibility for evil outcomes--disasters past, present, and future--such as calamitous computer mistakes and errors. I shall explain presently in more detail the concept of responsibility involved here and how it applies to the computer world. In the meantime, we may take the basic question to be about the ethics of what people unintentionally do to harm other people through the use of computers.

My procedure is as follows: First, I discuss how the problem arises and how it is generally handled. Second, I outline a revamped and relatively sophisticated conception of moral responsibility, which I put forward as a useful conceptual tool for understanding and dealing with a number of basic ethical issues connected with computers. Third, I introduce the concept of intermediaries as a complicating factor when responsibility is connected with technology, computers, and bureaucracies. Fourth, I compare and contrast human and computer control over intermediaries in order to bring out further facets of responsibility. I conclude the essay with two examples of how the concept of moral responsibility can be applied to concrete cases.

Responsibility in the World of Technology

The general area of concern in this chapter is a well-known problem connected with high technology in general, although more especially with computer technology; namely, How is it possible for particular individuals to have any moral responsibility at all for evil outcomes that are the compound product of complicated interacting processes that themselves apparently bypass human agency altogether? The question could be put in metaphorical terms by saying that there is such a long distance between the inputs of particular individuals and their significant outcomes, and there are so many different kinds of input from so many different sources (designers, operators, managers, and consumers), that as far as establishing human responsibility is concerned, we find ourselves adrift in a vast sea of anonymity where responsibility has become so diffused as to evaporate into nothingness.

The difficulty in relating responsibility to technology is due not only to technological and social complexity but also to the fact that multipurpose technology such as computers can be used both for good and for ill. Consequently, telephones, automobiles, and now computers must be ostensibly judged as good or bad by reference to the specific purposes for which they are used. When particular uses of computers are bad, we say that they have been misused or abused. The underlying assumption behind the use of terms like "misuse" or "abuse" is that computers, like telephones and automobiles, are essentially good and are evil only in exceptional cases that can easily be recognized.

The reliance on purpose and uses, good and bad, open and hidden, social and antisocial, as the primary standard for the moral evaluation of a particular technology or of a particular use of it becomes problematic as soon as we take into consideration, as we must, the unanticipated outcomes of the use of technology, such as accidents. Consider, for example, a nuclear accident, an airplane crash, or a police misidentification. Computers also crash--sometimes with disastrous results. In these cases, our focus shifts from purposes--what a computer is used for--to what it in fact <u>does</u>, the consequences of its operations. This aspect of computers is what I shall be concerned with in this chapter; the comprehensive concept of responsibility is designed to deal with problems of this type.

The Myth of Technological Neutrality

Underlying the problem of the moral evaluation of technologies--which in the present context involves such things as computer hardware, computer software, networks and their uses--is the generally unquestioned assumption that technology per se is <u>ethically neutral.</u> Examples abound: "Guns don't kill, only outlaws kill"; "Nuclear weapons aren't evil, only when used by evil people like the Russians are they evil"; or, closer to home, "'Matching' and 'Profiling' are not evil, only those who use them are evil" (e.g., the secret police). In other words, the moral acceptability or unacceptability of a particular technology depends on what it is used for and who uses it. Ethics and value questions are, as it were, external to computer technology. Doctrines like this, I shall argue, are an ethical cop-out.

The neutralist thesis, on analysis, is not as self-evident as it might at first seem to be. To begin with, it is quite obvious that technology changes our lives and therewith our ethics. A new technology makes certain modes of conduct easier and others more difficult; Saturday Night Specials facilitate, perhaps even encourage and invite, hold-ups. We are sucked in by new technologies, sometimes quite against our will and better judgment. It is clear that, like the Saturday Night Specials, computers facilitate, encourage, and invite new practices, such as matching and profiling, and along with them new types of surveillance. Thus, like other new technologies, computer technology has created new modes of conduct and new social institutions, new vices and new virtues, new ways of helping and new ways of abusing other people.

Ethical neutralism with regard to technology rests on a doctrinaire separation of means and ends, of tools and human well-being. I shall argue throughout this chapter that this separation is not only unrealistic but is also ethically mischievous; I shall try to show in particular that it leads to a serious misunderstanding of the nature of moral responsibility in relation to computers. Human agents are responsible not only for the outcomes of their actions and for their uses of technology but also for how the technology itself shapes our conduct, our attitudes, and our institutions. But the argument is complicated. It can only be understood by reference to a comprehensive conception of responsibility, which I shall now try to sketch.

A Comprehensive Concept
of Moral Responsibility

My purpose in introducing what I call a "comprehensive concept of moral responsibility" is to provide a more satisfactory conceptual tool for analyzing problems in computer ethics than other generally recognized concepts, such as rights or utility, can provide. At the outset, however, I should point out that the conception of responsibility that I have in mind departs in essential respects from the received notion discussed by philosophers under the heading of free will and determinism. Philosophical discussions of the latter are generally more concerned with defining the conditions of nonresponsibility (e.g., excusing conditions) than with giving an account of responsibility in a positive full-blown moral sense. Lawyers, for somewhat different reasons, are also concerned primarily with conditions of nonresponsibility; that is, conditions that exempt a person from criminal or civil liability.[1] In contrast to these notions, which I shall call "negative conceptions of responsibility," there is a broader, positive conception of moral responsibility that refers, for example, to a person's duties to others with whom he or she has a relationship, such as children, employees, or associates, and to a person's duty to have due regard for the consequences of his or her actions for the safety and welfare of others.

This positive sense of responsibility is partly captured by general terms like "social responsibility" and by other more specific terms like "family responsibility." It is also reflected in the use of "responsible" to stand for a virtue; that is, a character trait that persons ought to have and actions that ought to be done. In this sense, responsibility is contrasted with irresponsibility, and not being responsible means simply being irresponsible.[2]

It should be clear by now that the concept of responsibility involved here breaks the traditional ties between responsibility and liability (e.g., having to pay for damages) and between responsibility and punishability or blameworthiness. These other concepts can still be linked to the comprehensive concept of responsibility but only indirectly. The comprehensive concept focuses on what ought or ought not to be done, rather than on the responses that third parties, such as spectators and judges, are permitted to adopt in the form of disapproving, blaming, or punishing those who are on the giving or receiving end of transactions.

The positive conception of moral responsibility differs from the negative conceptions usually discussed by philosophers and lawyers in two basic respects: First, positive responsibility is nonexclusive. One person's being responsible does not entail that other persons

are not also responsible; hence, it is possible for a lot of people to be coresponsible
for something, although perhaps in varying
degrees. Second, responsibility need not always be direct and proximate; it may be and
more commonly is indirect and remote. Unlike
negative responsibility, which is character-
istically a black-and-white issue, positive
moral responsibility has no clear-cut borders
and, like a magnetic field, varies from point
to point in degrees of strength and strin-
gency. The advantage of the open-texture
quality of positive moral responsibility is
that it makes it possible to use sophisticated, complex, and multiple causal analyses
in detailing the moral responsibilities of
individual human agents in relation to particular untoward outcomes.[3]

In the comprehensive moral sense, responsibility expresses a certain kind of moral
and social relationship between persons. It
builds on the fact that human agents and other
human beings affected by the outcomes that are
the consequences of the agents' actions or
omissions. (The persons affected might be
called "victims" or "recipients.") The interpersonal relationship involved in responsibility has two sides: (1) a subjective (or mental) attitude, present or absent in the
agent(s), such as a concern (or lack of concern) for the safety or welfare of another
person; (2) an objective side, namely, a
causal connection between the agents' actions
(or omissions) and the unfortunate outcome for
the victim(s).[4] The first side, the subjective
attitude, can be illustrated by reference to
the tort of negligence, where the agent may be
reckless, careless, unconcerned, or plain
thoughtless about the consequences of his or
her actions (or nonactions) for the safety or
welfare of others (victims).[5]

The comprehensive concept of responsibility is intended to cover both retrospective
and prospective responsibility and so applies
both to past and to future actions and outcomes. Accordingly, it lays down moral
requirements about what people ought to have

done and about what people ought to do in the future. For example, a reckless driver who causes the death of another is retrospectively responsible for the outcome (liable) because he caused it by being reckless, and other drivers are prospectively responsible for preventing such outcomes and for being neither reckless nor a cause. The same thing, of course, could be said of a thoughtless programmer whose program has led or might lead to an accident. Because, as I have already pointed out, positive responsibility is nonexclusive, other people besides the driver or the programmer might also be either directly or indirectly responsible for preventing (or not having prevented) the accident.

Philosophically, one of the merits of the proposed comprehensive concept of moral responsibility is that, in current jargon, it is both "consequentialist" and "agent-relative." As such, it reflects the basic insights of the traditional concept of responsibility, which focuses on the moral linkage between outcomes, human agents, and human victims.[6] I shall now apply this notion to some of the ethical problems of responsibility that are connected with computers.

Intermediaries

Technology adds another element to the analysis of responsibility just outlined, namely, an intermediary. An intermediary provides the causal mechanism or causal structure that mediates between the actions of human agents and significant outcomes. In the case of the reckless driver, the technological intermediary is the automobile; in the case of the careless programmer, it is the technological process of running the program and tying it up with other parts of the system.

It is obvious that where complex technology is involved, the interposition of intermediaries of various sorts tends to make the assignment of responsibility for particular outcomes to particular agents diffi-

cult and ambiguous, simply because the causal
nexus is so complicated. To this difficulty
must be added the further difficulty that we
have a natural tendency to ignore the role of
intermediaries in determining responsibility
relations, because the technological infra-
structure that acts as intermediary is almost
always phenomenologically transparent. Thus,
we are hardly ever conscious of the part that
an automobile or a telephone system plays in
determining what we do when we use them or of
how they impose patterns of their own on our
actions and their outcomes.

By the same token, we tend to take for
granted ·the "ethical neutrality" of intermediaries, as I have already mentioned.
Occasionally, of course, we do take the
properties of a technological intermediary
into account; for example, as far as automobiles are concerned, experience has taught
us not only to drive carefully but also to
check on the condition of the machine, brakes,
tires, and so on. As far as other technologies
are concerned, we often have no way of assessing how and in what way they shape our actions and structure the outcomes. Presumably,
with computers, the complicated (and hidden)
nature of the technology reinforces our pro-
pensity to ignore our responsibility for the
outcomes of computer operations.

Needless to say, there are serious moral
objections to ignoring responsibility relations with respect to intermediary systems,
even where they are quite complicated. One
reason why we feel justified in doing so is
that we assume, falsely I have argued, that
moral responsibility must always be direct and
proximate. This assumption has its roots in
an oversimplified linear notion of causality,
which is fostered perhaps by the law, inasmuch
as law needs a standardized conception of
causal relations for the purposes of
establishing legal guilt and legal liability.[7]

Another consideration contributes to the
disavowal of responsibility: Where complex
technological systems are involved, the causal
contribution of any particular individual

agent to bringing about of a disastrous outcome may not be decisive and is usually
neither necessary nor sufficient. In fact, of
course, the precise causal nature of the contribution may not be known. Charles Perrow has
described in detail some of the disastrous
accidents that have taken place in complex
technological systems. He called them "normal
accidents."[8] In his detailed descriptions of
such accidents, he argued persuasively for the
conclusion that it is more plausible to attribute these industrial disasters to the complexities of the systems than to the failures
of human operators.

Nevertheless, the comprehensive conception of moral responsibility outlined above
implies that human agents are, in the final
analysis, responsible for the systems them-
selves--that is, for the way that intermediaries function--and that human responsibility for disasters (past and potential) is
not limited to the direct input of particular
individuals, such as operators. Responsibility
in the full moral sense covers indirect and
remote causal relations, partial and con-
tributory causes, as well as direct and
proximate ones; even though individual persons
are only indirectly or remotely connected with
the outcome, they are not freed from the
requirements of responsibility. However difficult it may be to determine, there is always
some sort of human responsibility for the outcome of even the most complicated intervening
technology.

The kind of indirect and diffused responsibility involved here is sometimes called
"collective responsibility." However, I
find this concept more confusing than helpful
because it diverts attention from the crucial
question about responsibility; namely, Which
people in particular are responsible? To
answer this question requires tracing the
causal connections and responsibility relations for outcomes to particular individuals
and to their individual failures stemming from
such things as self-centered projects, narrow
and single-minded interests, unconcerns, and

moral mindlessness.

So far I have addressed the role of an intermediary between agents and outcomes only in relation to technology and mechanical processes, but now I wish to extend the notion to apply to structured human processes, such as those found in formal organizations or bureaucracies. For, like machines, the latter act as a sort of conduit for individual human actions and decision-making. They are, in this sense, also intermediaries.

There is obviously an intimate connection between structured social processes and technology. It is usually difficult to separate them from each other; the relationship may be said to be "symbiotic." Consider, for example, the use of automated bank tellers, which employ new computer technology to execute financial transactions that themselves are defined through a complex set of social structures, processes, and practices.

The structured processes themselves, as adopted and employed in formal organizations, perform the role of intermediaries in a way that is comparable to the role of technological systems. Like machines, they are purported to be immune to imputations of responsibility on the grounds that they are ethically neutral. The imputation of responsibility to particular individuals in such systems is often difficult and almost always complicated. And, just as with machines, the social mechanism itself--in the cashing of checks, for instance--becomes phenomenologically transparent. The actions that we perform as "autonomous individuals" appear to be our own, although in fact their form, structure, and meaning are shaped by the social systems in which they take place, that is, by intermediaries.

In both types of intermediaries, however, individual human agents are not let off the hook as far as responsibility is concerned. The comprehensive conception of responsibility makes room for indefinitely large numbers of people to be morally responsible for an outcome, although their various contributions are at different levels and vary considerably in amounts and degrees.

As far as formal organizations (or bureaucracies) are concerned, I have argued at length elsewhere that it is both a conceptual mistake and a moral error to attribute moral responsibility to formal organizations as such, as is done in most of the literature on corporate responsibility.[9] To hold organizations as such morally responsible for untoward outcomes may be compared to holding a machine--for example, a robot that kills a person--morally responsible for homicide.[10] It is a bit of anthropomorphic nonsense to ascribe moral responsibility to systems, whether they be technological or social, in addition to or instead of to the individuals that make and use them. Questions about who was responsible for the Nazi holocaust are not simply answered by reference to the technological machinery involved or to the bureaucratic system that carried it out; rather, responsibility must be attributed to indefinitely large numbers of individuals who in one way or another contributed quite indirectly and remotely to the outcome.[11]

Individuals, whoever they are and however minor their contribution, cannot escape either their retrospective or their prospective moral responsibilities in an organization by appeal to the doctrine of respondeat superior.[12] For the same reason, computer professionals, users, operators, programmers, and managers cannot escape their responsibilities for outcomes by appeal to a doctrine of respondeat computer!

Computers as Metamachines

We come at last to the computer, which is typically a very special sort of machine: a metamachine. For, unlike other machines, computers are usually second-level machines that are used to control other machines. More generally, computer technology provides systems for controlling other systems, namely,

those that I have called "intermediaries."
Computers are, as it were, superintermediar-
ies. The intermediaries that are controlled
by computers may be either mechanical systems
or organizational systems; the latter are
controlled largely through networking.

In precomputer days, the intermediaries
and processes that are now controlled by
computers were and could only be controlled by
human beings. Now, computers have begun to
replace human beings in their capacity as
controllers, which is precisely the capacity
that makes human beings morally responsible
for outcomes. To put the point more pictur-
esquely, just as other machines (and tools)
have in the past been used to replace hands
(and bodies), so computers, the metamachines,
are now being used to replace brains. The
special responsibility problems raised by
computers are due, then, to the fact that they
are used to replace minds, or brains, which,
as I have said, are the source of human
responsibility.

It can be readily seen that the introduction of computers to replace human controllers of first level intermediaries complicates
an already complicated picture of moral responsibility. It sometimes appears to be the
case that we have "delegated" or "abdicated"
our decision-making powers to computers and
have made computers responsible for outcomes
for which human beings used to be responsible.
That is why it has become popular to "blame"
the computer for mistakes that were previously
blamed on human beings. In earlier days, if
one received a bill with an error in it, one
blamed a person; nowadays, one blames the
computer. Even though blaming a computer is
silly, the excuse for doing so is that computers now do the sort of thing that human
beings used to do and for which human beings
used to be responsible, such as carrying out
financial transactions, making reservations,
and landing aircraft. But being dumb machines,
when confronted with their mistakes, computers
do not answer with a polite, "I am sorry"
(unless they are programmed to do so). And

one soon concludes that it is not a violation of the rules of politeness to turn them off when they do not behave; for, after all, it is impossible to insult a computer.

Disregarding such anthropomorphic responses to computers, let us return to ethics, which is and must be grounded on realities rather than on fairy stories and mythologies. What happens then when computers take over peculiarly human functions? What ethical consequences does the replacement of human controllers by computer controllers have for the original responsibility functions of human beings? In other words, where a human being is replaced by a computer, what happens to the responsibility that the human being used to have?

The obvious answer to the question about responsibility is that, as with other intermediaries, human control and moral responsibility move to a third level. At that level, we have a new kind of control--control over computers--which itself is an example of indirect and less easily assigned responsibility. This move, however, leads to a whole new set of questions, issues, and problems relating to responsibility; namely, it leads to questions about the formerly human functions performed by computers and how computers perform them in specific instances. Do they perform them well or badly? And what kind of controls should be exercised over computers in order to obtain morally responsible outputs?

Responsibility and the Shift
from Human Control to Computer Control

The new set of issues raises questions about the ethically significant differences between human and computer control and about the effect of the shift from one kind of control to the other on the assignments of responsibility, especially as it relates to intermediaries at the first level. The shift to computers might be exemplified by controlled aircraft landing and computerized banking.

Both of these innovations have brought many benefits along with new hazards and, indeed, a number of disasters. In order to bring out the ethically significant aspects of this shift in control, we must examine more closely the similarities and differences between the two kinds of control.

There are, to begin with, certain obvious similarities between the jobs normally performed by human beings in controlling intermediaries and those performed by computers. As in human decision-making, computers make decisions based on the use of information processing. The decision-making process is structured through means-ends relationships of one sort or another. For computers, the ordering of means and ends is accomplished through the use of algorithms. In the cases under consideration here, the means consist of operations of intermediary systems, either mechanical or organizational.

The resemblance between the two types of decision-making or control may be seen by comparing, for example, a computer-directed operation with a human-directed operation such as the landing of an aircraft. As control centers, they both receive information and process it for the purposes of controlling the system, the intermediary, so that the latter will satisfactorily serve the purposes for which it is designed--in this case, flying and making a safe landing.

Inasmuch as computers, like human operators, operate at a second level--that is, they operate on other systems (intermediaries)--the final evaluation of their second-level operations is a function of how well or poorly the first-level controlled system performs. A good aircraft control system, whether human or computer, is one that flies and lands the airplane effectively and properly. What is important here is that neither human controllers nor computers produce their effects directly, whether good or bad, but only indirectly through the systems that they control. Hence, computers cannot be dangerous or safe in themselves but only on account of the inherent features of the systems (machines) they control. A computer-controlled nuclear power plant is dangerous because it involves nuclear processes, not because it involves computers. By itself, a computer is harmless or useless. As the value of computers--their programs and operations, both positive and negative--depends on the systems they are used to control, they could be said to be <u>parasites</u> from the value point of view. In the final analysis, as far as values are concerned, the outcome is what counts.

To pursue these similarities further, computers and human controllers are almost always superior to purely mechanical controls. They are more flexible, and they are responsive to different environments and varying sorts of data and information processing.[13] Such controls "monitor" changes in the environment and direct the systems they control (intermediaries) accordingly.

But here we begin to see differences between human and computer controls. On one hand, computers are in many respects clearly better than human beings are at controlling some systems because they have larger memories and can process information faster and more accurately, perhaps also more economically. They do not have to sleep or take coffee breaks. For these reasons, computer controllers are frequently and justly preferred to human controllers.

On the other hand, computerized controls are for certain purposes of limited value, either because they are ineffectual or because they are liable to error. They are limited for a number of reasons having to do with the peculiar properties of computers and how computer systems are coupled to other systems. Thus, computers are unable to deal with certain kinds of surprises and accidents. Their proneness to new and unexpected kinds of error may lead to disastrous results. It is unnecessary to repeat the horror stories.[14]

It is clear, therefore, that we need to ask which sort of control, computer or human, is best for a particular purpose and for a particular kind of intermediary, or more generally, we need to ask: What do computers do best and what do human beings do best? As we are concerned here with responsibility for avoiding disastrous outcomes, our answers must be framed with such outcomes in mind.

As a general principle the following seems most plausible: In situations where satisfactory controls require dealing only with closed systems of factors, data, or tasks, computers are probably superior; when the systems required are open-ended and fluid, human controllers are generally preferable. In an old-fashioned terminology, human beings are better than computers where "judgment" is required. Granting all this, however, we still have to answer crucial and controversial questions concerning which kinds of problems belong to each of these categories; more exactly, we must ask which parts of a problem belong in which of these categories.[15]

Given the difficulties created by the computer revolution, even after this general principle is accepted in the abstract, problems that properly belong to the open fluid category are likely to be handled as if they belonged to the other category. Thus, jobs will still be given to computers that they are intrinsically incapable of handling. Mismatching of this kind raises a new consideration: When, for some reason or other (such as incomplete or incorrect data or a rigid, inflexible program), the computer decision-making is defective, we need to have some way "to get out" and to revert to human controls. In order to do this, there needs to be a loose coupling between the computers and the systems they are controlling and between the latter and the production of outcomes. This kind of safety mechanism is especially necessary where there is a possibility that a computer error might lead to disastrous consequences.[16]

So there are at least two kinds of things that we, as responsible human beings, need to watch out for: first, not giving the computer control over jobs that it is unequipped to

handle, and second, providing some way to de-
couple from the computer if things go wrong.
Two examples will illustrate these points.

Lessons in Irresponsibility: Two Cases

There are a number of well-attested cases
of police misidentification based on computer-
based information (or disinformation) about
the identity of individual criminals being
searched for. These cases generally take the
same form; namely, from available databanks,
using matching and profiling techniques, the
inference is made that the wanted person has
certain identifying characteristics. An
individual is then found who by coincidence
happens to have a few or even most of the
characteristics in question. He or she is
then apprehended and perhaps falsely arrested
and in at least one case, even shot to
death.[17] The disastrous outcome in these cases
is the result of too tight coupling between
the computer-generated profile, bureaucratic
procedures (police protocols), and actions
directly affecting individual victims. (Often
the information in the databank is incorrect.[18]) This tight coupling might be said to
be the cause of the disaster, as in some of
the normal accidents described by Perrow.[19]

A second example is the tie-up of the
Bank of New York in November 1985 when a
computer foul-up prevented the bank from
delivering securities to buyers and making
payments to sellers. The system was down for
twenty-eight hours, and the bank had to borrow
$20 billion at an interest expense of about $4
million. A number of other financial losses
were incurred. A seemingly minor computer
error led to a near financial disaster.[20]
Again, we have a case of over-tight coupling
between the computer system and the intermediary, the Bank of New York and the Wall
Street financial system.

These two examples of overdependence on
computers may serve as illustrations of how
the framework of moral responsibility set

forth in this chapter could be applied to real situations. In particular, they show us how, as human agents, we must take moral responsibility for preventing the disastrous outcomes that computer operations can have for the safety, health, welfare, and moral integrity of innocent victims. Unless as citizens and responsible human beings we assume prospective responsibility of this kind--for example, for errors that might happen in the computer system that controls our nuclear arsenal--we may end up being retrospectively responsible for a nuclear holocaust and the end of civilization as we know it.[21] In view of the disastrous outcomes that may result in such cases, responsibility should be something to take seriously.

Notes

1. See the classic discussion by H.L.A. Hart, <u>Punishment</u> <u>and</u> <u>Responsibility</u> (New York: Oxford University Press, 1968).

2. G. Haydon, "On Being Responsible," <u>The Philosophical Quarterly</u> 28 (1979), pp. 46-57.

3. I have explained the present conception of responsibility in a number of other writings: "The Ethical Dimensions of the Concept of Action," <u>Journal of Philosophy</u> (4 November 1965), where I argue that responsibility applies to states of affairs rather than to actions; "The Ethics of Participation," in <u>NOMOS XVI: Participaition in Politics</u>, R. Pennock and J. Chapman eds. (New York: Atherton-Lieber, 1975), which contains arguments for a nonexclusive concept of responsibility; "Philosophical Remarks on Professional Responsibility in Organizations," <u>Applied Philosophy</u>, 1, no. 2 (Fall 1982); "Morality and the Ideal of Rationality in Formal Organizations," <u>Monist</u> (October 1970), where I argue that formal organizations as

such cannot have moral responsibilities; and, as a followup to the above, "Corporate Mythology and Individual Responsibility," Applied Philosophy 2, no. 1 (Fall 1984).

4. The comprehensive conception of responsibility also covers cases analogous to strict liability and vicarious liability, but I omit the discussion of them here.

5. William L. Prosser, The Law of Torts, 4th ed. (St. Paul, MN: West Publishing Co., 1971).

6. Thomas Nagel, "The Limits of Objectivity," in The Tanner Lectures on Human Values, vol 1, Sterling M. McMurrin, ed. (Cambridge: Cambridge University Press, 1980); Amartya Sen, "Rights and Agency," Philosophy and Public Affairs 2, no. 1 (Winter 1982), pp. 3-39.

7. In the law, the accepted principle is novus actus interveniens, which means that the causal chain can be broken by an intervening action. See H.L.A. Hart and A. M. Honore, Causation in the Law (Oxford: Clarendon Press, 1959), pp. 69 ff. My position, which is moral and not legal, rejects this notion. I am not alone in finding moral objections to it.

8. Charles Perrow, Normal Accidents (New York: Basic Books, 1984).

9. John Ladd, "Morality and the Ideal of Rationality in Formal Organizations," Monist 54, no. 4 (October 1970), pp. 488-516.

10. See "In the Lion's Cage," Forbes 136, no. 9 (7 October 1985), pp. 142-143.

11. Although it is not directly material to the present subject, one should remember that there is a subjective component to responsibility as well as the objective component we have been discussing. In the cases mentioned, there was a large amount of "unconcern" on the part of the general public--and not only in Germany--about what was going on in the concentration camps.

12. Hannah Arendt, Eichmann in Jerusalem (New York: Viking Press, 1963).

13. Nancy Leveson, "Software Safety: Why, Where, What?" (unpublished manuscript).

14. See newsletters of Computer Professionals for Social Responsibility and other CPSR material on computer unreliability (CPSR, P.O. Box 717, Palo Acto, CA 94301).

15. The following is an example provided by Richard van Slyke at the conference for which this essay was written.

16. Perrow, <u>Normal</u> <u>Accidents</u>.

17. The goriest case can be found in Jacques Vallee, <u>The</u> <u>Network</u> <u>Revolution</u> (Berkeley: And/Or Press, 1982), where the innocent victims were shot to death by the French police acting on a computer report.

18. An FBI audit of the National Crime Information Center showed that "the NCIC computer's responses include at least 12,000 invalid or inaccurate personal records each day." Ross Gelbspan, "Technological Surveillance: 1985 in the U.S.A.," <u>Computers</u> <u>and</u> <u>People</u> (March–April 1986), pp. 18-20.

19. Gary Marx, "Routinizing the Discovery of Secrets: Computers as Informants," <u>Software</u> <u>Law</u> <u>Journal</u> 1 (Fall 1985).

20. Phillip L. Zweig and Allanna Sullivan, "A Computer Snafu Snarls the Handling of Treasury Issues," <u>Wall</u> <u>Street</u> <u>Journal</u> (25 November 1985), p. 58.

21. Paul Bracken, <u>The</u> <u>Command</u> <u>and</u> <u>Control</u> <u>of</u> <u>Nuclear</u> <u>Forces</u> (New Haven: Yale University Press, 1983); See also, <u>Computers</u> <u>in</u> <u>Battle</u>, D. Bellin and G. Chapman, eds. (Boston, MA: HarcourtBrace Jovanovich, 1987).

12

Computer Crime: The Worm in the Apple

Rodney D. Andrews

With the advent of extensive computer use and the coming development of many types of networking, it is obvious that computers will be playing a major role in our future lives, going far beyond their initial use for carrying out calculations. They will be playing a social role, especially in communication in the broadest sense, including interpersonal communication, information and data storage, control of processes and operations, and financial accounting and the transfer of funds. They are being more and more extensively used in business, science and engineering, medicine, and national defense.

But with the unquestioned advantages of all of these developments, the opportunities for misuse of computers and computer systems will multiply correspondingly. Both the number of computers and the percentage of the population able to use them will increase dramatically as the young people now being taught computer skills in school and elsewhere grow to adulthood. Although the title of this chapter is "Computer Crime," a more general title of "Computer Misuse" might be more appropriate, because problems other than crime will also be discussed. The fact that there are such problems, and that these problems will undoubtedly increase, is reflected by the fact that the subject is even beign addressed in the popular media. For example, an article that appeared in <u>Time</u> magazine in November

230

1985[1] discussed this growing problem. And as the problem grows, the search for solutions must accelerate, as most of the good solutions are preventive ones.

Viruses and Other Parasitic Computer Programs

The _Time_ article mentioned a case early in 1984 in which someone (whose identity is still not known) inserted a small bit of false software coding (a "logic bomb") into the computer at the Los Angeles Department of Water and Power, that activated itself at a preassigned time and froze the utility's internal files. All work was halted until a team of experts, including the Los Angeles Police Department's newly formed computer crime unit, was able to uncover the destructive coding. Most such sabotage is apparently carried out by disaffected former employees, and the target can be any sort of organization. It is only necessary to gain access to the computer or computer system and have the necessary technical knowledge. Another type of parasitic program, which deletes particular portions of a computer's memory, is called a "worm" (which suggested this chapter's subtitle, although this particular type of worm could of course just as well be in an IBM or Commodore as in an Apple).

Another type of inserted program, which can replicate itself, is called a "virus" (or perhaps it could better be called a "cancer"). This "virus" continues to copy itself into the computer's memory until the memory becomes a shambles; in the case of a network, it can spread throughout the network and infect other computers. A January 1988 article in The New York Times[2] described how these viruses had been infecting computer systems around the world (in the United States, Israel, West Germany, Switzerland, Britain, and Italy) during the preceding nine months. Virus programs can be transmitted between computers over telephone lines or other network connections, and the infection can spread rapidly. Fred Cohen of the University of Cincinnati, who has been doing research on computer viruses since 1983, observed that most mainframe computers can be successfully subverted within an hour, and that networks--even a huge international network with thousands of computers spread over continents--can be opened up to illicit intrusion within days. Several American colleges have recently reported widespread viruses in the personal computers (these are the most easily infected) used on campus by students and faculty, and infections have been reported by other personal computer user groups in Florida, Colorado, New Jersey, and New York, as well as by business corporations (including IBM).

A particularly serious case occurred in Israel, where an infectious virus code that spread widely was apparently intended as a weapon of political protest. It contained a "time bomb" that was programmed to activate on May 13, 1988 (the fortieth anniversary of the last day of Palestine independence); it was designed to cause all infected programs to erase all their stored files. This virus was fortunately discovered before it could take effect, and an "immunity program" was circulated to "kill" the virus (remove it from memory storage). Such programs can neutralize a virus, but it is very difficult to prevent one from entering, as they are designed to jump the usual barriers to access.

Still another type of destructive program is known as a "Trojan horse" because it is sometimes let in by the unsuspecting victim. An example of such a program is given in the *Time* article: An engineer logged onto a computer "bulletin board," which offered what was purported to be a free program to improve the graphics capability of his home computer. But after a short while in which the screen remained blank, a message suddenly flashed on the screen: "Arf! Arf! Got you!" and the engineer found that nearly 900 files that he had stored in his machine containing accounting, word processing, and game data had all been completely erased.

Computer "Hackers"

The computer "hacker" phenomenon has received quite a bit of publicity[3] because it has a spirit of colorful banditry and illustrates what can be accomplished even by a single individual with initiative, cleverness, and the right degree of technical knowledge. These hackers are often young people looking simply for thrills and excitement, such as the group of thirteen-year-olds (the "Dalton Gang") at the Dalton School in New York City who used their classroom computers to carry out their exploits.[4] There was also the young man who, in 1983, using an ordinary modem and telephone, was able to penetrate the computer system at the Memorial Sloan-Kettering Cancer Research Center in New York City and gain access to private records.[5] He used a program called a "trapdoor," which collected users' passwords as they logged on. He was caught, but the majority of hackers are not. It has been estimated that hundreds, and more likely thousands, of such hackers have penetrated supposedly private computer systems all over the country.[6] And these hackers usually share information with each other through their computer bulletin boards on how different computer systems can be penetrated. In the summer of 1983 a number of people penetrated the Sloan-Kettering computer, including a famous group in Milwaukee, Wisconsin, consisting of young people aged fifteen to twenty-two (the "414's," named after their telephone area code).[7] This group also penetrated the system at Los Alamos Scientific Laboratory, a California bank, and some sixty other computer databanks around the country through the GTE Telenet national communications network. The FBI finally did close in on them. According to Broad,[8] "Computer experts say cracking a sophisticated computer network is far easier and has become far more common than has been generally believed. They say the recent intrusions by Milwaukee youths, for example, in no way represent an especially ingenious maneuver that could be achieved only by electronic wizards." There are many other examples. A group of students at Berkeley figured out how to enter the University of California's computer system,[9] but revealed their discovery to the administration; and a group of Cal Tech students gained brief control of the computer-operated scoreboard during the 1984 Rose Bowl game between Illinois and UCLA long enough to change the score temporarily to read "Cal Tech 38, MIT 9."[10] In most cases, these hackers seem to have no malicious intent but do it merely as sport and to show off their own cleverness. But they clearly demonstrate how vulnerable most computer systems are, and there is no guarantee that the individuals involved are only looking for fun. The front-page headline on the New York Post for July 24, 1987, was "Feds Crack High Tech Teens." The story inside detailed the capture of three Brooklyn teenagers who were members of a nationwide ring of computer hackers who had stolen millions of dollars of goods and services. The scheme involved penetration of the files of a credit card authorization center to obtain lists of credit card members, which were then used to make purchases.

On a happier note, the hacker phenomenon has even generated some literary works. A former MIT undergraduate hacker has written a book[11] concerning some of his own exploits and his general philosophy of hacking, which strongly emphasizes the positive side. And a play, Hackers, written by a graduate student in computer science from MIT, has been produced in regional theater to good reviews.[12]

Computer Crimes

In assessing the damage to computer systems all over the country, it is generally agreed that hackers are not the major problem. Most serious criminal acts are in fact "inside

jobs" carried out by employees who have legitimate access to the computer system used.
But even computer crime is not the most serious problem in financial terms: The problem
that causes the most financial loss to owners
of computer systems all over the United States
is simply human error.[13] Then comes crime by
insiders, particularly nontechnical people of
three types, according to Robert Courtney,
former chief of security for IBM and now a
security consultant: (1) single women under
thirty-five, generally clerical employees
whose boyfriends tell them to do it; (2) little old ladies fifty and over who give the
money to charity; and (3) older men in accounting who are disenchanted and feel unap-
preciated.[14] The acknowledged expert in the
field of computer crime is Donn Parker, who
has assembled case studies of computer crime
over a fifteen-year period and has written
several books on the subject.[15] An interesting
anecdotal compilation has also been given by
Whiteside.[16]

The spectrum of deliberate computer misuse thus runs all the way from simple pranks
to acts that could be extremely damaging. The
gradations could be described as pranks,
gamesmanship, vindictive hacking, crime itself
(often involving money), sabotage, and catas-
trophe. The boundaries between these categories are vague, but the existence of this
spectrum is clear. Effective means of dealing
with these different types of acts are also
different. Events of the catastrophic type
can easily be visualized in connection with
national security and the military, as more
and more advanced weapons systems are being
computer-controlled with a minimum of human
intervention. The movie War Games told a
story of a young computer "whiz kid" who
penetrated the national defense computer
system and nearly set off a nuclear war.
Although Pentagon spokespersons have said that
such a disaster would not be possible, everyone knows that, according to Murphy's Law,
since is always some way, in principle, to
subvert any system. It has been stated that

the Defense Department spends more than $50 million annually on security,[17] including research, hardware development and production, and even "Tiger Teams,"[18] whose sole responsibility is to try to break the codes and penetrate the system in any way.

A catastrophic act would have to be carried out only once, and legal deterrents would seem essentially useless. There would be little point in passing a law against starting World War III. The only solution is security systems.[19] And as computer networking is built into the defense system (and civilian systems as well) more and more, these systems will automatically become more and more vulnerable not only to system breakdown itself but to sabotage of an extremely serious nature. It will be an obvious goal of a future saboteur or terrorist to paralyze the computerized "nervous system" of an enemy.[20]

Computer technology itself has developed so rapidly that in the competitive rush to provide new functions and services, the development of adequate security systems has lagged far behind.[21] But as the need for such systems becomes more and more evident, new businesses are now springing up specifically to provide consulting services to clients on the security of their computer systems. It is interesting, and a little ironic, that the need for these services should sometimes provide good business opportunities for ex-computer criminals. A case in point is Stanley Rifkin, who embezzled $10.2 million from the Security Pacific National Bank in Los Angeles; he served less than three years of an eight-year sentence and now runs the computer system for a major organization.[22] Another young computer criminal, described by Parker,[23] stole a still undetermined amount of equipment from Pacific Telephone and Telegraph Company in Los Angeles through manipulation of its computer system and actually sold quite a bit of the equipment back to the same company as a demonstration of cool nerve. He was finally caught and sentenced to two months in a minimum security prison followed by three years of probation.

He served only forty days and paid a $500 fine, and on his release immediately set up a computer security consulting company in Los Angeles. The telephone company later sued him, however, and was awarded damages that he must pay to them over a period of time. Some insurance companies, incidentally, are now offering "computer crime insurance" as a new type of policy.[24]

Security Techniques

One primary tool in security systems is encryption and the use of codes. A semipopular description of some of the techniques used in such codes is given by Krauss and MacGahan,[25] and an additional discussion is given by VanDuyn.[26] These systems involve the use of a code-making algorithm and a key to provide access. By far the most widely used of these systems currently is the DES (Data Encryption Standard) developed by IBM and distributed by the National Bureau of Standards--since 1977 to government users and since 1980 to private users as well. This system encrypts data to be sent over a public channel, and it is used by the government for unclassified data. The equipment needed for encryption is relatively moderate in cost--about $5,000 per work station, and this cost will probably decrease with increased volume of use.[27] A recent development in this area is that the National Security Agency (NSA) proposes to supply new codes that will supersede the DES to both government agencies and private users, and these will be provided through intermediate manufacturing companies.[28] An interesting feature is that the codes will not be revealed to the users, which will also aid the problem of internal security. Both keys and the necessary computer hardware will be supplied. Walter Deeley at the NSA has said that the DES has been around too long and is now too widely used.[29] It is generally agreed that any code can, in principle, be broken if enough time and effort are put into the task,[30] so codes have a certain natural lifetime, and then new codes have to be developed. There seems to be an interesting analogy here to the development of synthetic antibiotics by the drug companies: As bacteria develop resistance to the current drugs, new drugs have to be developed at a pace at least as rapid as the bacteria are able to mutate and develop a new resistant strain. Lobel, who was manager of computer security for Honeywell Information Systems for twelve years, has stated that:

> System security and access control planning should be considered an ongoing activity. Computer abuse driven by constant technological change is a moving target. It must be challenged by an equally new and formidable security technology. . . . We can and should anticipate an increase in computer-oriented crimes (including malicious attacks) for economic, personal and even political reasons. . . . As businesses, government agencies and individuals have access to more powerful user-friendly systems, we will see far more sensitive and confidential data stored in computer databases. The targets will be more tempting.[31]

One interesting type of simple security system to foil the external "hacker"--who can perhaps discover the method of entering a system by considerable trial-and-error--is to use a two-step entry procedure. Such a procedure would allow the hacker to enter the first step but then prevent clearance of the second hurdle by not allowing a trial-and-error approach at that point: After two unsuccessful tries, the system would disconnect.

One of the major weaknesses of present computer systems, from a security standpoint, is that, generally, input cannot be traced. Data and programming can be put into the system and changes can even be made in stored data anonymously. This is just inviting trouble, obviously. In addition, it is pos-

sible to insert programming and then delete
any traces of it having been inserted. And
many systems are so complicated already, even
without networking, that they cannot be
analyzed to see what they contain. Consequently, there is no systematic way to detect
surreptitiously entered programming that could
be destructive; it would be detected only by a
lucky accident. The majority of computer
systems have been described as being like
Swiss cheese, with many empty holes in the
programming, into which parasitic programming
can be introduced that could change the operation of the system in ways limited only by
the ingenuity of the intruder.

Ethics in Computer Use:
Regulatory Laws and Education

The role of ethics in computer networking
is one of the particular areas of attention in
this chapter, and some discussion of ethics is
appropriate at this point. Ethics is an area
that is delimited by various sorts of boundaries. First, it is something that is specifically human, as the behavior of animals is not
considered to involve ethics. Second, ethics
is not invoked to cover the totality of human
behavior. Ethical issues arise only when someone is being hurt or could potentially be
hurt, and the purpose of ethics is to try to
avoid this harm. Third, for the most part,
ethics refers to conscious attitudes and conscious judgments and decisions (either the
actor or the observer must be conscious of the
ethical aspect of what is going on). Thus,
ethics is really the province of the morally
enlightened. Ethical attitudes are produced
in the individual mostly by upbringing and
training; they are the result of nurture
rather than nature; a baby is not born ethical. Ethics is an aspect of social interaction, and it seems that ethical principles
are most influential in human behavior when
they are applied in a limited social group,
that has enough power to enforce social codes

on its members. The concept of ethics actually covers two areas, one focusing on the individual and protection from harm and the other
focusing on society in terms of achieving "the
greatest good for the greatest number." These
areas could be referred to as "micro-ethics"
and "macro-ethics," to borrow from the econo-
mists.

In large groups, laws provide a codification of ethics with a built-in punishment
system for nonconformity, and such laws seem
necessary because of the fact that ninety-nine
people who follow ethical principles have no
inherent protection against the one person who
does not. Ethics as a social convention relates also to courtesy and in this sense has
the nature of a "gentleman's agreement" based
on the idea of mutual respect and mutual consideration. But ethics should come strongly
to the fore when laws are being formulated;
ethical insight and concern on the part of
lawmakers can have a very strong influence on
the creation of laws and perhaps are most effective in this context. It is perhaps ironic
that when public opinion polls are taken to
measure how people perceive different professions, politicians and lawyers seem to be
considered "least ethical" of all professions,
and yet they have the major responsibility for
the public codification of ethics in their
hands and seem to carry out this function
reasonably well. Those who make the laws and
the policy decisions can be educated through
consultants, just as the president has his
policy advisers. Such consultation is provided
by congressional hearings, many of which have
been held on computer crime. And scholarly
studies can also make their contribution to
this cause. Some consciousness raising is
obviously involved in any such education, and
this might be the major contribution of an
academic ethical analysis per se.

Competing Ethical Systems

Although the definition of ethics given

above might be regarded as a "classical" definition, one of the problems involved in
implementing it as a universal basis for
action is the existence of other competing
concepts of ethics (in the sense of codes
describing behavior that would be approved or
disapproved by others; such codes, therefore,
would be the controlling factor in determining
an individual's behavior). Examples of these
competing concepts would be the work ethic
(well symbolized by the German motto Arbeit
macht das Leben suss [Work makes life sweet.])
and its direct opposite, the leisure ethic, or
the dolce far niente (the sweetness of doing
nothing) point of view, which would be well
accepted by the jet set, and probably by many
others if they could afford it. There is also
the game-playing ethic, crystallized in the
famous statement of Vince Lombardi: "Winning
isn't the most important thing; winning is
everything." This ethic is closely related to
the success ethic (requiring the accumulation
of money, power, and the admiration of
others--perhaps even to the extent of becoming
a recognized public personality in the media).
A Harvard Business School professor has recently written a book for business executives
entitled Competitive Advantage.[32] This book
reflects the point of view of many business-
people that business is a game in which the
object is to "win out" over your competitors
by having an "edge" over them. Seeing business as a vicarious form of pro football, or
even economic war, undoubtedly tends to create
stimulation, excitement, and a maximum flow of
adrenalin, so that people will "give 110% to
win." But then the moral and ethical aspects
of business fade far into the background, as
well as the obligations of business to the
society in which it operates.

Then there is the obedience ethic, char-
acteristic of all military systems, in which
obeying the orders of a superior represents
the highest moral imperative. This authori-
tarian ethic often involves not only doing
what one is told to do but also believing what
one is told to believe. This ethic then comes

into direct conflict with the scientific ethic, which requires the scientist to always keep an open mind and not accept the authority of another person in regard to what he or she believes. There are obviously many other ethics as well, each with its own purpose and each establishing its own hierarchy of values (which creates a "bumping order" of priority when different values come into conflict--as they often do).

In view of these conflicting ethics, to what extent can "personal ethics" (based on the individual's own beliefs and enlightened attitudes) resolve the ethical problems to be faced in the computer age? The answer probably is that personal ethics can only solve these problems to a limited extent. Having an individual ethical point of view is often discouraged, and even punished, in our society and other societies as well. It is very often regarded as a destabilizing force, although it might be regarded with approval and even admiration where it does not seem to rock the boat. In cases where the individual is part of a group, he or she is usually expected to subordinate personal opinions to the opinions of the group. These group opinions are usually set by the leader of the group, who is in charge of "truth creation," where truth is defined as "what people believe." Usually the group members are given clear indications as to what they should believe and how they should act. And "to get along, you go along." This process is sometimes described as the "molding of opinion," or "the generation of group cohesiveness," and is often admired as a form of managerial skill.

Consider the case of a chemist synthesizing drugs in medical research who might accidentally find that one of his products is a potent nerve gas that permanently damages the nervous system of individuals or animals exposed to it. Could he take active steps, from strong personal ethical feelings and convictions regarding his own social and professional responsibilities, to make sure that the gas would never be used deliberately for that purpose? If he tried to take personal action in this regard, most organizations (i.e., their managers) would say that he was exceeding the limits of his authority and concerning himself with matters that were "not his business." This type of question, they would say, should be decided by company policy or by "a person with the authority to decide." This example bears directly on the question of whether a scientist should be held responsible, or should, from an ethical standpoint, assume responsibility, for the social consequences of his or her work. The answer is that the scientist is almost never allowed to do so. Where then does personal ethics enter the picture? The only possible response is that the scientist has the right to hold personal beliefs and can perhaps have an influence on others by his or her actions within the sphere allotted. There is a certain degree of freedom of speech allowed in our social system, but total freedom is not permitted without the potential of retaliation. Individual attempts to implement a personal ethics when it comes into conflict with any sort of organizational self-interest usually leads to forms of punishment sufficient to discourage the individual from proceeding. Or intimidation may be enough: Would the ethical issue be compelling enough to justify risking the loss of one's job? Individual ethics needs the protection of a social group when such actions are in conflict with group or organizational forces. Although personal ethics can make their contribution, it seems that they cannot by themselves be expected to provide a solution to the ethical problems to be encountered in the computer environment of the future.

Although personal ethics are not sufficient in themselves, they are still an essential component of an ethical environment, as the effectiveness of laws and a criminal justice system relies to a great extent on a stable and essentially ethical society in which most individuals are law abiding and obey accepted social norms. The criminal can only be handled as an exception to the general rule, and in fact can only be defined as an exception.   If indeed the computer will come to permeate our lives, and will be an instrument of contact and interaction with others, then it will be necessary for individuals to be taught rules of good behavior when the computer is being used--a sort of etiquette that will allow people to avoid unpleasant results of various sorts.   In the early days of the automobile, people learned a code of behavior when using an automobile, which was called "courtesy of the road," for much the same purpose, and this code was impressed on people consciously before it became absorbed into conventional social norms (largely regulated by state and local laws today). This sort of training will probably have to start at an early age in the case of the computer; it will be an educational process. There are indications that this process is already starting to take place. One newspaper article[33] reported that the superintendent of schools in the Red Bank, New Jersey, school system, which teaches computer use to grade school children, has incorporated some ethics of computer use ("computer responsibility") starting with their first exposure to the computer in the first grade (obviously the best of all methods). Encouraging signs can also be seen at the university level. Most universities with computer science curricula have courses that include material on the social and ethical aspects of computer systems. In some cases specific courses are given in this area, such as the course that has been taught by Professor John W. Snapper at Illinois Institute of Technology for several years on Moral Issues in Computer Science. A college-level textbook on the subject has also been coedited by Snapper and Johnson (of Rensselaer Polytechnic).[34] Another text has been prepared by Adams and Haden (of New Mexico State University).[35]

One other type of ethic, and one that is of special relevance here, is the professional ethic, which is often formalized as a "Code of Ethics" set up by a professional society as

guidance for its members. It is then natural
to ask: Would this sort of accepted ethic not
be sufficient to resolve the ethical questions
that arise in terms of computers and computer
networking, assuming that the professionals
involved are men and women of good will? Some
light can be cast on this question by a survey
carried out by the American Institute of Chemical Engineers (AIChE) a few years ago, in
which members were polled as to how they would
personally respond in a set of nine imaginary
but realistic cases of ethical problem situations involving chemical engineers as employees or independent consultants. The answers
showed mostly divided opinions; they had little relation to and showed little knowledge of
the official ethical code adopted by the society. The society representatives who conducted
the poll concluded that their official code of
ethics was not providing effective guidance
when ethical questions arose in real circumstances and that without some specification of
the order of priority of these principles in
cases where they came into conflict, the
ethical code as it was presently formulated
was "little more than a set of pious plati-
tudes."[36] In the computer field, where the
professional affiliation of individuals is
much more diverse, and where no single code of
ethics exists to cover this wide spectrum, it
seems safe to conclude that professional codes
of ethics are not sufficient to do the job.
Laws are needed, and these laws must be widely
known and understood. Although laws in turn
are not totally sufficient, they are an essential component in maintaining an ethical computer environment.

Laws and Gamesmanship

Most states have now passed laws concerning computer crime, but most of them have been
modifications of existing laws that simply
include mention of the computer aspects that
arise. Some do mention crimes against computers, computer systems, and software them-

selves. A review of the current status and nature of such state laws has recently been carried out by Jurkat.[37] At least forty-six states now have laws on their books concerning computer crime, but many of these have defects and are often awkward and difficult to implement. Special committee hearings of both the Senate and House have also been held, and testimony has been taken in these hearings regarding the need for federal laws regarding the computer, but this process has proceeded slowly and carefully at the federal level. This approach is probably a reasonable one because, as Parker has pointed out, many crimes that people describe as "computer crimes" are simply traditional crimes (such as embezzlement of funds from a bank) that happen to have involved computers or computer systems as an incidental factor. However, the need for such laws is clear and becomes more pressing with time. Bequai, a lawyer and law professor in Washington, D.C., specializing in this field, has given an informed book-length critique[38] of existing laws and currently admissible court procedures and has shown that the present legal system and legal philosophy are seriously inadequate for handling this type of crime. He said that there is still time to formulate such laws and develop new principles and procedures to handle the computer crime problem, but that time is running out. He has also written a second book[39] on the prevention of computer crime.

The deterrence aspect is feeble at this point, as the sentences given out for such white-collar crime have generally not been very severe. The problem is compounded by the unwillingness of banks and large corporations to report such crimes so that they can be prosecuted. Instead, they typically keep them secret and absorb the losses because they feel that making such incidents public would weaken confidence in the organization and reflect unfavorably on management. And there may be good reason for this feeling; Krauss and MacGahan[40] have pointed out that management sets the moral climate of a company and that employee dishonesty is a by-product of poor management, especially permissiveness and neglect by top management. A similar point is made by Van Duyn[41] who has pointed out that computer security is a management issue; that the most effective deterrent to computer crime is job satisfaction, as insiders are the greatest threat to a data processing system; and that a disgruntled employee is a potential computer criminal. Resentment is often as powerful a motivation to criminal acts as the desire for financial gain. Apart from the responsibility of management in the treatment of employees, there is also a responsibility of management to set a good example. As pointed out by Moffit, "Corporations can and do create a moral tone that powerfully influences the thinking, conduct, values, and even the personalities of the people who work for them. This tone is set by the men who run the company and their corruption can quickly corrupt all else."[42] These ideas are related to the social psychology of crime, as organizations are, in fact, miniature societies. Social influences and social pressures are certainly one of the prime factors determining the individual's behavior, and the individual often looks to those in authority positions for cues. A classical case is the group of Mafiosi sitting around a table when a joke is told--and their eyes all look at the boss to see if he laughs before they relax and laugh themselves. Speaking of the Mafia, a prominent consultant in the computer field recently stated that if he were a Mafia capo today, he would be sending his sons to college to study computer science. Even organized crime cannot afford to become technologically obsolescent. But in addition to ethical integrity, a good manager also requires information to implement good intentions with effective action. As most managers are not computer experts, specialized consulting services are now becoming increasingly available and books have been written specifically for managers on these problems, such as that by Schweitzer,[43] who developed and implemented a security program for electronic information at the Xerox Corporation.

It is also in limited societies where "gamesmanship" plays its greatest role. This behavior, although not illegal, is not quite ethical either in the idealistic sense; it is designed to allow the game player to "win out" in one way or another and still stay out of jail, so to speak. Here is another area where laws would not seem to be the solution to the problem. Laws seem to be most appropriate and effective in a range of intermediate seriousness, where specific types of illegal behavior can be codified. The game player always works inside the law and uses techniques that are often indirect. The game player is usually, like the hacker, proud of his or her own cleverness and skillful technique. The behavior involved does not have to be extreme; it simply has to be sufficient to win. What "winning" means depends on the situation--gaining or maintaining power over another individual or group of individuals would be a typical goal, and this goal may be a conscious or a subconscious drive. In either case, whatever means are at hand will be used by an unprincipled game player, including the computer. A recent advertisement for an in-house computer network provides an interesting example. The headline of the ad proclaimed: "Have your subordinates at your fingertips every moment of the day." The ad never appeared again--I suspect because of protests that this was too blatant an appeal to an executive's urge to domineer. The executive that the ad would appeal to would probably already be dominating his or her subordinates excessively and, with this technique available on the in-house computer network, would undoubtedly become intolerable.

The Computer and the Human Brain:
A Mismatch

Making use of the computer in other domination games can easily be visualized.

The computer and computer networks are outstanding in their ability to handle large
quantities of data at tremendous rates of
speed. Their communication power is truly
formidable--going far beyond human capacity to
do the same job. And here arises a serious
problem: The computer and the human brain are
mismatched. And although the human brain can
do many things that the computer cannot do,
the human brain is still sluggish in comparison and cannot keep up with the computer in
certain functions. The computer can communicate information far faster than the human
brain can assimilate it and in far greater
quantities than the human brain can absorb.
It is, therefore, easily possible to swamp
human thinking processes by use of the computer. (Was this possibility anticipated in a
physical form by the "feeding machine," in
Charlie Chaplin's Modern Times, which got out
of control and kept stuffing food faster and
faster into his mouth--too fast to chew and
swallow--while he desperately struggled to
escape from the chair that he was strapped
into?) The human attention span and intellectual energy are finite. People's thinking
processes will spontaneously turn off at a
certain point, when overloaded, as an in-
stinctual protection of the individual's
sanity (a fact that is used in professional
"brain washing").
　　Electronic mail systems already exist.
What is the likelihood of generating electronic "junk mail"? The computer may be able
to handle it, but can the human being absorb
it and deal with it? Because of the capacity
of the computer memory system, there will be a
temptation to introduce any and all data into
it, and the specter of an ever-increasing
quantity of "information" of ever-decreasing
quality and usefulness looms in the not-far-
distant future. Will computer networks carry
advertising? Setting up computer networks
will be expensive, and income from advertising
would be one way to defray the costs. Television and radio would probably not survive in
anything like their present form without their

deep involvement with advertising. Will the computer be used for political campaigning? This technique would offer a powerful way for candidates to "get their message to the people." The swamping of people's thinking processes by over-communication would be a very effective instrument of demagoguery and brainwashing. The technique is, of course, already used today in milder forms. In group meetings, there is usually someone who talks louder and longer than others and so dominates the meeting, the discussion, and often the decisions that are arrived at; these people "talk other people down" and dominate meetings by saturation of the air waves. Another example is the excessively fast-talking salesperson who doesn't allow people time to think. But with the computer, excessive communication will undoubtedly become easier and will become one of the most useful techniques in computer gameplaying. This point is not trivial, given that effective status can be achieved in this way. Psychological surveys carried out on more than one campus have shown that when students were asked to choose which of their fellow students had the greatest "leadership abilities," and the personal characteristics of the students in question were correlated with the responses, the perceived leaders were the students who talked the most and the most forcefully. The analogy to professional politicians and demagogues is obvious. Is this "unethical"? Most people would say no. And computers could enhance this ability. Will the future "leaders" be those who saturate their computerized communications network with the most relentless flow of "messages"?

The argument is often made that computers will make many jobs easier, but this may not always be the case. In fact, it could be anticipated that when an employee is given a computer, greater productivity will be expected and the employee will in fact be under pressure to produce faster and in greater quantity than before, because the manager who had the computer installed undoubtedly did it to "increase productivity." Human-computer interaction, which is being so strongly promoted today, would seem to inevitably produce some pressure for the human to "keep up." This increased pressure to work faster will probably produce new levels of job stress in many people, and perhaps psychological breakdowns of a new type, if care is not taken.

In a computer society, there will probably be more and more of a need for and admiration of people who can make quick snap judgments. There will also probably be more and more of a need for "hand waving," faking, and simulation, as there will not be enough time to do jobs properly, and yet people in general will want to retain their belief that continual progress is being made in working faster and more productively and at ever higher levels of quality. So the pace will be maintained, even at the expense of lack of content. It is often stated that humans use only about 5 percent of their total brain capacity; although it is not clear how such a figure is arrived at and whether or not the statement is true, it is not obvious how the computer or any other instrument will be able to activate that other 95 percent. So it is not clear how the human/computer mismatch can be rectified in any significant way. Administrators will simply have to use good judgment and not indulge in unrealistic dreams. So far, "ergonomics" has concerned itself more with how comfortable the chair is in front of the computer screen than with how much satisfaction the operator feels after a day's work in front of that screen. But that is just what future managers will have to worry about. If people come to feel that their computer is their slavemaster, then serious troubles can be anticipated.

Effect on Scientific Research

So the speed of the computer may not be an unmixed blessing. To cite another example, the current method of scientific publication is a very slow process, involving months, whereas computer networking would allow the possibility of almost instant publication or dissemination of scientific results. And yet there seems to be relatively little criticism or dissatisfaction among scientists with the current system and scientists do not seem badly frustrated by it. The reason is that the slow step in scientific progress is actually creative human thinking, and not the dissemination of results (contrary to what the nonscientist would probably believe). The human brain obeys its own laws. It is interesting to remember that Einstein's grade school teachers thought that he was stupid or perhaps mentally retarded because he seemed to think and work so slowly. But he was simply thinking deeply. The important ideas come slowly; trivial ideas can be handled quickly. There is a moral here for those who want to speed up science by computerization. The greatest value to research of the computer at present is in providing rapid retrieval of scientific information from databanks.

Another natural temptation in a highly computerized science environment would be for research contract monitors to ask for more frequent reporting, as it could presumably be done so easily and quickly and would also show how diligently the monitor was carrying out responsibilities. The problem is that this reporting procedure would in no way speed up the work itself. Anyone with long experience in contract research knows that even now, one of the problems that can occasionally crop up, research being what it is, is to write a quarterly progress report for a quarter in which little or no progress was made. Imagine the problem (or burden) of generating monthly progress reports (or weekly progress reports) on a true exploratory research project. Obviously, velocity and progress are two different things, and the distinction needs to be kept firmly in mind by all those responsible for directing or managing research. Dynamic productivity can often be simulated by moving at high velocity in a circle.

The Computer: Ethical or Unethical?

In summary, it is useful to remind ourselves that the computer is only an instrument and can only be the instrument of someone's wishes. The computer is morally and ethically neutral. It has no volition. It has no preferences. It will only do what someone has programmed it to do. People talk today about "artificial intelligence" (AI), but no one discusses "artificial ethics" (AE)--because it doesn't exist. So AE is unfortunately an acronym doomed to die, because although the computer can be programmed to mimic human logic, it cannot be programmed to duplicate human moral or ethical judgment. The human element cannot be replaced in this area because the subtleties remain too complex, and empathy (which the computer does not possess) is an important component of ethical judgments. And even when the computer mimics human thinking, by "smart programs," its intelligence is still the intelligence of the ventriloquist's dummy--there is always a human being behind it, and that is where the cleverness resides. So if the computer produces evil consequences, they can always be traced back to a human source who either had bad intentions or who failed to think about possible consequences.

The Frankenstein story is always with us and is an endless source of plots for science fiction writers. It is actually a morality play to remind us of an ever-present danger in a society devoted to technological progress. The key to the plot is the "turnaround point" where we lose control over the monster that we have created by our science and technology and it begins to control us. Some people have fears of this sort about the computer. But if we ever allow ourselves to become computer-controlled, then we will have simply bungled, from a managerial or political standpoint. No computer has the wish to control us, so we can only sabotage ourselves. Computers do not have any inherent ethical characteristics, and that simply means that the people who use them should realize their responsibility to make up that deficit.

This is not to say that formidable future problems will not exist. They will, but problems are always with us. Computer crime exists, but crime has always existed. We already have the means, with nuclear weapons, to destroy civilized life as we know it. People push ahead with the development of fusion energy, with its promise of an unlimited energy source. Will we know how to accommodate to such a situation if the effort is successful? Technology is continually presenting new ethical dilemmas. The possibility of genesplicing will present us with problems of the most serious magnitude. Will we be able to avoid the catastrophic possibilities? Humankind seems to be always living on the edge of disaster, and yet it survives--sometimes, it seems, like the Antrobus family in Thornton Wilder's play, by "the skin of its teeth." People are constantly testing the limits of the tolerable, or manageable, or possible, just catching themselves in time, and it may be that this hazardous process is the principal mechanism of human progress. We can, and do, constantly learn what corrective action to take to save ourselves, as we take each step forward at the edge of a slowly advancing cliff.

Certainly we should have no fears of the computer in any intrinsic sense. The computer is inert and we hold all the cards of power in our own hands. So it is up to us to learn to play them properly. The future does not yet exist, and we have the privilege of planning and working to create it in the form that we wish. What more can we ask?

Acknowledgements

I would like to thank Professor Carol Gould for her invitation to participate in this computer ethics project. Appreciation is also expressed to Professor M. Peter Jurkat and Dr. M. Alexander Jurkat for allowing the use of a manuscript copy of Reference 44 prior to publication, and for several additional literature references.

Note added in proof:

The "virus" problem continues to be reported.[44] But as in warfare (and this type of computer crime in fact somewhat resembles guerrilla warfare, which is a moving and shifting target), the invention of new aggressive weapons and strategies leads directly to the invention of new forms of defense. This is illustrated by a new computer program package called "Viralarm 2000", described in a recent article,[45] which is now commercially available. This is a set of programs which when put through the system will give a prescribed output when all is well. Any abnormality in the output indicates a spurious programming in the system, which the system operator can then locate and remove. This is, in fact, only one of several systems which have sprung up[44] in the attempt to cope with this problem, and still more are sure to appear. Several programs are now also available to remove viruses.

Notes

1. Jamie Murphy, "A Threat from Malicious Software," Time (4 November 1985), p. 94.
2. Vin McLellan, "Computer Systems Under Siege," The New York Times (31 January 1988), p. D1. See also John Markoff, "A 'Virus' Gives Business a Chill," The New York Times (17 March 1988), p. D1.
3. Frank Rose, "Joy of Hacking," Science 82 3 (November 1982), pp. 59-66; William D. Marbach, "Beware: Hackers at Play," Newsweek (5 September 1983), pp. 42-46, 48; "The World

of Data Confronts the Joy of Hacking," The New York Times (28 August 1983), Sect. 4, p. 20; and Mary Thornton, "Hackers Ignore Consequences of Their High-Tech Joy Rides," Washington Post (21 May 1984), p. A1.

4. Robert Friedman, "The Dalton Gang's Computer Caper," New York Magazine 13 (8 December 1980), pp. 65-75.

5. Murphy, "A Threat."

6. Joseph B. Treaster, "Hundreds of Youths Trading Data on Computer Break-ins," The New York Times (5 September 1983), pp. A1, A34.

7. Marbach, "Beware."

8. William J. Broad, "Rising Use of Computer Networks Raise Issues of Security and Law," The New York Times (26 August 1983), pp. A1, A15.

9. Gina Kolata, "Students Discover Computer Threat," Science 215 (5 March 1982), pp. 1216-1217; and Fredda Sacharow, "Computer Criminals: New Breed," The New York Times (4 April 1982), Sect. 11, pp. 1, 12.

10. Thornton, "Hackers Ignore Consequences."

11. Steven Levy, Hackers: Heroes of the Computer Revolution (Garden City, NY: Anchor/Doubleday, 1984).

12. Mike Eisenberg, Hackers, play produced at George Street Playhouse, New Brunswick, NJ, reviewed in Princeton (NJ) Packet, 10 December 1986.

13. Thornton, "Hackers Ignore Consequences."

14. Ibid.

15. Donn B. Parker, Crime by Computer (New York: Scribner's, 1976); Ethical Conflicts in Computer Science and Technology (Reston, VA: AFIPS Press, 1981); Fighting Computer Crime (New York: Scribner's, 1983); Managers Guide to Computer Security (Englewood Cliffs, NJ: Prentice-Hall, 1983); and Computer Crime: Computer Security Techniques (Rockville, MD: National Criminal Justice Reference Service, no date).

16. Thomas Whiteside, Computer Capers: Tales of Electronic, Thievery, Embezzlement,

and _Fraud_ (New York: New American Library, 1978).

17. Murphy, "A Threat."

18. Mary Thornton, "Age Of Electronic Convenience Spawning Inventive Thieves," _Washington Post_ (20 May 1984), p. A1.

19. "The World of Data Confronts the Joy of Hacking."

20. Mary Thornton, "Security is Often an Afterthought," _Washington Post_ (22 May 1984), p. A1.

21. Thornton, "Age of Electronic Convenience."

22. Richard Conniff, "Computer War," _Science Digest_ 90 (January 1982), pp. 14-15, 26, 28, 94.

23. Parker, _Crime by Computer_.

24. Thornton, "Age of Electronic Convenience."

25. Leonard I. Krauss and Aileen MacGahan, _Computer Fraud and Countermeasures_ (Englewood Cliffs, NJ: Prentice-Hall, 1979).

26. Julia Van Duyn, _The Human Factor in Computer Crime_ (Princeton, NJ: Petrocelli Books, 1985).

27. Ibid.

28. Gina Kolata, "NSA to Provide Secret Codes," _Science_ 230 (4 October 1985), p. 45.

29. Ibid.

30. Leonard I. Krauss and Aileen MacGahan, _Computer Fraud and Countermeasures_ (Englewood Cliffs, NJ: Prentice-Hall, 1979), p. 210.

31. Jerome Lobel, _Foiling the System Breakers: Computer Security and Access Control_ (New York: McGraw-Hill, 1986).

32. Michael Porter, _Competitive Advantage_ (Glencoe, IL: The Free Press, 1985).

33. Vivian Aplin-Brownlee, "Ethical Questions Arise from Computers Biting into Privacy," _Washington Post_ (23 May 1984), p. A1.

34. Deborah G. Johnson and John W. Snapper, eds., _Ethical Issues in the Use of Computers_ (Belmont, CA: Wadsworth, 1985).

35. J. Mack Adams and Douglas H. Haden, _Social Effects of Computer Use and Misuse_ (New

York: Wiley, 1976).

36. Roy V. Hughson and Philip M. Kohn, "Ethics," Chemical Engineering (22 September 1980), p. 132.

37. M. Alexander Jurkat, "Computer Crime Legislation: Survey and Analysis," Annual Survey of American Law 3 (1986), p. 511.

38. August Bequai, Computer Crime (Lexington, MA: D. C. Heath, 1978).

39. August Bequai, How to Prevent Computer Crime (New York: Wiley, 1983).

40. Krauss and MacGahan, Computer Fraud.

41. J. Van Duyn, The Human Factor in Computer Crime (Princeton, NJ: Petrocelli Books, 1985).

42. Donald Moffit, ed., Swindled! (Princeton, NJ: Dow Jones & Co., 1976), p. 46.

43. James A. Schweitzer, Computer Crime and Business Information: A Practical Guide for Managers (New York: Elsevier, 1986).

44. John Markoff, "A 'Virus' Gives Business a Chill," New York Times, (17 March 1988), p. D1. Eliot Marshall, "The Scourge of Computer Viruses," Science 240 133 (1988). See also Computers and Security (New York: Elsevier Science Publications, April 1988).

45. Sarah Fryberger, "Take Two Aspirins and Call It Up in the Morning," New Jersey Monthly (September 1988), p. 11.

13

The Ethics of Voluntary and Involuntary Disclosure of Company-Private Information

Donn B. Parker

A position of trust implied or stated in most business employment agreements or contracts makes unauthorized disclosure of sensitive information a violation of ethics. Computer security technologists possess information of the greatest sensitivity--information concerning the protection of their employers' vital business information. Disclosure of such information and compromise of information on mergers, acquisitions, litigation, or research could do irreparable harm to a competitive business. The subject of this chapter is the ethics of revealing an employer's sensitive security information and of using deception, or spoofing, to obtain sensitive information to gain advantage over a business organization.

Change in the Nature of Communication

Computers and computer networks are changing the ways in which employees and competitive businesses communicate and providing new and easier means of disclosing and obtaining sensitive information. These technologies have introduced hybrids of spoken and written communications. An example is voice mail, a service that conveys spoken store-and-forward messages privately from person to person, within a conference of several people, or from one person to many people. Another example is electronic mail, whereby written store-and-forward messages are similarly conveyed. Whereas an etiquette has developed for conversations, face-to-face communications, and letter writing, none has yet evolved for these new systems.

With the new communication technologies, bilateral verification of identities is impossible and the receiver cannot determine what the sender's state of mind and values were at the time the message was created.[1] Such easily created and transmitted messages tend to be cryptic and created on-the-fly as urges to communicate arise. The sender may expect his electronic mail to simply be flashed on a screen momentarily to be read and then erased by a receiver, whereas in fact it may be viewed by many people, kept in computer storage for later use, or printed out in a permanent form. Voice mail, likewise, may be recorded and played back several times. Misunderstanding of the message communicated and its context may result from a lack of parallel "messages" such as tone of voice or parenthetical commentary, which provide clues to the meaning of the message content.

For example, the sender may wish to tease the recipient of an electronic mail message by including the statement, "Your password is a dirty word. I guessed it. You had better change it." This would usually be taken as a friendly suggestion. If the sender recasts the statement to read, "You use dirty words for passwords. Clean up your act," the receiver would wonder whether the sender meant it as friendly advice or had some undercurrent of malice. The sender may decide to be even more brief, merely saying, "You have a dirty mind. Replace your password," thinking that this was still a friendly remark. The receiver, however, is very likely to take offense at what he believes is a pernicious statement. These kinds of misunderstandings can be quite severe in groups of technologists who share computer resources.

Very soon, digitized voice communications, digital signatures with legal accep-

tance, and laser optics memory of a nonde-
structible form may be available. These
advances will exacerbate such communications
problems unless etiquette and ethics are
applied in creating messages.

Proliferation of Information

Even though new technologies are being
introduced, we still drag our old technologies
along with us so that the new adds to, rather
than replaces, the old. For example, five
years ago the paperless society was predicted
with the advent of computer terminals. Today,
the paper manufacturing industry reports that
its production is growing 9 percent per year.
We are producing more information on paper
than we ever have throughout history. Attached
to the millions of microcomputers that were to
produce the paperless society are high-speed
printers that can collectively print at hitherto unimaginable speeds.[2] Such devices
have given employees not only access to more
information but also more free time to disseminate and receive information. Information
is now the dominant raw material asset and
product of most business organizations. Computers and computer networks, therefore, now
have strategic competitive roles in businesses
rather than simply passive service roles and
directly affect earnings. For example, retail
food manufacturers, commercial banks, and
insurance companies are enticing their whole-
salers and sometimes retail customers to enter
orders for products or services directly from
their terminals into the suppliers' computers.
The purpose, in addition to reducing costs of
order entry and processing, is to capture
customers by making them dependent on a single
supplier's computer systems. These computers
store electronic mail, bank account balances,
manufacturers' sales data, and insurance companies' claims experience data. The whole-
salers (and among them direct and indirect
competitors), retailers, and retail customers
are all in mutually adversarial business re-

lationships, and adequate control of the flow
of information in their computers is not possible with today's security technology. In
such sensitive situations, information must be
protected not only by technical methods but
also by applying constraints on the people who
have access to it.[3]

Two Information Security Problems

Two problems are associated with the
security of information. One is the problem of
the computer security technologist who voluntarily discloses business secrets concerning
his work. Prompted by their dedication, en-
thusiasm, and search for new information,
technologists may naively convey information
to other technologists without considering the
sensitivity of the information. For example,
a technologist may disclose details pertaining
to an employer's information security
controls--either at professional and trade
conferences or in casual conversations with
others who are unauthorized to receive such
information. The admonishment of World War II
that "Loose Lips Sink Ships" addressed the
same type of problem. Questionnaires mailed
to computer security technologists by survey
companies often request detailed answers to
sensitive questions and names and addresses
for the return of compiled results. Even
within a company, task forces established to
solve particular problems in several departments may result in the disclosure of vulner-
abilities and details of control to task force
members who have no functional need to know
such information. Visitors and vendor personnel given the freedom to move about technical
staff offices have the opportunity to learn
sensitive information from computer security
technologists. Sensitive information is also
freely disclosed in newsletters, training
courses, and system manuals. Even the information banners appearing at computer terminal
log-on often reveal unneeded sensitive information to users.

The second problem is computer security technologists' involuntary disclosure of security secrets. This situation occurs when computer media documents containing sensitive security information are stolen from them or when an unauthorized person copies such information. Another example is overt espionage designed to obtain sensitive information from technologists. Spoofing as a form of deception is a common method hackers and "phone phreaks" use to obtain technical information from unsuspecting technologists. In this case, the hackers deceive the technologists through the use of flattery and familiar jargon that implies that the hackers are authorized to receive additional similar information. These techniques are increasingly being made easier, as previously indicated, by such services as voice mail and electronic mail.

Guidelines for Information Sensitivity

Computer security technologists in particular, and computer technologists in general, must have guidance to distinguish between sensitive information that must be held secret and other technical information that they are free to disclose or exchange. The following sensitivity test can be taught to employees entrusted with technical business information:

1. If the information is already generally or publicly known, it may be disclosed. (An exception to this rule is that if the information is generally known but disclosure of the source may present a vulnerability, it should not be disseminated from the identifiable source. Also, further disclosure is not advised if it provides no useful benefit to the discloser.) If the information is not generally or publicly known, proceed to rule 2.
2. Information may be disclosed if it

3. would not aid an adversary. (The adversary must be carefully defined as being anyone without an explicit need to know.) If this rule does not result in a final decision, proceed to rule 3.

3. Disclosure is acceptable if it will result in a net benefit--what is received in exchange is at least as valuable as what may be lost by disclosure of the information. However, all the benefits and values may be extremely difficult to determine, and the assistance of others may be needed to make this determination. If the question of disclosure is not resolved by this rule, proceed to rule 4.

4. If the information can be disclosed anonymously, and if the source cannot be identified in any practical way or harmed by the disclosure, the information may be disclosed. Otherwise, proceed to rule 5.

5. If authorization can be obtained from a higher accountable authority, information may be disclosed. In this way, the computer security technologist can obtain informed consent to reveal information, and the burden of responsibility can be placed on higher management, where it most likely belongs. As implied, however, the approval must be based on provision of all known factors to the deciding authority.

Although computer security technologists will most likely not remember all these rules in practical situations, periodic reminders should prompt them to remember and apply them, resulting in an incremental increase in security.

Controls and Practices
Against Voluntary Disclosure

A number of generally accepted controls and practices are prudent to prevent harmful voluntary disclosure of information.[4] First, company policy must be established to define or classify sensitive information, and top management must give direction and motivation for this task. In addition, trusted employees must be provided with due notice of this policy, preferably periodically so that they will not forget it. A code of conduct should be promulgated.[5] In all fairness, such a code should indicate both what is expected of employees in the protection of information and what management is accountable for in providing employees with adequate instructions regarding the disclosure of information. A system of rewards and penalties must also be established in order for the code of conduct to be more than merely a set of guidelines. Employees and managers should be required to sign confidentiality and avoidance of conflict of interest agreements.[6] Procedures should be established for obtaining approval of information dissemination. Safe and fair hiring and termination procedures should be established. Periodic training programs should be conducted to teach the good practices and rules described above. Minimal computer terminal screen prompting should be applied to avoid revealing sensitive information, especially before log-on has been completed. Although many more controls and practices could be instituted, these provide a starting baseline for good disclosure prevention.

Controls and Practices
Against Involuntary Disclosure

The following controls and practices can be used to enhance prevention of involuntary disclosure when an adversary actively seeks information. Spoof proofing of employees can be accomplished through training programs to identify potential adversaries and their methods and through provision of examples of information that may or may not be revealed. The usual security practices should also be applied--separation of employees' duties, dual control over tasks, and access isolation of sensitive information sources such as high-speed printers. The many controls and practices for physical and logical protection of information should be invoked, such as use of locked cabinets for paper and diskettes, cryptographic protection of information, and the use of secret passwords and other techniques for bilateral verification of authorized parties and systems. Copies of sensitive documents can be controlled through labeling, numbering, requiring receipts for delivery, and limiting the numbers of copies, as well as providing means for safely discarding them. Logging of documents and periodic inventorying can control document distribution. Warning signs should be placed near copy machines, and strict rules about copying should be promulgated. Carrying sensitive information during business travel requires special procedures, including continuous personal possession, use of safe deposit boxes in hotels, limiting the use and storing of sensitive information to the confines of secure business offices, and locking sensitive materials in the trunks of cars.

Special Considerations

Some employees may be responsible for attempting to obtain important information about competing business organizations.[7] This can be a legitimate business activity, provided the principle of informed consent is applied. The competing business organization representatives should knowingly consent to disclose the information and should understand the identity of the receiving parties. Any activities beyond this limit would be unethical, unless a higher ethical principle prevailed, such as obtaining information about the misconduct of a competing business organization to report it to legal authorities. In such cases, however, the array of legal and criminal constraints and rules of evidence must be applied, and corporate legal counsel should be sought for advice and instructions.

Conclusion

Without doubt, the advancement of computer and network technology is facilitating the ease of communication and increasing the kinds and volume of sensitive information. At the same time, it is also facilitating new and more effective controls and practices. However, with each type of advance, the ethical values of the past must be carried over to the new technology to ensure their preservation.

Notes

1. Norman Z. Shapiro and Robert H. Anderson, _Toward an Ethics and Etiquette for Electronic Mail_ (Santa Monica, CA: The Rand Corporation, 1985).

2. In my consulting work, I recommend that for each high-speed printer the user should also obtain a shredder, with the additional facetious advice that as the paper is printed it be automatically fed into the shredder; only by exception would it be removed before shredding. (I have failed so far to interest printer manufacturers in developing a new integrated printer/shredder product!)

3. Donn B. Parker, _Fighting Computer Crime_ (New York: Charles Scribner's Sons, 1983).

4. Donn B. Parker, _Computer Crime_:

Computer Security Techniques (Gaithersburg, MD: National Criminal Justice Resource Service, 1984).

5. Douglas W. Johnson, Computer Ethics (Elgin, IL: The Brethren Press, 1984).

6. Thomas J. Smedinghoff, The Legal Guide to Developing, Protecting, and Marketing Software: Dealing with Problems Raised by Customers, Competitors and Employees (New York: John Wiley and Sons, 1986).

7. Richard M. Greene, Jr., Business Intelligence and Espionage (Homewood, IL: Dow Jones-Irwin, 1966).

Contributors

<u>Rodney D. Andrews</u>, Chemistry, Stevens Institute of Technology

<u>Robert J. Baum</u>, Philosophy, University of Florida, Gainesville

<u>Frank T. Boesch</u>, Electrical Engineering and Computer Science, Stevens Institute of Technology

<u>Carol C. Gould</u>, Philosophy, Department of Humanities, Stevens Institute of Technology

<u>Deborah G. Johnson</u>, Philosophy, Department of Science and Technology Studies, Rensselaer Polytechnic Institute

<u>M. Peter Jurkat</u>, Computer Science, Department of Management, Stevens Institute of Technology

<u>John Ladd</u>, Philosophy, Brown University

<u>I. Richard Lapidus</u> (1935-1988), formerly Professor of Physics, Stevens Institute of Technology

<u>James H. Moor</u>, Philosophy, Dartmouth College

<u>James W. Nickel</u>, Philosophy, Center for Values and Social Policy, University of Colorado, Boulder

<u>Donn B. Parker</u>, Computer Science, Stanford Research Institute International

<u>John W. Snapper</u>, Philosophy, Department of Humanities, Illinois Institute of Technology

<u>Arnold B. Urken</u>, Political Science, Department of Humanities, Stevens Institute of Technology

Index